D1526778

Handbook of Carbon Offset Programs

Handbook of Carbon Offset Programs

Trading Systems, Funds, Protocols and Standards

Anja Kollmuss, Michael Lazarus,
Carrie Lee, Maurice LeFranc and
Clifford Polycarp

publishing for a sustainable future
London • Washington, DC

First published in 2010 by Earthscan

Earthscan Ltd, Dunstan House, 14a St Cross Street, London EC1N 8XA, UK
Earthscan LLC, 1616 P Street, NW, Washington, DC 20036, USA
Earthscan publishes in association with the International Institute for Environment and Development

For more information on Earthscan publications, see www.earthscan.co.uk or write to earthinfo@earthscan.co.uk

ISBN: 978-1-84407-929-2 hardback

Typeset by Domex e-Data, India
Cover design by Yvonne Booth

A catalogue record for this book is available from the British Library

Library of Congress Cataloging-in-Publication Data

Handbook of carbon offset programs : trading systems, funds, protocols and standards / Anja Kollmuss ... [et al.].
    p. cm.
  Includes bibliographical references and index.
  ISBN 978-1-84407-929-2 (hbk.)
  1. Carbon offsetting. 2. Emissions trading. I. Kollmuss, Anja.
  HC79.P55H36 2010
  363.738'746–dc22   2009033839

Mixed Sources
Product group from well-managed forests and other controlled sources
www.fsc.org Cert no. SGS-COC-2482
© 1996 Forest Stewardship Council

Contents

List of Figures, Tables and Boxes

Figures

Tables

Boxes

Acknowledgements

The authors greatly appreciate the time taken by the many individuals listed below for their clarifications and enrichment of specific report sections, and for their suggestions that improved the overall organization and framing of this document. The authors extend particular thanks to Derik Broekhoff of the World Resources Institute, whose unpublished survey of standards and programs, conducted with support from the World Economic Forum, provided a helpful guidepost for this effort. We acknowledge the World Wildlife Fund for their support of earlier research, which helped to build a strong foundation for this book.

Edwin Aalders, Voluntary Carbon Standard
Heather Angstrom, Stockholm Environment Institute, Intern
David Antoniolli, Voluntary Carbon Standard Association
Aaron Atteridge, Stockholm Environment Institute
Andrew Aulisi, US Environmental Protection Agency
Nicholas Bianco, World Resources Institute
Adam Bless, Oregon Department of Energy
Pierre Boileau, Canadian Standards Association
Martina Bosi, World Bank Carbon Finance Unit
Derik Broekhoff, Climate Action Reserve
Meinrad Buerer, Gold Standard
Phil Carver, Oregon Department of Energy
Marsha Cheddi, International Standards Association TC/207 SC7
Marzena Chodor, European Commission
Thomas Claßen, TÜV SÜD Industrie Service GmbH
Nathan Clark, Chicago Climate Exchange
James Colman, Massachusetts Department of Environmental Protection
Nathalie Dault, European Commission, DG Environment
Bill Drumheller, Oregon Department of Energy
Joanna Durbin, Climate, Community and Biodiversity Alliance
Allen Fiksdal, Washington Energy Facility Site Evaluation Council
Rob Fowler, Booz and Company
Gary Gero, California Climate Action Registry
Mary Grady, Winrock Internatinal
Isabel Hagbrink, World Bank Carbon Finance Unit
Ray Hammarlund, Kansas Corporation Commission
Josh Harris, Voluntary Carbon Standard
Judith Hull, Environment Canada
Jasmine Hyman, Gold Standard
Toby Janson-Smith, Conservation International
Mark Kenber, Voluntary Carbon Standard

Grant Kirkman, UNFCCC
Kimberly Klunich, US Environmental Protection Agency
Lars Kvale, Center for Resource Solutions
Suzanne Loney, Environment Canada
Damien Meadows, European Commission, DG Environment
Cecilia Michellis, Social Carbon
David Moffat, Pacific Carbon Trust
Alexa Morrison, Plan Vivo Foundation
Allison Myers Crimmins, Stockholm Environment Institute Intern
Shahyar Niakan, World Bank Carbon Finance Unit
Juan Simon, International Organization for Standardization
Gordon Smith, Ecofor LLC
Dean Stinson O'Gorman, Environment Canada
Manuel Oliva, Climate Leaders, US Environmental Protection Agency
Steven Panfil, Climate, Community and Biodiversity Alliance
Navena Pingarova, TÜV SÜD Industrie Service GmbH
Andy Ridge, Alberta Environment
Robert Savage, Alberta Environment
Michael Schlup, Gold Standard
Kai-Uwe Barani Schmidt, UNFCCC CDM Secretariat
Jerry Seager, Voluntary Carbon Standard Association
Chris Sherry, New Jersey Department of Environmental Protection
William Space, Massachusetts Department of Environmental Protection
Caitlin Sparks, Gold Standard
Scott Subler, Chicago Climate Exchange
Jim Sullivan, Climate Leaders, US Environmental Protection Agency
Jane Valentino, Center for Resource Solutions
Jennifer Weiss, Climate Action Reserve
Melissa Weitz, US Environmental Protection Agency
Rich Wong, Pembina Institute
World Bank Carbon Finance Unit's Operations Team

List of Acronyms and Abbreviations

AAU	Assigned Amount Unit (Kyoto Protocol)
ACESA	American Climate and Energy Security Act
ACP	Abatement Certificate Provider
ACR	American Carbon Registry
ACT	Australian Capital Territory
AIE	Accredited Independent Entity
ALM	agricultural land management
BAU	business-as-usual
BC	British Columbia
BER	Baseline Emission Rate
BioCF	BioCarbon Fund
CAR	Climate Action Registry
CARS	carbon asset registry system
CCAR	California Climate Action Registry
CCBA	Climate, Community and Biodiversity Alliance
CCBS	Climate, Community and Biodiversity Standards
CCEMA	Climate Change and Emissions Management Act
CCX	Chicago Climate Exchange
CDM	Clean Development Mechanism
CDM EB	CDM Executive Board
CEEM	Center for Energy and Environmental Markets
CER	Certified Emission Reduction
CFB	Compact Fluorescent Bulb
CFI	Carbon Financial Instrument
CFU	Carbon Finance Unit
CH_4	methane
CITL	Community Independent Transaction Log
CMAC	Climate Marketers Advisory Committee
CO_2	carbon dioxide
CO_2e	carbon dioxide equivalent
COP	Conference of Parties
COUP	Intertribal Council on Utility Policy
CRS	Center for Resources Solutions
CRT	Climate Reserve Tonne
CSR	corporate social responsibility
DFID	UK Department for International Development
DFP	Designated Focal Point
DNA	Designated National Authority
DOE	Designated Operational Entity
ECCM	Edinburgh Centre for Carbon Management

ECOSUR	EI Colegio de la Frontera Sur
EIA	Environmental Impact Assessment
EIT	economy in transition (e.g. Eastern Europe)
EPA	US Environmental Protection Agency
EPC	Emission Performance Credit
ER	emisssion reduction
ERPA	Emission Reduction Purchase Agreement
ERT	Emission Reduction Ton
ERT	Environmental Resources Trust
ERU	Emission Reduction Unit
ESC	Energy Saving Certificate
ESS	Energy Savings Scheme
EU ETS	European Union Emission Trading System
EUA	EU ETS allowance
FPO	Forward Purchasing of Offsets
FSC	Forest Stewardship Council
GGRTA	Greenhouse Gas Reduction Targets Act
GHG	greenhouse gas
Green-e CPRE	Green-e Climate Protocol for Renewable Energy
GS	Gold Standard
GS TAC	Gold Standard Technical Advisory Committee
GWh	gigawatt hour
GWP	global warming potential
HFC	hydrofluorocarbon
IAE	Independent Accredited Entity
ICAP	International Carbon Action Partnership
lCER	long-term CER
ICRC	Independent Competition and Regulatory Commission
IE	Instituto Ecológica
IETA	International Emissions Trading Association
IFM	Improved Forest Management
IMP	Inventory Management Plan
INCIS	International Carbon Investors and Services
IPART	Independent Pricing and Regulatory Tribunal
IRP	Integrated Resource Planning
IRR	internal rate of return
ISO	International Organization for Standardization
ITL	International Transaction Log
JI	Joint Implementation
JISC	JI Supervisory Committee
LDC	least developed countries
LULUCF	land use, land-use change and forestry
MA	Massachusetts
MassDEP	Massachusetts Department of Environmental Protection
MDG	Millennium Development Goals
MGGRA	Midwestern Greenhouse Gas Reduction Accord

MmtCO$_2$e	million metric tons of CO$_2$ equivalent
MOU	memorandum of understanding
MRET	Mandatory Renewable Energy Target
MstCO$_2$e	million short tons of CO$_2$ equivalent
MW	megawatt
N$_2$O	nitrous oxide
NAP	National Allocation Plan
NEM	National Electricity Market
NGAC	NSW GHG Abatement Certificate
NGO	non-governmental organization
NSW GGAS	New South Wales Greenhouse Gas Abatement Scheme
ODA	official development assistance
ODS	ozone depleting substance
OR	Oregon
OSQP	Offset System Quantification Protocol
PDD	Project Design Document
PFC	perfluorocarbon
PIN	Project Idea Note
ppb	parts per billion
ppm	parts per million
pre-CER	pre-registered Emission Reduction
PSEG	Public Service Enterprise Group
PV	photovoltaic
RAO	Regional Administrative Organization
REC	Renewable Energy Credit
REDD	reduced emissions from deforestation and degradation
RF	radiative forcing
RGGA	Regional Greenhouse Gas Initiative Allowance
RGGI	Regional Greenhouse Gas Initiative
RGGI COATS	RGGI CO$_2$ Allowance Tracking System
RIT	Registration and Issuance Team
RMU	Removal Unit
RPS	Renewable Portfolio Standard
SC	Social Carbon
SCM	Social Carbon Methodology
SDI	sustainable development indicators
SEI	Stockholm Environment Institute
SF$_6$	sulphur hexafluoride
SSCWG	Small Scale Working Group
TAG	Technical Advisory Group
tCER	temporary CER
TCG	The Climate Group
tCO$_2$e	tons of CO$_2$ equivalent
UNDP	United Nations Development Programme
UNFCCC	United Nations Framework Convention on Climate Change
USDA	US Department of Agriculture

VCS	Voluntary Carbon Standard
VCS AFOLU	VCS Agriculture, Forestry and Other Land Use
VCSA	Voluntary Carbon Standard Association
VCU	Voluntary Carbon Unit
VER	Verified or Voluntary Emission Reduction
VERR	Verified Emission Reduction/Removal
WA	Washington
WBCSD	World Business Council for Sustainable Development
WCI	Western Climate Initiative
WEF	World Economic Forum
WRI	World Resources Institute
WWF	World Wildlife Fund

1

Introduction to Carbon Offsetting

Current climate science suggests that global greenhouse gas emissions must decline by as much as 80 per cent by mid-century to avoid unacceptably high risks. To achieve this goal, we must dramatically transform how we produce and use energy, manage land and value the climate in our economic system. Such a transition will require far-reaching local, national and international climate policies, with support and participation by businesses and communities.

What role can carbon offsets play in meeting this profound challenge?

Carbon or greenhouse gas (GHG) offsets have long been promoted as an important element of a comprehensive climate policy approach. By virtue of enabling emission reductions to occur where costs may be lower, offset projects and programs can reduce the overall cost of achieving a given emission goal, a finding supported by many economic analyses. Furthermore, offsets have the potential to deliver sustainability co-benefits, to spur technology development and transfer, and to develop human and institutional capacity for reducing emissions in sectors and locations not included in a cap-and-trade or a mandatory government policy.

With increasing attention on tackling the challenge of climate change, it is no surprise that interest in carbon offsets is blossoming. Increasingly, individuals, organizations and policy makers are considering carbon offsets to be a key element in their strategies to address GHG emissions.

As experience with offset markets grows, however, a number of risks have become more widely apparent and have caught the attention of the mainstream media. Most fundamentally, offsets can pose a risk to the environmental integrity of climate actions, especially if issues surrounding additionality, permanence, leakage, quantification and verification are not adequately addressed. Depending on how offsets are used, they could delay investment and innovation in lower-emitting technologies in key sources and sectors of the economy (e.g. those covered by a cap-and-trade). They may provide desirable near-term cost advantages, but at the risk of 'locking-in' higher emission infrastructures and higher costs in the longer term. Where the cost of implementing offset projects is significantly lower than the market price of offsets, as is the case for many non-carbon dioxide (CO_2) projects such as hydrofluorocarbon (HFC) incineration, offsets may provide a useful transition mechanism; ultimately, however, other polices such as direct incentives or regulation could achieve deeper reductions more rapidly and at lower cost.

The challenge for policy makers is clear: to design offset programs and policies that can maximize their potential benefits while minimizing their potential risks

Given the number and complexity of offset issues and interactions, this challenge is considerable. At the same time, well-designed offset programs may be one way out of the conundrum of needing to achieve steep global emission reductions while at the same time supporting development in less affluent regions. The climate imperative calls for steep domestic reductions in wealthier nations and historical responsibility to reduce emissions, as well as significant financial flows to support the low-carbon transition in nations lacking capacity.

Offset programs can also tap mitigation opportunities from sources, such as on-farm manure management, that are otherwise difficult to address through traditional policy mechanisms. In so doing, offset markets can develop the knowledge and institutional capacity needed to transform management and investment practices or to set the stage for more comprehensive strategies in the longer term. To maximize their effectiveness, offsets will need to be rigorous, regulated and defined broadly to support local programs and policies, not just individual projects.

Analysis of experience with current offset markets and standards can offer important insights and lessons for participants and designers of offset programs

Apart from a few reviews of the voluntary carbon market (Hamilton et al, 2007; Trexler, 2007; Kollmuss et al, 2008), there is a general lack of publicly available reports that compile and compare the key features of the broad array of mandatory and voluntary offset programs. Much of the available literature on offsets focuses on individual programs or on specific aspects of the offset market, such as economic impacts, accounting protocols and co-benefits. (The World Bank's annual *State of the Carbon Market* series (Capoor and Ambrosi, 2008) provides an excellent, albeit summary review of the broad trends and figures in the carbon market generally, and the offsets market specifically. Some proprietary publications, such as *Point Carbon*, provide ongoing assessments of offset market activities.) Numerous leading actors in offset markets that we interviewed suggested that a general offset program review is both currently lacking and much needed.

To fill this gap, we have designed a systematic review of domestic and international offset programs. Our intended audience includes parties interested and involved in the development of mandatory compliance systems and of voluntary offset programs and standards. The goal of this review is to provide an analysis of the most influential offset programs and activities, to reflect on lessons learned, and thus to inform participants and designers of current and future offset programs. Our intention is to stay up-to-date with ongoing developments and to make this information more accessible (see our website at www.co2offsetresearch.org).

This book reviews offset programs that meet one or more of the following criteria:

- a significant volume of credit transactions occurring or anticipated;
- an established set of rules or protocols; and
- path-breaking, novel or otherwise notable initiatives or important lessons learned.

Recent trends

The landscape of domestic and international project-based emission reduction or 'offset' programs is evolving rapidly. While the global economic slump dampened activity in 2008, the global value of primary offset transactions had grown to US$7.2 billion in 2008, representing more than ten-fold growth from 2004 levels (Capoor and Ambrosi, 2009). European governments and companies continue to be major buyers of both Kyoto and voluntary offsets. While these programs and players are likely to continue to dominate the global offset market for some time, recent developments suggest that this pattern may be starting to shift, particularly in North America.

In July 2007, Alberta launched an offset system for its regulated large GHG emitters, and in March 2008 the Canadian Government launched its design for a federal offset program. In the US, the eastern states' Regional Greenhouse Gas Initiative (RGGI) formally began in January 2009 as North America's first regional GHG cap-and-trade market with the first government-regulated offset program in the US. In September 2008 and June 2009, respectively, the Western Climate Initiative (WCI) and Midwestern Accord released design recommendations for regional emission trading systems, with the broadest coverage of any cap-and-trade system to date. These initiatives, which encompass 70 per cent of Canada's population and half of the US's, are actively developing their own offset programs. These initiatives each cover nearly 90 per cent of regional emissions by encompassing the residential, commercial, industrial and transportation sectors in addition to electricity.

As we go to press, the biggest news is the passage of cap-and-trade legislation by the US House of Representatives, which foreshadows a massive expansion of offset market activity. The American Climate and Energy Security Act (ACESA) establishes emission targets of 17 per cent below 2005 levels in 2020, and 83 per cent below 2005 by 2050, with offsets as the most prominent mechanism for containing costs of compliance. The bill allows for covered emitters to use up to 2 billion tons in domestic and international offsets for compliance each year. Were the full 2 billion tons of offsets to be used, which is unlikely for some time, it would require a four-fold increase in the global volume of offset created as compared with current levels. Accordingly to modelling projections (Congressional Budget Office, 2009), this increase would come largely from offset projects that reduce deforestation and degradation in developing countries, a project type yet to be established in existing carbon markets and one which faces considerable barriers. The US Environmental Protection Agency (EPA) projects that under ACESA the value of offsets would be in the order of US$20 billion per year in 2020 (1.2 billion tCO$_2$e (tons of CO$_2$ equivalent) at \$17/tCO$_2$e) and US\$40 billion by 2030 (1.4 billion tons at \$27/tCO$_2$e) (US EPA, 2009c).

The fate of US cap-and-trade legislation and the outcome of international climate negotiations, together with the timing of a global economic recovery, appear from today's perspective to be the major uncertainties that will drive offset markets in the years to come.

Voluntary market offset programs, as described in this book, could prove influential in the design of a federal US offset market, as well as in the reform of Clean Development Mechanism (CDM) and Joint Implementation (JI). Private companies are increasing their investment in the voluntary market in anticipation that voluntary offsets will have greater value in future mandatory systems, but surveys suggest that corporate social responsibility and public relations are still the main drivers of voluntary offset purchases today (Hamilton et al, 2009). Some predict that the voluntary market could rival today's CDM market within five years, with over half of this activity in the US (ICF International, 2006 and Trexler, 2007 as cited in Broekhoff, 2007a). The lack of common rules, transparent procedures and overall rigour in the voluntary market has led to increasing concerns about the credibility of the offset market. With legitimacy of carbon offset projects more frequently debated, we are currently seeing the greater use and development of recognized offset standards, third-party verification and offset registries.

Note to readers

As you review the material in this report, bear in mind that:

- Program reviews are organized by program type. However, the order of program reviews within each program type (e.g. mandatory cap-and-trade systems) has no implications.
- Some program reviews contain more limited discussion of the lessons learned (selected issues). It is our aim to provide a consistent level of detail and information across all program reviews; however, this is challenged by the imbalance in the published literature in favour of a select number of offset programs as well as the fact that experience and attention is concentrated in a handful of programs. This is especially the case for the CDM, which as the most mature and dominant offset program operating in the carbon market has been reviewed by many more publications than any other program. This is reflected in the CDM program review in this report, which has a more in-depth selected issues section than exists for any of the other programs.
- Offset programs and standards are quickly evolving. For up-to-date information on the programs detailed in this book, please visit our website: www.co2offsetresearch.org

2
A Comparison of Offset Programs

Rising concern over the threat of climate change has led to an expanding number of mandatory and voluntary greenhouse gas (GHG) emission reduction programs and activities, of which offsets are a common feature.

Every mandatory GHG emission trading system to date has allowed for the use of offsets by regulated entities to meet their compliance obligations. Mandatory compliance regimes such as the Kyoto Protocol, the European Union Emission Trading System (EU ETS) and, to a lesser extent, regional programs in Australia, the US and Canada have been the principal drivers in the creation of project-based emission reduction offsets. These regimes and programs are responsible for well over 90 per cent of the financial transactions and offsets generated to date. Most of the transactions and offsets have been generated from projects in developing countries through the Clean Development Mechanism (CDM).

The design features of, and the experience and lessons learned from, the CDM are thus of central importance to participants in and designers of current and future offset programs. Although dominant, however, the CDM is not by any means the only program to learn from.

Chapter 2 provides a summary comparison of the key features of the programs reviewed in detail in the main body of the book. The book reviews the key design elements and experience of over 27 major programs and efforts to create and guide offset markets across the world: mandatory compliance programs that drive the demand for offsets; offset programs designed for this mandatory compliance market; voluntary compliance and emission trading programs; and 12 different voluntary offset protocols and standards.

The five tables in Chapter 2 compare the programs' key features and help the reader to assess how they differ in terms of market size and scope, project eligibility, additionality and quantification procedures, and project approval processes, program administration and authority. Each table is introduced with a brief overview and comments on some of the key features.

General features of offset programs

Table 2.1 summarizes the general features of offset programs, including the regional scope, type of program and the start of program.

Mandatory systems require regulated emission sources, by national, regional or provincial law, to achieve compliance with GHG emission reduction requirements. For regulated emission sources, offsets serve as an alternative compliance mechanism to allowances or direct emission reductions that emission sources can use to meet these requirements. In most cases, these sources are regulated under cap-and-trade emission trading regimes, such as the Regional Greenhouse Gas Initiative (RGGI) or the EU ETS.

The two international mandatory project-based offset mechanisms established under the Kyoto Protocol, the CDM and JI, were established in 2001 and began issuing registered offsets in 2005. The participants in the EU ETS, the governments of the EU member states and the Japanese Government and industry are the principal buyers of CDM and JI offsets. The remaining mandatory programs that use offsets are located in North America and Australia. Many of these programs only recently got under way or are still under development. A notable exception is the New South Wales Greenhouse Gas Abatement Scheme (NSW GGAS), which has operated since 2003.

The voluntary offset market includes a wide range of programs, entities, standards and protocols. Voluntary emission reduction programs such as EPA's Climate Leaders and the Chicago Climate Exchange (CCX) set participating entities' emission targets, which can partly be met through offsets certified through their respective protocols.

Offsets generated through voluntary markets, known as Verified or Voluntary Emissions Reductions (VERs), have been promoted as an opportunity for experimentation and innovation. They have the advantage of generally lower transaction costs than offsets generated for use in mandatory compliance programs. However, the lack of quality control – and the resulting attention attracted by substandard offset credits in the voluntary market – has generated concern from the wider offset market.

In response, carbon market actors along with key business and environmental interests have launched several efforts to create standards and protocols to improve the quality and credibility of voluntary offsets. These standards and protocols differ significantly in their goals and the services provided. At one end are complete standards that provide rules and administrative bodies for accounting, quantification, monitoring, verification, certification and registration of offsets. These fully fledged standards tend to build on existing rules and procedures in compliance markets, most notably the CDM. These standards are designed to provide offset providers with quality assurance certification for their products and offset consumers with greater transparency and confidence in the credibility and integrity of certified offsets.

At the other end are offset protocols that are more limited in scope, such as the International Organization for Standardization (ISO) standard 14064 and the World Resources Institute (WRI) GHG Protocol for Project Accounting. These protocols provide common definitions, accounting frameworks and quantification options that can be adopted or adapted by individual offset programs or standards. In this sense, these protocols can be viewed as building blocks for the development of offset standards and programs. There are other institutions, standards and criteria that provide a mix of services for designing, screening, certifying or registering offsets. The Green-e Climate Program audits and certifies carbon offset retailers and ensures that their marketing claims are truthful. Other standards, such as the Climate, Community and Biodiversity Standards provide design criteria to ensure robust project design and, particularly in this case, local community and biodiversity benefits.

The proliferation of standards, protocols and other programs reflects the significant flux and experimentation in today's voluntary offset market. Some consolidation of standards may occur in future years. At the same time, because of the differing objectives of many voluntary market participants, especially with respect to the local impacts and benefits of offset projects, multiple standards and screens are likely to remain lasting features of the voluntary market.

Table 2.1   *General features of offset programs*

Name of program	Regional scope	Type of program	Start of program
International offset mechanisms			
Clean Development Mechanism	International (covers all countries that have ratified the Kyoto Protocol)	Project-based offset mechanism under the Kyoto Protocol	General rules established in 2001, first offset issued in 2005
Joint Implementation	Annex-1 parties to the Kyoto Protocol	Project-based offset mechanism under the Kyoto Protocol	General rules established in 2001
Offset features of mandatory cap-and-trade systems			
European Union Emission Trading System	27 EU member states, as well as Norway, Iceland and Liechtenstein	Mandatory cap-and-trade program with offsets as a limited compliance mechanism	Started in 2005
Regional Greenhouse Gas Initiative	Northeast US states: CT, DE, ME, NH, NJ, NY, VT, MA, RI and MD	Regional cap-and-trade with offsets as limited compliance mechanism	Started in 2009
Western Climate Initiative	Western states (AZ, CA, MT, NM, OR, UT, and WA) and Canadian provinces (BC, MB), Ontario and Quebec	Under development. Regional cap-and-trade system with offsets as potential compliance mechanism	Start expected in 2012
Midwest Greenhouse Gas Reduction Accord	6 Midwest US states (IA, IL, KS, MI, MN, WI) and one Canadian province (Manitoba)	Under development. Regional cap-and-trade system with offsets as potential compliance mechanism	Start expected in 2012
Canada's Offset System for Greenhouse Gases	Canada	Under development. National emission reduction targets with offsets as proposed compliance mechanism	Under development

Table 2.1   *Contd.*

Name of program	Regional scope	Type of program	Start of program
Australian Carbon Pollution Abatement Scheme	Australia	Under development. National cap-and-trade system proposed with offsets as potential compliance mechanism	Start expected by 2010
New South Wales Greenhouse Gas Reduction Scheme	NSW, Australia	State per capita-based cap-and-trade system with offsets as unlimited compliance mechanism	Started in January 2003
Offset features of mandatory cap-and-trade systems			
Chicago Climate Exchange	Originally only in the US but has been expanded. International membership now possible	Voluntary compliance cap-and-trade with offsets as unlimited compliance mechanism	Launched in 2002
Offset features of other GHG systems			
Alberta Offset System	Canadian province of Alberta	Provincial intensity-based emission regulations allow for unlimited offsets as a compliance option	Started in July 2007
State power plant rules (OR, WA, MA)	Oregon	Legislated emission standard	OR: Started in 1997
	Washington	Legislated emission standard	WA: Started in 2003
	Massachusetts	State cap with offsets as limited compliance mechanism	MA: Started in 2006
British Columbia Emission Offset Regulation	British Columbia	Provincial compliance program for the public sector with offsets as unlimited compliance mechanism	Started in 2008

Table 2.1   *Contd.*

Name of program	Regional scope	Type of program	Start of program
Climate Leaders	Primarily US	Voluntary compliance program with offsets as unlimited compliance mechanism	Launched in 2002
GHG accounting protocols			
WBCSD/WRI GHG Protocol for Project Accounting	Not defined	GHG project accounting protocol	Published in 2005
ISO 14064–2	Not defined	GHG project accounting protocol	Launched in 2006
Voluntary standards for offset projects and retailers			
Climate Action Reserve	US (mainly California)	Full-fledged voluntary GHG offset project standard	Active since 2008 (its predecessor, the California Climate Action Registry (CCAR), was established in 2002)
Gold Standard	International	Full-fledged voluntary GHG offset project standard	Launched in 2003
Voluntary Carbon Standard 2007	International	Full-fledged voluntary GHG offset project standard	VCS Version 1 launched in 2006
VER+	International	Full-fledged voluntary GHG offset project standard	Launched in 2007
American Carbon Registry	International	Voluntary GHG offset project standard	Active since 2008 (its predecessor, the GHG Registry, was launched in 1997)
Climate Community and Biodiversity Standards	International	GHG offset design project for standard biosequestration projects with focus on co-benefits	Launched in 2005

Table 2.1   *Contd.*

Name of program	Regional scope	Type of program	Start of program
Plan Vivo	Developing countries	Voluntary GHG offset project standard with focus on co-benefits	First project started in 1994
Social Carbon Methodology	Developing countries (currently Brazil only)	GHG offset project design standard with focus on co-benefits	First project started in 1998
Green-e Climate Protocol for Renewable Energy	US	Voluntary GHG offset project design standard for renewable energy projects	Launched in 2007
Green-e Climate Program	US focus/ International	Voluntary certification program for retailers	Launched in 2007
Carbon finance funds			
World Bank Carbon Finance Funds	International	Offset Fund	Launched in 2000

Market size and scope

The landscape of domestic and international project-based emission reduction or offset programs is evolving rapidly. While the global economic slump dampened activity in 2008, the global value of primary offset transactions had grown to US$7.2 billion in 2008, representing more than ten-fold growth from 2004 levels (see growth in CDM trading volumes, Figure 2.1). Primary transactions represent the flow of new project-based emission reductions to the market. The secondary market, which involves the resale of offset commodities, as well as options, futures and spot transactions, grew by 350 per cent in 2008 to over US$25 billion, indicative of the growing sophistication and maturity of this market (Capoor and Ambrosi, 2009).

This large growth has been due largely to the main offset mechanisms of the Kyoto Protocol: principally, the CDM and to a much lesser extent, JI. The CDM, which enables the financing of offset projects in developing countries, accounts for 90 per cent of offset project transaction volumes and value. JI, the mechanism supporting offset projects within countries that are parties to the Kyoto Protocol, accounts for another 5 per cent. The voluntary offset market accounted for the remaining 5 per cent. In contrast to declines in primary transactions for both JI and CDM, the voluntary market continued to post double-digit growth in 2008.

Despite the continued growth of the carbon market, the ultimate fate of the offset market is far from clear. If and when project types, sectors and countries become increasingly covered by emission caps or other regulations, the market for offsets could

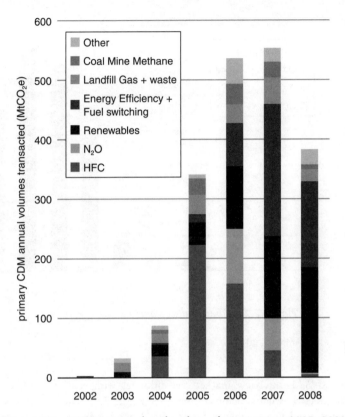

Figure 2.1 *CDM: Annual trade volumes by project type 2002–2008*

Source: Capoor and Ambrosi, 2009.

begin to decline as allowance allocation and trading or other policy instruments take on a greater role. It will depend on the role policy makers assign to offsets in an efficient, equitable and effective policy regime that comprehensively addresses the climate change challenge.

Figure 2.2 compares the market size and scope of various offset programs and providers, to the extent that information could be compiled. Compiling estimates of the size or volume of the offset market is challenging because metrics vary and information is often proprietary, especially within the voluntary market. Some figures for offset market activity represent total offset transactions in a given year, including both primary (by original offset providers) and secondary (resold offsets) transactions, some are for primary transactions alone, while others represent the total offsets registered or certified (which may include expected offsets generated in future years) or issued during a given year. The resulting estimates of the 'size of the CDM market' can thus vary by as much as an order of magnitude. For example, slightly over 100 million Certified Emission Reductions (CERs) have been issued to date, while other figures refer to the 1.2–2.6 billion CERs registered and in the 'pipeline', that is, that could be issued cumulatively by 2012 if projects registered, and those under development, yield credits as expected.

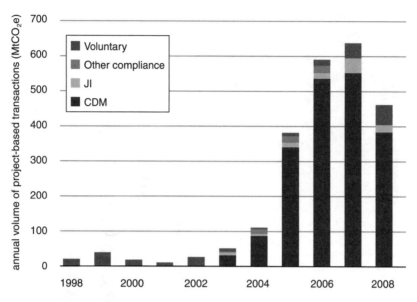

Figure 2.2 *Annual offset trades by type of market*

Source: Capoor and Ambrosi, 2009.

Readers should thus view market size estimates with caution, and with careful attention to precisely what is being counted (see Figure 2.2). Those interested in more detailed and up-to-date assessments should consult market analyst publications such as those produced by *Point Carbon, New Carbon Finance* and *Ecosystem Marketplace*, as well as the annual *State of the Carbon Market* review published by the World Bank.

Compliance (mandatory) markets

Only offsets generated from the CDM and JI project-based mechanisms are eligible for compliance under the EU ETS and for compliance with the Kyoto Protocol, which makes such offsets by far the largest component of the compliance offset market. Demand from the EU ETS, as the largest mandatory cap-and-trade system, has dominated the purchasing of offsets in recent years. European buyers account for over 80 per cent of CDM and JI purchases to date (Capoor and Ambrosi, 2009).

Voluntary markets

Estimates of the size of the voluntary offset market vary widely and sales information from retail offset providers can be difficult to track. For example, according to Hamilton et al, 2009 the global voluntary market grew by 87 per cent in 2008 to 123MmtCO$_2$e. The Chicago Climate Exchange accounted for 56 per cent of these voluntary transactions and over-the-counter purchases made up the remaining 44 per cent. The total value of the voluntary market in 2008 was over US$700 million (Hamilton et al, 2009). The

Table 2.2 *Market size and scope*

Name of program	Tradable unit name and acronym	Participants/ buyers	Unit of measurement	ERs to date (Mmtco₂e)*	Projected ERs by 2012 (Mmtco₂e)*	Indicative prices (US$/metric ton)[1]
International offset mechanisms						
Clean Development Mechanism	Certified Emission Reduction (CER)	Public and private entities within the jurisdiction of Kyoto Protocol member countries; other entities may use/retire them under voluntary offset programs	metric	286 (5/09)	>2,900	2008 average price US$16.78 (€11.46) 16% increase over 2007 prices

Primary and secondary CER prices converged in 2009[2] |
| Joint Implementation | Emissions Reduction Unit (ERU) | Same as CDM | metric | 1.2 (7/09) | 342 | 2008: average ERU price US$14.56 (€9.95)[2] |
| *Offset features of mandatory cap-and-trade systems* | | | | | | |
| European Union Emission Trading System | EU Allowances (EUA) and CERs and ERUs | Public and private entities within the jurisdiction of the EU ETS | metric | N/A | N/A | EUAs in 2008/9 highly volatile: 8/08: €28.73; 2/09: €7.96 2009 average: €10–15[2]

For offset prices, see CDM and JI |

Table 2.2 *Contd.*

Name of program	Tradable unit name and acronym	Participants/ buyers	Unit of measurement	ERs to date (Mmtco$_2$e)*	Projected ERs by 2012 (Mmtco$_2$e)*	Indicative prices (US$/metric ton)[1]
Regional Greenhouse Gas Initiative	RGGI Allowances (RGGA) and CO$_2$ Offset Allowances	Compliance entities in the region	short	n.d.	n.d.	RGGA: US$3.90 per short tCO$_2$e[2] n.d. for offset prices
Western Climate Initiative	Under development	Under development. Expected to be compliance entities in the region	Not yet specified	n.d.	n.d.	n.d.
Midwest Greenhouse Gas Reduction Accord	Under development	Under development. Expected to be compliance entities in the region	Not yet specified	n.d	n.d.	n.d.
Canada's Offset System for Greenhouse Gases	Offset credit	Compliance entities in the nation and/or for the voluntary market	metric	n.d.	n.d.	n.d.
Australian Carbon Pollution Abatement Scheme	Under development	Under development. Expected to be compliance entities in the nation	metric	n.d.	n.d.	Prime Minister Rudd announced 4 May 2009 AU would set fixed allowance price of AU$10 (about US$7)

Table 2.2 *Contd.*

Name of program	Tradable unit name and acronym	Participants/ buyers	Unit of measurement	ERs to date (Mmtco$_2$e)*	Projected ERs by 2012 (Mmtco$_2$e)*	Indicative prices (US$/metric ton)[1]
						for first year of operation (2011)[2]
New South Wales Greenhouse Gas Reduction Scheme	NSW GHG Abatement Certificates (NGACs)	Compliance and elective entities in the state	metric	90 (5/09)	n.d.	Prices declined from AU$7–8 autumn 08 to AU$3 spring 09[2]
Offset features of voluntary cap-and-trade systems						
Chicago Climate Exchange	Carbon Financial Instruments (CFI)#	CCX members and non-members such as offset brokers	metric	registered 60 (3/09)	n.d.	CFI prices: 2008 average: US$4[5] 5/08:US$7.00 9/08: US$2[6]/09: US$0.9–1.2[3]
Offset features of other GHG systems						
Alberta Offset Exchange	Alberta-based offset credit	Compliance entities in the province	metric	2.75 (3/09)	n.d.	n.d.
State power plant rules (OR, WA, MA)	Oregon: CO$_2$ offsets	Compliance entities in the state	short	OR: 1.5	n.d.	OR: US$1.40
	Washington: Carbon credits					WA: US$1.60

Table 2.2 *Contd.*

Name of program	Tradable unit name and acronym	Participants/ buyers	Unit of measurement	ERs to date (Mmtco₂e)*	Projected ERs by 2012 (Mmtco₂e)*	Indicative prices (US$/metric ton)[1]
	Massachusetts: GHG Credits					MA: US$5
British Columbia Emission Offset Regulation	Emission reductions and removals	Provincial public sector organizations	metric	0	0.3 (until 2014)	n.d.
Climate Leaders	External GHG reductions	Climate Leaders partners	metric	n.d.	n.d.	N/A
GHG accounting protocols						
WBCSD/WRI GHG Protocol for Project Accounting	N/A	N/A	N/A	N/A	N/A	N/A
ISO 14064-2	N/A	N/A	N/A	N/A	N/A	N/A
Voluntary standards for offset projects and retailers						
Climate Action Reserve	Climate Reserve Tonnes (CRTs) 'Carrot'	Individuals, nonprofit organizations, government agencies and businesses	metric	6/09: 75 total projects, including 51 registered, 9 listed (accepted by the Reserve as eligible)	N/A	CRT prices 2008/09: US$5.00–14.00[2] 2008 average: US$8.9[5]

Table 2.2 Contd.

Name of program	Tradable unit name and acronym	Participants/buyers	Unit of measurement	ERs to date (Mmtco₂e)*	Projected ERs by 2012 (Mmtco₂e)*	Indicative prices (US$/metric ton)[1]
Gold Standard	GS CER and GS VER	Offset retailers, providers, individuals, organizations and businesses	metric	Retired VER credits as of 3/09: 0.45MmtCO₂e	n.d.	Average premium GS VERs: 20–100% above comparable VERs GS; CERs: 5–25% above regular CERs 2008 average: US$14.4[5] 4/09 price GS VER: €8.38 (07/08 vintage); €5.75 (future vintages)[4]
Voluntary Carbon Standard 2007	Voluntary Carbon Unit (VCU)	Voluntary offset retailers and providers, individuals, organizations and businesses	metric	n.d.	10–20	2008 average: US$5.5# 4/09 price VCU: €2.75 (07/08 vintage, industrial) – €4 (future vintages, renewables)[2]
VER+	VER	Voluntary offset retailers and providers, organizations and businesses	metric	n.d.	n.d.	2008 average: US$5.8[5]

Table 2.2 *Contd.*

Name of program	Tradable unit name and acronym	Participants/ buyers	Unit of measurement	ERs to date (Mmtco$_2$e)*	Projected ERs by 2012 (Mmtco$_2$e)*	Indicative prices (US$/metric ton)[1]
						4/09 price VER+: €3.25 (07/08 vintage)[2]
American Carbon Registry	Emission Reduction Tons (ERTs)	Corporate pre-compliance buyers, hedge funds, carbon retailers and nonprofits	metric	30 (1997–2008)	n.d.	2008 average: US$3.8[5]
Climate Community and Biodiversity Standards	N/A	Individuals, nonprofit organizations, and businesses	metric	n.d.	n.d.	2008 average: US$9[5]
Plan Vivo	Plan Vivo Certificates	Individuals, nonprofit organizations, and businesses	metric	n.d.	n.d.	2008 average: US$5.6[5]
Social Carbon Methodology		Individuals, nonprofit organizations, and businesses	metric	n.d.	n.d.	2008 average: US$7.4[5]
Green-e Climate Protocol for Renewable Energy	VER	Offset retailers, individuals, organizations and businesses	metric	n.d.	n.d.	n.d.

Table 2.2 *Contd.*

Name of program	Tradable unit name and acronym	Participants/ buyers	Unit of measurement	ERs to date (Mmtco₂e)*	Projected ERs by 2012 (Mmtco₂e)*	Indicative prices (US$/metric ton)[1]
Green-e Climate Program	VER and CER	Carbon offset retailers	(varies by program certified)	n.d.	n.d.	Varies by offset retailer
Carbon finance funds						
World Bank Carbon Finance Funds	CER and ERU	Government agencies and private sector companies	metric	6.9	300	n.d.

Notes: *Values in these columns are estimates of cumulative ERs generated. Refer to sections for discussion. Estimates may not be fully comparable.

[1]Indicative prices are from 2008 and 2009; when available several sources are listed; prices may fluctuate significantly, especially those linked to trading markets.

[2]Capoor and Ambrosi, 2009.

[3]CCX Report June 09 reference.

[4]*Carbon Finance*, April 2009.

[5]Hamilton et al, 2009

n.d. no data readily available.

N/A not applicable.

Units are denominated in 100 metric tons of CO₂.

World Bank on the other hand reported that the voluntary market in 2008 grew by only 26 per cent to 54MmtCO$_2$e, with a reported value of a little under US$400 million (Capoor and Ambrosi, 2009). It is unclear why the reported numbers differ so much.

Offset prices

Offset prices tend to vary based on the project type, its location, the market demand and the stringency of the offset program requirements. Offset prices in the compliance market are driven primarily by the supply of and demand for offsets and allowances. Demand drives prices for offsets. It is therefore not surprising that offsets for the mandatory market fetch considerably higher prices than voluntary offsets. This is most apparent when comparing the price of CDM offset credits with those available on the voluntary offset market, as shown in Table 2.2.

These price estimates should be viewed with caution, since they represent only a brief snapshot of an often volatile market. Nonetheless, they illustrate that prices vary by an order of magnitude depending on the program, its requirements and, perhaps most importantly, the markets in which the offsets are sold. For example, prices for CDM and JI offsets are linked to the broader markets for EU ETS and Kyoto allowances. Depending on the extent to which delivery of CERs and JI Emission Reduction Units (ERUs) is guaranteed, they can garner upwards of 100 per cent of the trading price of EU allowances. Even though in principle CERs, ERUs and EU allowances are fully fungible, countries have 'supplementarity' limits on the amount of CERs and ERUs they can purchase to meet their compliance obligation. To the extent that these limits are expected to be binding, and thus that the supply of CERs and ERUs is expected to exceed allowable demand under the supplementarity limits, CERs and ERUs are expected to trade for prices lower than allowances. It is not clear whether this will occur in the period to 2012.

Prices for voluntary offset credits vary significantly based on the standards used, project types, project locations, offset quality, delivery guarantees and contract terms. No readily available metrics currently exist for consumers to determine either how the price of offset credits sold in the voluntary market is determined, or the role the offset price has on the quality of the offset purchased.

Offset project eligibility

Table 2.3 shows offset eligibility requirements for each offset system or program. These requirements reflect the specific context and objectives of each system. Restrictions on project location or type are usually defined so as to direct offset investments to favoured regions, project types or technologies. Some offset programs and standards also include environmental and social objectives – commonly referred to as co-benefits or secondary benefits – as project eligibility criteria.

In general, offset programs tend to focus on either encouraging regional investment in developed nations or supporting sustainable development and providing financial flows to developing economies. While sustainable development and technology transfer to developing countries was an explicit design goal of the CDM and the Kyoto Protocol, many of the regional and provincial mandatory compliance programs outside the Kyoto Protocol prefer to maintain benefits and build support through investment in local or regional communities and enterprises.

Project location

Table 2.3 shows the eligible project locations but not the distribution of offset project activities to date under each program. The distribution of project locations and project types reflects not only where market opportunities lie (e.g. the supply of low-cost emission reductions), but also the capacity of national and local institutions to engage in the offset market, as well as the transaction costs and other barriers they may face. For instance, in the CDM 84 per cent of offset project transactions in 2008 were for projects located in China, but only 4 per cent in India, 5 per cent in Latin America, 2 per cent in Africa and 4 per cent in the rest of Asia (Capoor and Ambrosi, 2009). China has an increasingly well-developed infrastructure for developing and approving offset projects and also has abundant low-cost opportunities to reduce emissions of so-called high global warming impact 'industrial gas', in particular HFC-23 and nitrous oxide (N_2O) produced as the unwanted by-products of refrigerant and chemical manufacturing, respectively. In recent years, China increasingly has added renewable energy projects to its CDM portfolio: of the 800 Chinese projects entered in the CDM pipeline since January 2008, the largest volumes of annual emission reductions have come from hydro and wind projects. Yet, wind and hydro projects in China face increasing scrutiny over their additionality claims.

In the voluntary market, 45 per cent of all offsets sold in 2008 originated from projects located in Asia and 28 per cent from projects located in North America (Hamilton et al, 2009).

Project type

Whereas offsets from industrial gas projects have dominated the CER market up until 2006, their market share has dropped significantly in 2007 and are now virtually absent from the primary markets. With 45 per cent of CER volumes, renewable energy is currently the largest project type in the CDM, followed by energy and fuel switching (37 per cent) (see Figure 2.3). Less common offset project types include, among others, methane capture and biological carbon sequestration – ranging from forestry and agricultural activities to avoided land-use change (Capoor and Ambrosi, 2009).

In the voluntary market (excluding CCX transactions), offsets from renewable energy projects also dominated the market in 2008 with over half the market share, followed by landfill methane (16 per cent) and biosequestration projects (16 per cent) (see Figure 2.4) (Hamilton et al, 2009).

Bottom-up or top-down approaches

In addition to the relative cost of implementing projects, the availability of program-approved methodologies for quantifying emission reductions or removals is a key determinant of the mix of project types in the market today. In general, offset programs

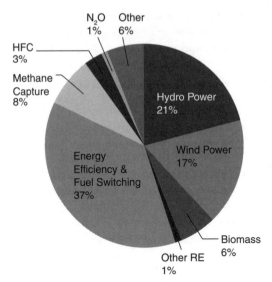

Figure 2.3 *CDM market: Total volume traded in 2008: 552MtCO₂e*

Source: Capoor and Ambrosi, 2009.

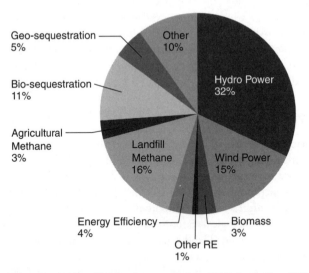

Figure 2.4 *Voluntary market: Total volume traded in 2008 (excluding CCX): 54MtCO₂*

Source: Hamilton et al, 2009.

have developed two different approaches to determining offset project-type eligibility. At one end is the bottom-up approach used under the CDM, where project types are considered, as submitted by the project developers, and approved if deemed adequate by the administrative body or program authority (CDM Executive Board, CDM EB). At the other end is a top-down approach, such as that taken by RGGI, which spelled out in its 'Memorandum Of Understanding and Model Rule' precisely which project types would be eligible, and which methodologies applicable, from the outset of the project (although other project types would be considered).

Project start date

The project start dates listed in Table 2.3 refer to the cut-off date for project commencement. In principle, a project type that has commenced prior to the start date would be considered ineligible, although precise definitions of start-up vary among programs. The typical rationale for setting a start date is to help to ensure that offset programs actually lead to a project happening, that is, that they are additional. Therefore, the project start date is generally linked to the timing of the launch of the overall offset program. The start dates of some programs, such as the CCX, pre-date the start of the offset program launch and reflect the grandfathering of offset credits created through other certification programs (e.g. Renewable Energy Credits (RECs)).

Additionality and quantification procedures

Table 2.4 shows the different approaches to additionality assessment and quantification procedures across various offset programs.

The design elements most fundamental to ensuring that offset projects are 'real' and 'quantifiable' have also been the most contentious. In theory, additionality answers a very simple question: 'Would the activity have occurred, holding all else constant, if the activity were not implemented as an offset project?' In practice, however, determining whether an offset is 'real' through additionality requirements presents a significant design challenge. Quantification of an offset project's GHG benefits relies on the development of a baseline scenario, a *hypothetical* scenario of emissions that would have occurred had the activity *not* been implemented as an offset project. By definition, this baseline scenario will never occur; instead, the offset credits generated from a project are quantified with incomplete certainty, based on the difference in emissions between the offset project and the baseline scenario.

Offset programs and standards differ in their overall approaches to additionality and quantification procedures. Top-down programs tend to provide specific detailed accounting rules upfront, while bottom-up programs tend to offer only general guidelines for project GHG accounting and instead evaluate projects on a case-by-case basis.

Project-based versus standardized additionality testing

There are two broad design approaches to evaluating additionality and the closely linked process of determining baselines: *project-specific* and *standardized* (often called 'performance standards'). The project-specific approach involves the evaluation of individual projects based on one or more additionality tests. These project-specific additionality tests are commonly based on the 'CDM additionality tool' (see Figure 2.5), which evaluates whether the offset project is dependent on offset project revenue ('investment test') or whether it has overcome significant implementation barriers ('barriers test'). In addition, the CDM tool requires that the technology or practice used by the project must not be in common use ('common practice test'). Most programs also require projects to be 'regulatory surplus', that is, that they exceed existing legal requirements.

Due in part to concerns regarding the partly subjective nature of some project-based methods, several offset programs and protocols incorporate or rely exclusively on standardized methods to assess additionality. Standardized methods include, among others, performance thresholds (emission rates or other characteristics defined based on similar activities) and clearly defined common practice tests (e.g. lower than a specified level of market penetration for similar activities). Standardized approaches have the advantage of streamlining the process and increasing transparency. The disadvantage of standardized approaches is that they are less flexible and do not allow site-specific conditions to be taken into account. This means, the broader these standardized project protocols are defined (e.g. geographic scope) the more generalized the conditions they apply will be (e.g. forestry conditions in California can expected to be quite distinct from forestry conditions that are generalized for the whole of the US). Also, depending on how rigorous the parameters of standardized protocols are, they may allow a non-trivial number of free-riders (non-additional offsets) to enter the offset project stream.

Climate Leaders, Climate Action Registry (CAR), CCX, RGGI and NSW GGAS are among the programs and protocols that rely more heavily on standardized approaches. The GHG Protocol for Project Accounting and ISO 14064 standards provide guidelines for both approaches.

Investment analysis

Revenue from the carbon offsets must be a primary driver for project implementation; *or*

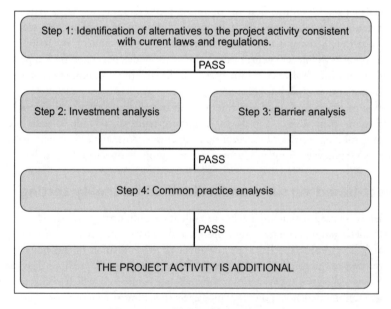

Figure 2.5 *CDM additionality tool*

Table 2.3 *Offset project eligibility*

Name of program	Eligible project locations	Eligible project types	Project start date
International offset mechanisms			
Clean Development Mechanism	Developing (non-Annex-I) countries where Designated National Authorities (DNAs) are established	All eligible except nuclear energy, new hydrochlorofluorocarbon (HCFC)-22 facilities or avoided deforestation	1 January 2000
Joint Implementation	Annex-I countries that are signatories to the Kyoto Protocol with capped emissions	Same as CDM plus forest management, cropland management and grazing management, ineligible under JI CDM are eligible under JI	1 January 2000
Offset features of mandatory cap-and-trade systems			
European Union Emission Trading System	CDM and JI restrictions apply	All eligible except nuclear energy, new HCFC-22 facilities and LULUCF	CDM and JI requirements apply
Regional Greenhouse Gas Initiative	Within RGGI participating states or other approved jurisdictions; if emission allowances exceed the Stage 2 trigger price (US$10), the eligible project location is expanded to include offsets from any governmental mandatory program outside the US with a tonnage limit on GHG emissions	Landfill methane capture and destruction; Reduction in emission of sulphur hexafluoride (SF_6) Sequestration of carbon due to afforestation; Avoided/reduced natural gas or oil combustion due to end-use energy efficiency in the building sector;	20 December 2005

Table 2.3 *Contd.*

Name of program	Eligible project locations	Eligible project types	Project start date
		Agricultural manure management operations;	
		Continued development of additional eligible project types expected	
Western Climate Initiative	WCI may approve certified offsets from projects in the US, Canada and Mexico; and CDM offsets, subject to added criteria or standards	Under development. Priorities for protocol investigation and development include: Agriculture (soil sequestration and manure management);	Under development
		Forestry (afforestation/reforestation, forest management, forest preservation/conservation, forest products); and	
		Waste management (landfill gas and wastewater management)	
Midwest Greenhouse Gas Reduction Accord	Not yet specified	Not yet specified	Not yet specified
Canada's Offset System for Greenhouse Gases	Canada	Project types to be reviewed for consideration include: afforestation, landfill gas capture	1 January 2006

Table 2.3 *Contd.*

Name of program	Eligible project locations	Eligible project types	Project start date
		and combustion, reduced or no tillage, wind, forest management, wastewater management and anaerobic biodigesters	
Australian Carbon Pollution Reduction Scheme	Under development. Design recommendations include both domestic and international offset projects	Under development. Design recommendations have prioritized the following project types: land use, forestry, wood products, avoided deforestation and carbon geosequestration	Under development
New South Wales Greenhouse Gas Reduction Scheme	Within New South Wales only, except for electricity generation projects, which can be within the Australian National Electricity Market	Additional electricity from low emission sources (including use of RECs as compliance units); Supply-side energy efficiency at existing power stations; Demand-side energy efficiency; Industrial on-site emission reductions; Forest carbon sequestration (afforestation or reforestation)	Electricity generation: 1 January 2003; Demand-side management: 1 January 2002 in NSW and 1 January 2004 in the Australian Capital Territory (ACT); Carbon sequestration: 1 January 2003

Table 2.3 *Contd.*

Name of program	Eligible project locations	Eligible project types	Project start date
Offset features of voluntary cap-and-trade systems			
Chicago Climate Exchange	Any country except European Union Emission Trading System member countries or Annex 1 countries that are signatories to the Kyoto Protocol	Energy efficiency and fuel switching, coal mine methane, agricultural methane, agricultural soil carbon, rangeland soil carbon, forestry carbon, landfill methane, ozone depleting substance (ODS) destruction and renewable energy	All projects except: 1 January 1999; Forestry projects: 1 January 1990; ODS projects: 1 January 2007
Offset features of other GHG systems			
Alberta Offset System	Alberta only	Acid gas injection, anaerobic wastewater treatment, beef feeding, beef-feed days, beef lifecycle, biofuel, biogas, biomass, compost, energy efficiency, enhanced oil recovery, streamlined enhanced oil recovery, landfill bioreactor, landfill gas, modal freight, non-incineration of thermal waste, pork, road rehabilitation, run-of-the-river electricity systems, solar electricity systems, tillage, waste heat recovery, streamlined waste heat recovery and wind-powered electricity systems	1 January 2002

Table 2.3 *Contd.*

Name of program	Eligible project locations	Eligible project types	Project start date
State power plant rules (OR, WA, MA)	Oregon: Any location	OR: No limitations or specifications	OR: Within 2 years of new project
	Washington: Not specified	WA: No limitations or specifications with approval	WA: 1 July 2004
	Massachusetts: Anywhere in the US or US coastal waters. Approved EUAs and CERs have no restrictions	MA: Any except nuclear power generation, underwater and underground sequestration	MA: 1 January 2006
British Columbia Emission Offset Regulation	British Columbia	No current restrictions	29 November 2007
Climate Leaders	Protocols applicable to US projects. Project developers that are able to develop a performance standard and country-specific data for an international project type can propose an international project	Current eligible projects: landfill methane collection and combustion; manure management (dairy or swine); captured methane end use; transit bus efficiency; industrial and commercial boilers; afforestation/reforestation projects. Additional project types eligible with protocol approval by US Environmental Protection Agency (EPA)	20 February 2002
GHG accounting protocols			
WBCSD/WRI GHG Protocol for Project Accounting	Not defined	Project guidance can be applied to any project type. Specific guidelines have been developed	Not defined

Table 2.3 *Contd.*

Name of program	Eligible project locations	Eligible project types	Project start date
		for grid-connected electricity and LULUCF projects	
ISO 14064	Not defined	Not defined	Not defined
Voluntary standards for offset projects and retailers			
Climate Action Reserve	US	Current eligible projects: conservation-based forest management; reforestation; avoided conversion; tree planting projects by municipalities, utilities and universities; livestock and landfill methane capture	Carbon sequestration: 1 January 1990; Methane capture: 1 January 2001
Gold Standard	All locations, except in countries with emission caps unless Gold Standard (GS) Verified Emission Reductions (VERs) are backed by permanently retiring Assigned Amount Units (AAUs)	Renewable energy and energy efficiency projects. Additional rules and requirements for hydropower larger than 20MW	1 January 2006
Voluntary Carbon Standard 2007	All locations, except in countries with emission caps unless Voluntary Carbon Units (VCUs) are backed by permanently retiring AAUs	All project types eligible with VCS-approved methodology, except projects from new industrial gas facilities	1 January 2002; Future restrictions: start date must be within 2 years of validation date
VER+	All locations, except in countries with emission caps unless VERs are backed by permanently retiring AAUs	VER+ accepts all project types except HFC projects, nuclear energy projects, large hydropower projects	1 January 2005. Retroactive crediting limited to 2 years before registration date

Table 2.3 *Contd.*

Name of program	Eligible project locations	Eligible project types	Project start date
		over 80MW. Hydro projects exceeding 20MW have to conform with World Commission on Dams rules. LULUCF projects, including reduced emissions from deforestation and degradation (REDD), are accepted if implemented with a buffer approach to address the risk of non-permanence	and will be phased out by the end of 2009
American Carbon Registry	No restrictions on project location	No restrictions. All projects that meet the ACR Technical Standard are eligible for registration	Non-LULUCF projects: 1 January 2000 LULUCF projects: 1 November 1997. Earlier start date evaluated on a case-by-case basis
Climate, Community and Biodiversity Standards	All locations	Biosequestration projects, including: primary or secondary forest conservation; reforestation or revegetation; agro-forestry plantations;	No restrictions on project start date

Table 2.3 *Contd.*

Name of program	Eligible project locations	Eligible project types	Project start date
		densification and enrichment planting;	
		introduction of new cultivation practices;	
		introduction of new timber harvesting and/or processing practices (e.g. reduced impact logging);	
		reduced tillage on cropland;	
		improved livestock management, etc.	
		actions to reduce emissions from deforestation and degradation (REDD)	
Plan Vivo	Developing countries	Biosequestration projects:	No restrictions on project start date
		forest restoration;	
		agroforestry/small plantations;	
		forest protection and management;	
		soil conservation and agricultural improvement	
Social Carbon Methodology	Developing countries	Eligible project types not defined	No restrictions on project start date
Green-e Climate Protocol for Renewable Energy	US	Renewable energy projects: wind, solar, hydropower (up to 5MW; additional specifications),	1 January 2005

Table 2.3 *Contd.*

Name of program	Eligible project locations	Eligible project types	Project start date
		geothermal, methane capture, ocean thermal, wave and tidal; new project types evaluated on case-by-case basis	
Green-e Climate Program	Specified by applicable offset standard	CDM standard requirements except LULUCF and hydropower >10MW excluded; all VCS 2007 except hydropower >10MW and additional native species requirement for carbon sequestration projects	1 January 2000
Carbon finance funds			
World Bank Carbon Finance Funds	No limitations beyond CDM and JI restrictions. Requirements can vary by fund	CDM/JI requirements apply. Additional limitations vary by fund	CDM/JI requirements apply

Barriers analysis

Project implementation must require the ability to exceed implementation barriers, such as local resistance, lack of know-how and institutional barriers; *and*

Common practice analysis

Projects must employ technology that is not commonly used.

Baselines and quantification procedures

Offset programs also differ significantly in how emission reductions or removals are quantified for individual offset projects. The expansion of offset programs in recent years has led to a proliferation of baseline and monitoring quantification protocols, which are now far too abundant for them all to be described in detail here. For example, the CDM includes over 70 approved methodologies for different project types. Table 2.4 therefore focuses on the process by which quantification protocols are developed. Approved methodologies include project-specific baselines developed from the bottom up by project participants and developers, the performance standard approach developed from the top down by program administrators and authorities, or some hybrid of the two. Programs designed to accommodate an expanding set of offset project technologies have tended to opt for a bottom-up approach, the CDM being the classic example. Others, such as RGGI, have incorporated a significant body of existing work on protocol developments, and have opted for a more top-down prescriptive approach. Both top-down and bottom-up programs vary in their use of project-specific or performance standard approaches to determining baselines.

Table 2.4   *Additionality and quantification procedures*

Name of program	Additionality and related requirements	Quantification (baseline/ monitoring) protocols
International offset mechanisms		
Clean Development Mechanism	Project specific CDM additionality tool:	
	• Step 1: Identification of alternatives to the project activity consistent with mandatory laws and regulations • Step 2: Investment analysis or • Step 3: Barrier analysis,	Baselines defined by methodologies (proposed by project proponents, reviewed by Methodology Panel), many using standardized equations, some based on project-specific parameters No standardized protocol for monitoring. Monitoring

Table 2.4   *Contd.*

Name of program	Additionality and related requirements	Quantification (baseline/ monitoring) protocols
	• Step 4: Common practice analysis Steps 1, 4 and either 2 or 3 must be fulfilled	is done in accordance with the process laid out in the registered Project Design Document (PDD)
Joint Implementation	Either the same as CDM requirements, or can be demonstrated by: • Using an approved CDM baseline and methodology • Applying the CDM additionality tool • Providing information on a previously 'successfully determined' comparable project that has already been implemented	CDM principles and process for quantification apply
Offset features of mandatory cap-and-trade systems		
European Union Emission Trading System	CDM and JI requirements apply	CDM and JI requirements apply
Regional Greenhouse Gas Initiative	• Regulatory surplus test • No credits for electric generation unless legal rights to renewable energy credits are transferred to RGGI • No funding from any system or customer benefit fund • No credits or allowances awarded under any other mandatory or voluntary GHG program	Standardized approach: Baseline and monitoring protocols are outlined in detail for each eligible offset project type in the RGGI Model Rule
Western Climate Initiative	Under development	Under development
Midwest Greenhouse Gas Reduction Accord	Recommended requirements:	Standards-based quantification protocols recommended

Table 2.4 *Contd.*

Name of program	Additionality and related requirements	Quantification (baseline/ monitoring) protocols
	• Regulatory surplus test • Reductions/removals must exceed baseline scenario	
Canada's Offset System for Greenhouse Gases	• Regulatory surplus test • Reductions/removals must exceed baseline scenario	Standardized approach, all projects must be quantified using protocols that are pre-approved by Environment Canada
Australian Carbon Pollution Abatement Scheme	Under development	Under development
New South Wales Greenhouse Gas Reduction Scheme	Performance standard approach, based on positive technology list and established baseline scenarios	Standardized approach: Explicit rules and instructions for baseline quantification provided in GHG Benchmark Rules for each type of project activity
Offset features of voluntary cap-and-trade systems		
Chicago Climate Exchange	• Regulatory surplus test • Defined as new project • Common Practice test	Standardized approach: CCX-developed predefined baselines and methodologies for each specific project type
Offset features of other GHG systems		
Alberta Offset System	• Regulatory surplus test • Real (specific and identifiable actions that reduce or remove GHGs) • Demonstrable (demonstrate a net reduction in GHGs) • Quantifiable	Quantification protocols are developed by Alberta Environment or proposed by project developers and reviewed and approved by Alberta Environment
State power plant rules	• Regulatory surplus test • Offsets must be 'real'	Regulation provides guidance for required documentation for quantification yet no specific requirements
British Columbia Emission Offset Regulation	• Baseline scenario must include consideration of regulatory requirements and incentives • Financial barriers analysis	Quantification protocols from recognized protocols may be proposed. BC-specific protocols are expected to be developed

Table 2.4   *Contd.*

Name of program	Additionality and related requirements	Quantification (baseline/ monitoring) protocols
Climate Leaders	• Regulatory surplus test • Performance standard approach	Standardized approach: Baseline and monitoring protocols are outlined in detail for each eligible offset project type
GHG accounting protocols		
WBCSD/WRI GHG Protocol for Project Accounting	Project-based and performance standard approaches guidelines provided. No requirements	Generic guidelines for project-specific and performance standard baseline quantification and monitoring protocols. No requirements
ISO 14064–2	Project-based and performance standard approaches guidelines provided. No requirements	General guidance offered for baseline quantification and monitoring protocols. No requirements
Voluntary standards for offset projects and retailers		
Climate Action Reserve	• Performance standard approach where possible • Regulatory surplus test	Performance standards used where possible and general project-specific monitoring protocols developed
Gold Standard	• CDM additionality tool (latest version) and • Previous announcement checks	GS CERs: all methodologies approved by CDM EB GS VERs: all methodologies approved by CDM EB, Small Scale Working Group (SSCWG), United Nations Development Programme (UNDP) Millennium Development Goals (MDG) Carbon Facility. New methodologies must be approved by GS Technical Advisory Committee
Voluntary Carbon Standard 2007	• Regulatory surplus test • Implementation barriers test • Common practice test Performance-based and positive technology list-based approaches will be eligible in the future. No performance tests or technologies have yet been approved by VCS	All CDM methodologies approved. New project-specific quantification protocols must be independently approved by two different auditors

Table 2.4   *Contd.*

Name of program	Additionality and related requirements	Quantification (baseline/ monitoring) protocols
VER+	Project based: • Follow specific additionality rules of an approved CDM methodology, *or* • In all other cases, apply the most recent version of the CDM Additionality Tool	All CDM-approved baselines and methodologies are allowed. The latest versions of the CDM methodologies must be used. New methodologies are reviewed on a project-by-project basis. Project methodologies must be based on 'guidance on criteria for baseline setting and monitoring' as defined for JI activities
American Carbon Registry	Either performance-based and regulatory additionality test or project-based test: • Exceed regulatory/ legal requirements; • Go beyond common practice; • Overcome 1 of 3 barriers: institutional, financial or technical	CDM, EPA Climate Leaders, and VCS protocols approved ACRs own protocols Include: a forest carbon project standard and project-specific protocols for landfill methane, livestock waste management (biodigester) and industrial gas substitution. Several other sector standards and protocols in various stages of development New protocols are reviewed on a project-by-project basis
Climate Community and Biodiversity Standards	Project-based, specified by individual methodologies • Regulatory surplus test • Barriers test	Relies on methods and tools developed by other organizations and standards for their baseline calculations. Projects must use '2006 Guidelines for National Greenhouse Gas inventories, Volume 4 Agriculture, Forestry and Other Land Use' (IPCC, 2006) or a more robust and detailed methodology, i.e. updated from IPCC GPG
Plan Vivo	Project-based: Barriers test	Baselines are calculated at the project level and also modelled at the regional scale.

Table 2.4   *Contd.*

Name of program	Additionality and related requirements	Quantification (baseline/ monitoring) protocols
		Methodologies for the carbon potential of each land-use system are commissioned by the Plan Vivo Foundation
Social Carbon Methodology	No definition of additionality criteria	Relies on methods and tools developed by outside standards
Green-e Climate Protocol for Renewable Energy	• Regulatory, legal, institutional surplus test and; • Timing test (project start date) • Technology test and performance test	Standardized methodologies
Green-e Climate Program	Requirements of each approved standard apply	Requirements of each approved standard apply
Carbon finance funds		
World Bank Carbon Finance Funds	CDM and JI requirements apply	CDM and JI requirements apply

Program administration and authority

Table 2.5 lists the actors responsible for regulating various key aspects of each offset program: overall administration, validation and/or verification, and project approval and registration.

All offset programs include some form of administrative body to oversee the project approval process to ensure that the offset projects developed meet established program requirements. Although there are several common components of the project approval process, programs have developed varied approaches to confront key quality-assurance concerns.

- *Validation requirements* provide *ex-ante* assessment and confirmation of offset project eligibility as defined by the rules of the program or standard.
- *Verification* requirements provide *ex-post* assessments and confirmation of quantification of the volume of emission reductions or removals that have been produced from an offset project across a certain period of time.
- *Registries* are used to reduce concerns regarding double counting by tracking information regarding ownership and development of the offset projects and the credits generated.

- *Third-party auditors* are required by some programs to help limit any potential conflict of interest between offset project developers and buyers, which both have financial incentives for inflating the volume of offset credits generated.
- *Project approval* requirements vary among standards. Some programs have a decision-making body that approves offset projects after documentation is submitted by auditors/project developers. Other programs use the auditors to approve the projects and there is no additional project approval step.

The structure of program administrators varies by program type and design (see Table 2.5). Compliance programs are generally administered by either an existing regulatory agency, as in the case of state regulatory agencies under RGGI, or an administrative body established exclusively for the offset program, as in the CDM EB. Voluntary offset providers are managed by a mix of Boards of Trustees, advisory committees and paid staff.

Nearly all programs require some form of project validation and verification. Increasingly, programs require verification to be conducted by an approved third-party auditor independent of either the program administrator or the project developer. Exceptions include the NSW GGAS, which assesses the need for project verification on a case-by-case basis, and the Climate Leaders program, which recommends but does not require third-party verification.

Some programs and standards give their auditors the decision-making power to approve or reject a project. Others have a separate body to evaluate and approve projects. Such a program or standard-based decision-making body adds another layer of quality control, as well as an administrative burden.

Offset programs have incorporated the use of carbon offset registries to keep track of offset ownership and to minimize the risk of double counting. A registry assigns a serial number to each verified offset and once the offset is 'used' to claim emission reductions, the serial number is retired, preventing the credit from being resold. No universal registry exists for either the compliance or voluntary offset markets, limiting their utility for minimizing double counting across the offset market. Instead, different registries have been developed; some tied to specific retailers, standards or compliance programs, as in the case of the CDM Registry and the CCX Registry, and others that function independently.

Table 2.5 *Program administration and authority*

Name of program	Who administers?	Who validates/ verifies?	Who approves?	Name of registry
International offset mechanisms				
Clean Development Mechanism	CDM Executive Board	Designated Operational Entities (DOEs)	CDM Executive Board	CDM Registry http://cdm.unfccc.int/Registry
Joint Implementation	JI Supervisory Council	Accredited Independent Entity (AIE) Provisionally DOEs currently serve as auditors	AIE unless a review is requested, in which case the JI Supervisory Council approves the project	Offset credits tracked in respective National Registries
Offset features of mandatory cap-and-trade systems				
European Union Emission Trading System	European Commission and National administrators	CDM and JI requirements apply	CDM and JI requirements apply	Community Independent Transaction Log (CITL) for allowances; for CERs and AIEs see above
Regional Greenhouse Gas Initiative	State regulatory agencies	State-accredited independent verifier	State regulatory agencies	RGGI CO$_2$ Allowance Tracking System (RGGI COATS) www.rggi-coats.org/eats/rggi
Western Climate Initiative	WCI partner jurisdictions	Under development	Under development	Under development
Midwest Greenhouse Gas Reduction Accord	Accord partner jurisdictions	Under development	Under development	Under development

Table 2.5 *Contd.*

Name of program	Who administers?	Who validates/verifies?	Who approves?	Name of registry
Canada's Offset System for Greenhouse Gases	Minister of the Environment	Accredited third-party verifier	Environment Canada	Under development
Australian Carbon Pollution Abatement Scheme	Under development	Under development	Under development	Under development
New South Wales Greenhouse Gas Abatement Scheme	Independent Pricing and Regulatory Tribunal of NSW (IPART)	Approved third-party auditor in Audit and Technical Services Panel	IPART	NSW GGAS Registry www.ggas-registry.nsw.gov.au
Offset features of voluntary cap-and-trade systems				
Chicago Climate Exchange	CCX Committee on Offsets	CCX-approved verifiers	CCX Committee on Offsets	Chicago Climate Exchange Registry www.chicagoclimatex.com
Offset features of other GHG systems				
Alberta Offset System	Alberta provincial government	Third-party verifier	Alberta Environment	Alberta Emissions Offset Registry www.carbonoffs etsolutions.ca/aeor/
State power plant rules (OR, WA, MA)	OR: Energy Facility Siting Council	OR: Program administrator	OR: Program administrator	OR: None
	WA: Energy Facility Site Evaluation Council	WA: Independent entity	WA: Program administrator	WA: None

Table 2.5 *Contd.*

Name of program	Who administers?	Who validates/ verifies?	Who approves?	Name of registry
	MA: Dept of Environmental Protection	MA: Dept of Environmental Protection	MA: Dept of Environmental Protection	MA: GHG Registry
British Columbia Emission Offset Regulation	BC Ministry of Environment	Validation and Verification body (accreditation required after 1 July 2010)	Verification body	Pacific Carbon Trust
Climate Leaders	US Environmental Protection Agency (US EPA)	US EPA	US EPA (Third-party verification encouraged)	Recommends use of independent registry, although not required
GHG accounting protocols				
WBCSD/WRI GHG Protocol for Project Accounting	N/A	N/A	N/A	N/A
ISO 14064–2	N/A	N/A	N/A	N/A
Voluntary standards for offset projects and retailers				
Climate Action Reserve	Board of Directors	American National Standards Institute (ANSI)-accredited independent verifiers approved by the Reserve	State of California and the Climate Action Reserve	Climate Action Reserve administered by APX Inc: www.apx.com/environmental/ carbon-market-infrastructure.asp
Gold Standard	Gold Standard Foundation, GS Secretariat, Foundation	DOEs	GS TAC, GS Secretariat, GS NGO Supporters	Gold Standard VER Registry administered by APX Inc: http://goldstandard.apx.com

Table 2.5 *Contd.*

Name of program	Who administers?	Who validates/ verifies?	Who approves?	Name of registry
	Board, GS Technical Advisory Committee (GS TAC), GS non-governmental organization (NGO) supporters			
Voluntary Carbon Standard 2007	VCS Association	Accredited VCS auditors	Accredited VCS auditor	Launched 17 March 2009 VCS Project Database (www.vcsprojectdatabase.org) and approved registries: • APX Inc (www.vcs registry.com) • Caisse des Dépôts • Markit Environmental Registry (formerly TZ1) (www.tz1market.com/registries.php)
VER+	TÜV SÜD certification body 'climate and energy'	CDM- and JI-accredited auditors	CDM- and JI-accredited auditors	BlueRegistry (www.blue-registry.com)

Table 2.5 *Contd.*

Name of program	Who administers?	Who validates/ verifies?	Who approves?	Name of registry
American Carbon Registry	Winrock, ACR Director	ACR-approved verifiers or verifiers approved under CDM, JI, VCS and the Climate Action Reserve. Starting 10 2010, verifiers must be ANSI-certified	ACR-approved verifiers	ACR, soon to be listed with Markit Environmental Registry (formerly TZI)
Climate, Community and Biodiversity Standards	CCB Alliance (CCBA)	DOEs or evaluators who are accredited under the Forest Stewardship Council	Third-party auditors	N/A
Plan Vivo	Plan Vivo Foundation	Plan Vivo Foundation	Plan Vivo Foundation	Markit Environmental Registry (formerly TZI) (www.tz1market.com/plan vivo.php)
Social Carbon Methodology	Ecológica Institute (Brazil)	Certifying entities: DOEs or auditors from full standards approved by SCM and auditors that have 'proven experience in the validation/verification of projects [...]'	Certifying Entities	Markit Environmental Registry (formerly TZI) (www.tz1 market.com/social.php)
Green-e Climate Protocol for Renewable Energy	Center for Resources Solutions (CRS)	Green-e CPRE, administered by CRS	Green-e CPRE, administered by CRS	Use of electronic tracking systems for Renewable Energy Certificates is required. Registry not specified

Table 2.5 *Contd.*

Name of program	Who administers?	Who validates/ verifies?	Who approves?	Name of registry
Green-e Climate Program	Center for Resources Solutions (CRS)	Green-e Governance Board/Accredited third-party auditor	See requirements of approved standards under Green-e Climate	Required. Registry not specified
Carbon finance funds				
World Bank Carbon Finance Funds	World Bank: Carbon Finance Unit	CDM and JI requirements apply	CDM and JI requirements apply	CDM and national registries

3

International Offset Mechanisms

The Clean Development Mechanism (CDM) and Joint Implementation (JI) are project-based offset mechanisms under the Kyoto Protocol, a legally binding international treaty to reduce global greenhouse gas (GHG) emissions that was negotiated in 1997 and which entered into force in 2005. Under the treaty, a group of industrialized countries and countries with economies in transition (EIT) have legally binding commitments to reduce their overall GHG emissions to 5 per cent below 1990 levels during the period 2008–2012. Each country within the group also has a separate target that ranges between an 8 per cent reduction to a 10 per cent cap on increases in emissions (UNFCCC, 1997).

JI is the instrument for offset projects taking place within countries with binding emission commitments under the Kyoto Protocol, while the CDM is for offset projects in countries without such commitments, that is, most developing countries. Both the CDM and JI provide Kyoto countries with the flexibility to meet a part of their emission target obligation in a more cost-effective manner by purchasing offset credits generated by GHG abatement projects in other Kyoto countries. However, the Kyoto Protocol requires that the use of the offset and other flexible mechanisms such as emission trading be supplemental to domestic action taken by countries to meet their commitments, and it is left to each country to decide the extent to which these mechanisms may be used (UNFCCC, 1997). Furthermore, in addition to the objective of economic efficiency, the CDM has the objective of promoting sustainable development and technology transfer in host countries.

Clean Development Mechanism (CDM)

http://cdm.unfccc.int

Unless referenced otherwise, the information in this section is based on the above website, personal communications and the following sources: UNFCCC (1992); UNFCCC (1997); UNFCCC (2006a); Pearson (2007); Sutter and Parreño (2007); UNFCCC (2007d); Point Carbon (2008b); UNFCCC (undated g).

Overview

Type of standard and context

The Clean Development Mechanism (CDM) is a project-based GHG offset mechanism under the Kyoto Protocol. The scheme aims to assist Annex-I parties (industrialized countries with binding emission reduction targets) to cut global GHG emissions in a more cost-effective manner by allowing them to invest in offset projects in non-Annex-I parties (developing countries without binding targets). The CDM also aims to assist non-Annex-I parties achieve sustainable development, to contribute to the ultimate objective of the treaty, to stabilize GHG concentrations in the atmosphere at a level that would prevent dangerous anthropogenic interference with the climate system within a time frame that allows ecosystems to adapt naturally, and to ensure that food production is not threatened and that economic development proceeds in a sustainable manner.

The parties to the United Nations Framework Convention on Climate Change (UNFCCC) negotiated and adopted the Kyoto Protocol in 1997. Initially, they only sketched out the basic features of the offset mechanism. In 2001, following a series of negotiations, the rules governing the operation of the mechanism were fleshed out in what are now known as the Marrakech Accords. The first CDM project was registered in 2004, and in the following year, after Russia's ratification of the Protocol saw it enter into force, the first emission reduction credit was issued to a project. Since then, the scheme has grown rapidly and now dominates the offset market. Since September 2007, the CDM has self-financed its regulatory functions through fees charged to projects and no longer relies on grants from Annex-I countries.

Standard authority and administrative bodies

The CDM Executive Board (EB) consists of ten members and ten alternate members representing different UN regions and interest groups under the Kyoto Protocol. The EB oversees the functioning of the CDM. The EB is ultimately accountable to the governing body of the Kyoto Protocol Conference of the Parties – Meeting of the Parties (COP-MOP), which includes representatives of all the countries that have ratified the treaty. The EB is supported by expert panels, which focus on specific tasks:

The Accreditation Panel oversees the accreditation of designated operational entities or auditors.

The Methodologies Panel (Meth Panel) reviews the methodologies for setting the baseline for projects and monitoring them. The Meth Panel also considers revisions and improvement to the over 100 approved methodologies.

The Registration and Issuance Team (RIT) is responsible for reviewing requests for project registration and issuance.

Within each member country, a *Designated National Authority (DNA)* is required to issue letters of approval to projects confirming their voluntary participation in the CDM, and host countries must confirm that the activity assists the country to achieve sustainable development.

Designated Operational Entities (DOE) are UNFCCC-approved auditors who validate and verify CDM projects.

Regional scope

The scope of the CDM is international, involving all countries that have ratified the Kyoto Protocol.

Recognition of other standards/links with other trading systems

Although the tradable units of other schemes cannot be used as CDM credits, several other compliance programs and voluntary standards either already recognize and accept Certified Emission Reductions (CERs) or plan to do so in the near future. Such schemes or standards include the EU ETS, the Regional Greenhouse Gas Initiative (RGGI), Canada's Offset System for Greenhouse Gases, the Voluntary Carbon Standard (VCS), and the Green-e Climate Program. The Gold Standard certifies projects that use CDM methodologies and also comply with additional Gold Standard criteria.

Market size and scope

Tradable unit and pricing information

The tradable unit under the CDM is a Certified Emissions Reduction (CER). Each CER is equal to 1 metric ton of CO_2e emissions abated. In 2008 the average CER price was US$16.78 (€11.46), a 16 per cent increase over 2007 prices (Capoor and Ambrosi, 2009).

Participants/buyers

Both public and private entities develop CDM projects and sell or buy the generated CERs to comply with their domestic or international emission reduction targets. Under the CDM, the project must be based in a non-Annex-I (developing) country, but the project developers, CER buyers and other participants may be based in any country, provided they are authorized to participate in the project by the project host country's DNA. Other parties involved in project development and the CER trade include intermediary buyers, such as private carbon trading firms (e.g. EcoSecurities, Tricorona Carbon Asset Management, EDF Trading, etc.) or public institutions (e.g. the World Bank). CERs can also be sold into the voluntary market. About 16 per cent of voluntary offsets traded (by volume) were CDM and JI credits (Hamilton et al, 2008).

Current project portfolio

There were a total of over 4000 projects in the CDM pipeline in July 2009; of those almost 1700 projects are registered and almost 200 are in the registration process. For up-to-date information, see UNEP Risø Centre (http://cdmpipeline.org) and UNFCCC CDM Statistics (http://cdm.unfccc.int/Statistics/index.html).

The distribution of CDM project types shown in Figure 3.1 shows the dominance of renewable energy and methane projects. Whereas offsets from industrial gas projects dominated the CER market until 2006, their market share dropped significantly in 2007 and they are now virtually absent from the primary markets. Nevertheless, industrial gas CERs are expected to make up about one third of all CERs generated until 2012. Renewable energy projects make up another third, followed by methane projects (see Figure 3.2).

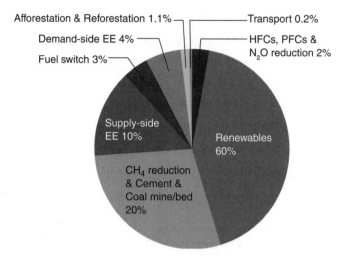

Figure 3.1 *CDM projects by project type*

Source: UNEP Risoe Centre, July 2009, http://cdmpipeline.org.

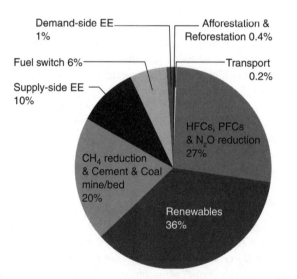

Figure 3.2 *Total expected CERs until 2012 by project type*

Source: UNEP Risoe Centre, July 2009, http://cdmpipeline.org.

Offset project eligibility

Project types

Any project is eligible that reduces or avoids emissions of one of the six Kyoto GHGs below the level projected in the absence of the registered activity with the following exceptions:

- Nuclear energy projects are excluded under the Kyoto Protocol.
- New HCFC-22 facilities, avoided deforestation and carbon capture and storage are currently excluded but are still under debate.

Purchasing countries may impose additional unilateral project-specific restrictions on CERs. For example, the EU ETS does not currently allow the use of offsets generated from forestry projects. Also, buyers may put additional restrictions on hydropower projects to ensure that they meet the requirements of the World Commission on Dams.

Project locations

A CDM project must be located in a non-Annex-1 country that has ratified or acceded to the Kyoto Protocol.

Project size

The only specific project-size limitations are for small-scale renewable energy projects, which must have a maximum output capacity of 15MW, energy savings from energy efficiency projects of up to 60GWh per year; or reduce or sequester a maximum of 60,000 tons of CO_2e (UNFCCC, 2008).

Start date

Only projects that started on or after 1 January 2000 are eligible for consideration. The earliest possible start date for the crediting period is the start date of the project or the registration date of the project, whichever is later. If a project generated emission reductions before it was registered, then those emission reductions are not eligible to be issued as CERs. However, some of these ineligible emission reduction credits are being sold as VERs on the voluntary market (often called pre-registration credits). Similarly, some projects that have failed to qualify under the CDM are finding their way to the carbon market as VERs.

Crediting period

The crediting period for all CDM projects, except afforestation and reforestation projects, can be either:

- seven years with the option of up to two renewals of seven years each if the project baseline is still valid or has been updated with new data; or
- ten years with no renewal option.

For afforestation and reforestation projects, the choice is between:

- twenty years with up to two renewal periods of 20 years each; or
- thirty years with no renewal.

Co-benefit objectives and requirements

While there are no explicit guidelines for the environmental or social co-benefits of CDM projects, the Kyoto Protocol requires that CDM projects assist the host country in achieving sustainable development. The sustainable development criteria for evaluating CDM projects are accordingly set by each host country and may include social benefits such as improvements in the quality of life, alleviation of poverty and greater equity, as well as environmental benefits such as conservation of local resources, removing pressure on local environments, health benefits and compliance with domestic environmental policies. Some countries levy taxes on CDM activities that have no apparent direct sustainable development impacts in order to re-channel funds into activities that assist them with achieving sustainable development (e.g. China places a levy on several project types).

Additionality and quantification procedures

Additionality requirements

Each CDM project must demonstrate that the CDM was essential to bringing the project to fruition, or that in the absence of the CDM, the project would either not have gone ahead or have used an inferior technology, resulting in higher GHG emissions. Baseline methodologies incorporate these additionality requirements, which usually involve three of the four steps outlined in the 'CDM Additionality Tool' (see also Figure 2.5):

1   *Identifying alternatives*: identification of realistic and credible alternatives to the proposed project activity that are compliant with current laws and regulations;
2   *Investment analysis*: determination that the proposed project activity is not the most economically or financially attractive;
3   *Barrier analysis*: analysis of barriers that prevent the implementation of the proposed project activity or do not prevent the implementation of one of the alternatives;
4   *Common practice analysis*: analysis whether the proposed project activity is 'commonly practised' by assessing the extent of diffusion of the proposed project activity.

Steps 1 and 4 are required for all projects, whereas project developers have a choice of either step 2 or step 3 to fulfil the additionality requirement. It is important to note that the additionality tool is not compulsory unless specified in a methodology.

Quantification protocols

The CDM uses a bottom-up approach. Project developers propose new methodologies and once these methodologies are reviewed and approved, they can be used to approve other projects of the same type. New methodologies are first reviewed by a Designated Operational Entity (DOE), an independent CDM-accredited auditor, on behalf of a project developer. The methodology is then reviewed and assessed by the CDM Methodology Panel, incorporating expert input and public comments. Finally, it is approved or rejected by the CDM EB.

Existing methodologies have been amended and refined over time as new projects have been proposed and approved with amendments to existing methodologies. Furthermore, similar methodologies for certain types of project, such as landfill gas projects or grid-connected renewable energy electricity projects, have been consolidated into single methodologies to make them applicable to a broad range of projects. The CDM EB has issued tools that developers can draw on to address common methodological features when proposing new methodologies.

Leakage and permanence

The baseline methodologies for afforestation and reforestation projects must account for leakage by including information on the sources of leakage and how they will be accounted for. The information submitted must specify the relevant leakage calculations, indicate how the values will be obtained and describe the uncertainties associated with key parameters. Furthermore, if some leakage sources are not accounted for, the Project Design Document (PDD) must explain why these sources were excluded. The requirement for addressing leakage applies to other project categories also but is most relevant for land use, land-use change and forestry (LULUCF) projects. International leakage and market shifting do not need to be accounted for.

The risk of carbon being re-released into the atmosphere by forest destruction is addressed by requiring forestry CDM projects to produce temporary emissions credits referred to as either 'temporary CERs' (tCERs) or 'long-term CERs' (lCERs). Both types of CER have expiry dates, after which they must be replaced by another tradable emission unit under the Kyoto Protocol. The tCERs and lCERs may be cancelled if verification reveals that the stored carbon for which they were issued was released back into the atmosphere. On cancellation, they must be replaced by another Kyoto Protocol emission trading unit.

Project approval process

Validation and registration

The validation and registration processes for project developers involve several steps. It starts with the preparation of a PDD detailing the project activities, the baseline methodology used to quantify the emission reduction, the monitoring process and information relating to the local stakeholder process that the project proponent conducts. The document is then made publicly available for comment. The PDD and the public comments are then reviewed by a CDM-approved auditor (a DOE). This may involve visits to the project site and consultations with the local stakeholder. Once the review is complete, the DOE prepares a Validation Report confirming that the project is a valid CDM project.

Prior to registration, the CDM Designated National Authority (DNA) in the country hosting the project needs to provide a letter of approval. The DNA will issue such a letter confirming its approval of the project if the project meets the host country's sustainable development criteria, complies with the country's laws and regulations and fulfils any other requirement specified by the DNA. In some countries the validation report referred to above is a prerequisite for the host country to assess the activity.

Following host nation approval, all the documents are then submitted to the CDM EB for registration and made publicly available. The project is registered if, within an eight-week period (four weeks for small-scale projects), there are no objections from either the member countries involved in the project or three or more EB members.

Monitoring, verification and certification

Once the project is operational, it must be monitored periodically in accordance with the monitoring plan. A Monitoring Report has to be prepared recording the CERs generated, which is made public at the start of the DOE assessment process. Once again, the DOE must verify this report, and based on its assessment prepare a Verification Report and a Certification Report, confirming the emission reductions achieved. The same auditor who validates the project cannot serve as the verifier except in the case of small-scale projects.

The Monitoring, Verification and Certification Reports are submitted to the CDM EB requesting the issuance of CERs for the amount of emission reduction achieved and verified. The Registration and Issuance Team assists the EB in the review process. As with the registration process, the request for issuance will be executed after 15 days, unless a member country involved in the project or at least three members of the EB request a review of the project during this period.

Registries and fees

The CDM Registry is administered by the UNFCCC secretariat. On instruction by the EB to issue CERs for a project activity, the secretariat forwards the issued CERs to the relevant holding accounts. Project participants may have a holding account in either the CDM Registry or the National Registry of an Annex-1 country.

For the CERs to be transferred from the CDM Registry account to a National Registry account, they must pass through the International Transaction Log (ITL). The first transfers to the New Zealand, Swiss and Japanese registries have been completed. The ITL will record transactions of CERs from the CDM registries to the Annex-I National Registries. Once the CERs are received in a National Registry account they can either be traded or used for compliance with national targets or regional targets, as is the case with the EU, by retiring the CERs within the registries. At present, CERs cannot be transferred between National Registries, but internal transfers within a National Registry are possible.

The CDM fee structure is as follows:

- A fee of US$1000 is charged for a new methodology submission, which, if the methodology is approved or consolidated, is considered as a down payment on the registration fee.
- A registration fee, a down payment accounted for at the time of the first issuance, of US$0.10 per CER is charged for the first 15,000 CERs issued in a given calendar year A charge of US$0.20 per CER is made for every additional CER issued up to an upper limit, which is set at US$350,000. No registration fee is charged if the average annual emissions over the crediting period amount to less than 15,000tCO$_2$e. If the project is not registered, then any amount above US$30,000 is reimbursed to the project developer. Project activities located in the least developed countries (LDCs) do not have to pay a registration fee or a share of the proceeds.

- An issuance fee of 2 per cent of the CERs from each issuance is charged to cover administrative expenses and adaptation costs.

Selected issues

The CDM dominates overall offset activity, and is the most mature of all offset schemes in the carbon market. As a result, there have been more issues identified, lessons learned and remedies suggested for the CDM than for any other offset mechanism. This section reviews eight specific issues raised in CDM-related publications, as well as the remedies proposed by various authors. At the time of writing, these and other issues are among the elements of CDM under current UNFCCC negotiation for a post-2012 agreement.

Weakness of long-term market signal

Hepburn (2007) notes the widely recognized constraint of the Kyoto Protocol: that currently there are no binding targets and timetables, and thus there is no firm market for the CDM beyond 2012. Uncertainty about future markets leads to a transfer of risk from the government to the private sector. Numerous countries and regions, including the EU and several US states, have made emission reduction commitments to 2020 and beyond, many of which are established in legislation and refer directly to the use of offsets from developing countries, but these alone are insufficient to provide investor certainty in the CDM market.

Proposed remedies
- Secure a strong post-2012 agreement. International negotiators and domestic constituencies are working on proposals to ensure an efficient, effective and fair post-2012 agreement.
- Contractually bind governments to their long-term goals; set up authoritative agencies to advise governments on achieving their 2050 targets and report annually on progress (Hepburn, 2007).

Ability to finance high capital cost, longer payback investments

Ellis and Kamel (2007) highlight the challenge of securing financing for projects with high initial investment costs, such as renewable energy systems and re/afforestation activities. Such projects can involve a long project lead time, and are perceived by financing sources as high-risk projects compared to conventional projects, such as coal- or gas-fired plants. Additionally, power generation projects are usually appraised on the basis of the installation cost (cost per kW installed) rather than the life cycle cost of production of electricity (cost per kWh), an approach that favours conventional technologies with low capital cost requirements.

Proposed remedy
- Increase certainty of demand (and price) for CDM credits post-2012
- Implement tax/incentive structures in host countries that facilitate initial capital investments (Ellis and Kamel, 2007).

Profits and perversities associated with low-cost non-CO_2 projects

Several project types that dominated the early CDM market – most notably, the destruction of high global warming potential (GWP) gases (HFC-23 and N_2O) – present very low GHG abatement costs (less than US$1/$tCO_2$e), high profits and little sustainable development benefit (Hepburn, 2007; Schneider, 2007; Wara and Victor, 2008). Furthermore, CER revenues can provide the incentive to increase production of high GWP gases, for example, at refrigerant (HCFC-22) manufacturing facilities where the high GWP gas HFC-23 is a by-product. Current CDM rules aim to limit this potentially perverse impact by disallowing CERs for production levels that exceed historical levels (at existing facilities) and by disallowing CDM projects at new HCFC-23 facilities (an option still under consideration).

Proposed remedies

- Establish separate mitigation regimes for non-CO_2 gases, and create a funding mechanism whereby industrialized countries pay directly for the actual costs of high GWP gas destruction, modelled along the lines of the Multilateral Fund under the Montreal Protocol (Wara, 2008).
- Restrict the CDM to CO_2 and methane, and provide countries with other financial incentives to mitigate other GHGs (Hepburn, 2007).
- Use ambitious benchmarks (emissions per unit of production) to reduce the number of CERs issued while still providing sufficient financial incentives (Schneider, 2007).

Potential for offsets to deter the adoption of government policies

Schneider (2007) and Hepburn (2007) suggest that the CDM can create a perverse incentive for governments in developing countries to avoid enacting or implementing policies that result in emission-reducing activities, since doing so might reduce opportunities to garner CER revenues.

Proposed remedies

- Enable policy-based crediting. The CDM is currently limited to project-based activities; a broader scope could allow developing country governments to garner CERs for the introduction of policies to reduce emissions (Hepburn, 2007). However, Schneider (2007) points out that a policy-based CDM approach raises concerns regarding the assessment of additionality, as there are several motivations for the adoption of policies, and GHG mitigation may only be one of them. Schneider (2007) suggests that policies and measures could be credited indirectly through sectoral approaches.
- Foster sectoral approaches. Under the sectoral approach, a baseline is established for an entire sector (e.g. cement, electricity, aluminium) and emission reductions below this baseline are credited. Many variants of sectoral (and policy-based) crediting – such as sectoral no-lose targets or sectoral benchmarks – are under active discussion in international negotiations. Under sector-wide approaches, governments themselves would receive the credits if emissions fall below a sectoral target or

benchmark, and governments could in turn transfer credits or provide financial incentives or regulations that would spur individual facilities and the private sector to achieve emission reductions.

High transaction costs

Cosbey et al (2005), Ellis and Kamel (2007) and Hepburn (2007) point out that the high transaction costs of CDM projects pose a common hurdle for many project developers, especially for small-scale projects and in poor developing countries. Though transaction costs typically represent less than US$1 per tCO_2e when averaged over the life of a project (Antinori and Sathaye, 2007), these costs are incurred upfront, while CDM revenue is only generated once a project is registered and credits are issued (Ellis and Kamel, 2007). Cosbey et al (2005) further points out that high transaction costs may disproportionately affect projects with significant development benefits.

Proposed remedies

- Reduce the costs associated with validation and verification. Fees paid to DOEs make up a sizable portion of project transaction costs. The establishment and training of developing country DOEs might lower these costs as host country offices are likely to offer a more attractive fee schedule than their northern counterparts (Cosbey et al, 2005).
- Create alternative financing mechanisms to cover transaction costs. Some emission reductions buyers, especially large institutional or national carbon funds, have been offering different types of advance payments to project developers in order to help them overcome the burden of the project's transaction costs. One model involves offering grants, separate from the funds used by the buyer, to purchase emission reductions. Another model is to pay part of the price for the purchased CERs in advance before the project's inception (Ellis and Kamel, 2007).
- Reduce barriers for programmatic CDM to better support energy efficiency and transportation investments that currently face significant transaction costs due to the small scale of individual activities (Hepburn, 2007).

Quality of validation and verification

As Schneider (2007) and Schneider and Mohr (2009) observe, a weak threat of sanctions coupled with increasing competition between DOEs, can lead to a 'race to the bottom' in the quality of the validation and verification processes. In 2008 and 2009, an increasing proportion of CDM projects were rejected by the CDM EB, and spot checks at validators and verifiers (DOEs) revealed serious shortcomings (CDM Pipeline: http://cdmpipeline.org/overview.htm).

Proposed remedies

- Develop a policy framework to address validator/verifier non-conformities and non-compliance in a systematic manner, including criteria for the suspension or withdrawal of accreditation as well as other sanctions. Strengthen the liability of validators/verifiers (DOEs) by requiring them to replace any excessive CERs issued (Schneider, 2007).

- Reduce the potential conflict of interest for validators/verifiers by paying them through the CDM, for example from proceeds to cover administrative expenses, instead of directly through project developers. This would also be beneficial to small-scale projects as it reduces transaction costs (Schneider, 2007).

Contribution to sustainable development

Cosbey et al (2005), Olsen (2007) and Schneider (2007) highlight the limited role that sustainable development objectives play in directing CDM investments. While rhetorically mandated in the Kyoto Protocol, sustainable development criteria vary greatly among host countries. In most countries, projects need only comply with one of many sustainable development criteria to be approved. The result is a CDM project portfolio largely determined by economic attractiveness, potential and risk (Schneider, 2007).

Proposed remedies

- Foster NGO involvement. Premium markets, such as the Gold Standard, can help bring value to sustainable development achievements. NGOs and research institutions could play a more proactive role in promoting co-benefits by monitoring the results of CDM projects (Cosbey et al, 2005).
- Develop clearly defined criteria and guidelines for establishing sustainable development criteria in host countries. Strengthen the capacity-building efforts of DNAs to help them enforce clear definitions of sustainable development (Schneider, 2007).
- Establish minimum quotas for projects with high sustainability benefits. Industrialized (Annex I) countries could commit themselves to purchasing a minimum quota of projects with a high level of sustainable development benefits (Schneider, 2007).

Demonstration of additionality

The issuance of CERs to non-additional projects increases global GHG emissions. Schneider (2007) analysed 93 CDM projects and found that 43 per cent of the projects that claimed barriers as a rationale for additionality did not provide evidence of their existence. A survey revealed that 71 per cent of the participants thought that 'many CDM projects would also be implemented without registration under CDM' and 85 per cent felt that 'in many cases, carbon revenues are the icing on the cake, but are not decisive for the investment decision'.

Proposed remedies

The following are among the measures Schneider (2007) suggests to improve the assessment of additionality:

- Establish ambitious and dynamic benchmarks to be used to assess additionality in industries where the data are available (e.g. using the performance of the top plants in the industry as the benchmark).

- Provide clear, explicit guidance for demonstrating additionality, especially for small-scale projects.
- Eliminate the use of highly subjective and company-specific barriers.
- Require investment analysis for all large-scale projects. The use of barrier analysis can be less credible given the scale of investment involved. Investment analysis could be mandatory for such project types, and more specific guidance should be provided to reduce the risk of gaming.
- Introduce quantitative thresholds for some sectors to make common practice analysis more objective.

Joint Implementation

http://ji.unfccc.int

Unless referenced otherwise, the information in this section is based on the above website, personal communications and the following sources: UNFCCC (2006b); UNFCCC (2006c); Cames et al (2007); Gaye (2007); MOE (2007); Salay (2007); Schlamadinger and O'Sullivan (2007); UNFCCC (2007b); UNFCCC (undated a); UNFCCC (undated b); UNFCCC (undated c); UNFCCC (undated d).

Overview

Type of standard and context

Joint Implementation (JI), like the CDM, is a project-based mechanism under the Kyoto Protocol. It is limited to transactions between industrialized countries and countries with economies in transition (EIT) that have commitments to limit or reduce their GHG emissions under the Protocol. The goal of the program is to increase market efficiency by allowing industrialized countries to meet a part of their obligation by investing in GHG abatement projects in another industrialized or EIT country if the cost of abatement is lower in the other country.

Like the CDM, the JI mechanism was negotiated in 1997 as a part of the Kyoto Protocol. Its goal is to combat climate change using a flexible GHG trading mechanism. JI grew out of a pilot program which began in 1995. Most of the pilot projects cannot be converted into JI emission reduction credits because they started before 1 January 2000, which precludes them from being considered under the JI mechanism (UNFCCC, 2006a).

Although the program became officially operational after the entry into force of the Protocol in 2005, the final determination (similar to registration) of the first JI project was only completed in March 2007. This was because the JI Supervisory Committee (JISC), the governing authority for the JI program, was not established until December 2005, and the verification procedure under the committee was only finalized in October 2006. The program entered its first commitment period under the Kyoto Protocol in January 2008 and is expected to show better growth in 2008–2009.

The administrative and regulatory functions of the JI will be funded by the fees charged to project participants, and by the core and supplementary budgets of the UNFCCC. However, the funds generated from fees are not expected to accumulate to adequate levels until 2010, so reliance on industrialized and EIT country funding contributions will continue at least until the end of 2009 (UNFCCC, 2007a).

Standard authority and administrative bodies

The JI program is supervised by the JISC, a ten-member team with voting rights that represent the EIT countries, the industrialized countries, developing countries and the small island nations. There are ten additional members without voting rights who represent the same country groups as the voting members. They participate in all JISC meetings and share the work responsibilities of the JISC. The JISC is supported by an expert panel for the accreditation of independent auditors (JI Accreditation Panel) and is ultimately accountable to the governing body of the Kyoto Protocol, which includes representatives of all countries that have ratified the treaty. Within each industrialized and EIT country, there is a Designated Focal Point (DFP) that serves as the nodal agency responsible for administering JI activities within its jurisdiction.

Regional scope

The JI scheme is international in its scope, but only industrialized and EIT countries that have ratified the Kyoto Protocol can host JI projects and issue the Emission Reduction Units generated from the projects.

Recognition of other standards/links with other trading systems

As in the case of the CDM, although the emission reductions of other schemes cannot be used under the JI program, other compliance programs, including the EU ETS, and RGGI, and some voluntary standards either recognize and accept JI emission reductions under their schemes or plan to do so in the near future.

Market size and scope

Tradable unit and pricing information

The tradable unit under the JI program is an Emission Reduction Unit (ERU). Each ERU is equal to one metric ton of carbon dioxide equivalent ($mtCO_2e$). According to the 2009 World Bank report on the carbon markets, ERUs were transacted at an average price of US$14.56 (€9.95) in 2008 (Capoor and Ambrosi, 2009).

Participants/buyers

JI project participants include public or private entities based in industrialized and EIT countries that have ratified the Kyoto Protocol, or other legal entities that are approved by the project's host country DFP to participate in the project. Approved entities may develop JI projects, sell the emission reduction generated, or buy ERUs to comply with their domestic and international obligations. To avoid the double counting of units, if industrialized or EIT country participants sell the JI emission reductions generated, they cannot count these reductions towards meeting their own targets. Buyers from other voluntary programs may also purchase JI Emission Reduction Units.

Current project portfolio

As of 1 July 2009 there were a total of 209 JI projects in the pipeline (UNEP RISØ Centre, 2008). JI distinguishes between Track 1 and Track 2 projects. Of the projects currently in the pipeline, 180 are following Track 2 verification procedures and 28 are following Track 1. Track 2 projects must be approved by the JISC. Track 1 projects, on the other hand, are approved by their respective host countries. Track 2 projects are located in countries that either do not fully comply with the eligibility requirements for participating in the JI program, or meet the eligibility requirements, but have voluntarily chosen to use the Track 2 verification procedure under the JISC. Projects that follow the Track 1 verification procedure established by their respective host country governments are located in countries that meet all the eligibility requirements for participating in the JI program and are thus authorized to verify projects. ERUs are issued and transferred by the host country under both the Track 1 and Track 2 verification procedures.

The JI projects in the pipeline have been dominated by methane reduction projects, which make up 34 per cent of projects, followed by 29 per cent from renewable energy projects (UNEP RISØ Centre, 2009).

Of the 209 JI projects in the pipeline Track 2 projects: one has been rejected by the JISC; six projects' determination reports, similar to a validation report under the CDM, have been assessed by the JISC and secured a 'final determination', which is similar to registration under the CDM. To date almost 1.2 million ERUs have been issues and all these projects are expected to generate 342 million ERUs by 2012 (UNEP RISØ Centre, 2009).

Although projects may be developed in any industrialized or EIT country, in practice most of the projects are currently located in Eastern European countries and in the countries of the former Soviet Union. The portfolio illustrates this trend: the majority of the JI projects are being developed in Russia and Ukraine, which had proposed 102 and 34 projects, respectively, as of 1 July 2009 (UNEP RISØ Centre, 2009). Of the remainder of the JI projects, 59 are proposed for Eastern Europe, followed by 14 projects proposed in other regions including Germany, France and New Zealand (UNEP RISØ Centre, 2009).

The buyers of primary CDM and JI tend to be dominated by private sector companies from Western Europe (Capoor and Ambrosi, 2009). These private sector buyers have slightly less than 80 per cent of the volumes contracted; even amid the economic downturn it was reported that European utilities were active buyers (Capoor and Ambrosi, 2009). In 2008 20MmtCO$_2$e in ERUs, down from 41MmtCO$_2$e in 2007, was transacted, worth US$294 million (Capoor and Ambrosi, 2009).

Updated information on JI project numbers, type and location can be found at the following website: http://cdmpipeline.org/ji-projects.htm#4,

Offset project eligibility

Project types

The project types eligible under JI are the same as those under the CDM. The only difference is that while only afforestation and reforestation LULUCF projects are eligible under the CDM, other LULUCF project types, including forest management, cropland management and grazing management, are eligible under JI (UNFCCC, undated e).

Project locations

A JI project can be located in any industrialized or EIT country that has ratified the Kyoto Protocol and has GHG emission limitations under the treaty.

Project size

The only specific project size limitations are for small-scale renewable energy projects which cannot exceed an output capacity of 15MW (UNFCCC, 2007c).

Start date

The project start date for eligibility is 1 January 2000.

Crediting period

The crediting period for a JI project must begin after 1 January 2008 and end in 2012. However, the length of the crediting period can be extended beyond 2012 up to the operational life of the project if it is approved by the JI DFP in the country hosting the project (UNFCCC, undated f).

Co-benefit objectives and requirements

Like the CDM, there are no explicit guidelines on the environmental or social co-benefits of JI projects. Unlike the CDM, JI projects are not required to assist countries with achieving their sustainable development goals, and projects do not have to be assessed based on any sustainable development criteria (UNFCCC, 1997).

Additionality and quantification procedures

Additionality requirements

Like the CDM, every JI project must demonstrate that without JI, either the project would not have gone ahead, or it would have used an inferior technology resulting in higher GHG emissions. A JI project can demonstrate additionality in one of the following ways:

*   using an approved CDM baseline and monitoring methodology;
*   applying the most recent version of the 'Tool for the demonstration and assessment of additionality' or any other method approved by the CDM EB;

- providing traceable and transparent information showing that the project's baseline was identified on the basis of conservative assumptions, that the project scenario is not part of the identified baseline scenario and that the project will lead to reductions in anthropogenic emissions or enhancements of net removals; or by
- providing traceable and transparent information on a previously 'successfully determined' comparable project implemented under comparable circumstances, and justifying why it is relevant to the proposed project under consideration.

Quantification protocols

The basic principles and the processes that apply in the quantification of emission reductions in CDM projects are the same for JI projects.

Project approval process

Validation and registration

Under JI, the validation stage is referred to as the determination. The determination of a JI project is carried out by an independent auditor (an Accredited Independent Entity, AIE) accredited by the JISC. There are no accredited auditors under the JI program as yet, so the CDM auditors (DOEs) are serving as provisional auditors for determining JI projects. The acceptance of the auditor's determination report by the JISC, referred to as final determination, is similar to the registration of the project under the CDM. This is only required for Track 2 projects as Track 1 projects are not assessed by the JISC.

Like the CDM, the project developers have to develop a project design document, which the AIE reviews to confirm that the project is eligible, additional and compliant with national laws and environmental requirements. The AIE also solicits public comments through the UNFCCC and then prepares a Final Determination Report, which is made public through the JISC. Like the CDM registration process, unless a party involved in the project or three members of the JISC request a review of the project, the AIE's determination report is accepted and the project secures a final determination from the JISC. If a review is requested, the JISC must make a final decision no later than six months or at its second meeting after the review was requested.

Monitoring, verification and certification

The monitoring and verification processes for JI projects under its Track 2 procedure are similar to that of the CDM projects. It requires the preparation of a Monitoring Report by the project developer, verification with possible site visits, and the preparation of a Verification Report by the accredited auditor. Both the documents are made public through the UNFCCC secretariat. If the JISC is not asked to review the auditor's verification, then the assessment is made final and the project host country can issue ERUs equivalent to the amount of emission reductions approved by the JISC. The ERUs are converted from Assigned Amount Units (AAUs) or from Removal Units (RMUs, from LULUCF activities). There is no certification procedure for JI projects.

Registries and fees

There is no JI registry. ERUs are issued to the national registries of the industrialized and EIT countries hosting the projects. ERUs may be transferred from one national registry to another if the ERUs are purchased by an entity authorized by an industrialized or EIT country DFP. The JI fee structure is as follows:

- Independent auditors applying for JI accreditation are required to pay a one-time non-reimbursable fee of US$15,000 in addition to any direct costs incurred by the team assessing its application.
- A progressive fee based on the volume of emission reduction or removal is charged for processing verification reports. The fee is US$0.10 per metric ton of CO_2e for the first 15,000 units generated in a year, and US$0.20 for each additional unit.
- The fee is charged as an advance at the time of applying for final determination by the JISC. The advance is adjusted against actual payments due at the time of verification. Small-scale projects with emission reductions of less than 15,000tCO_2e are exempted from paying in advance, but are required to pay the fee at the time of verification.
- Up to US$30,000 of the amount paid in advance is non-reimbursable if the project does not secure a final determination by the JISC.

Selected issues

JI projects face many risks similar to those faced by CDM projects, such as uncertainties surrounding national approval and validation and registration processes, the potential for technical failure, and the demand for JI credits post-2012 (Cames et al, 2007). The status of JI in some countries is still unclear; in these countries, implementation rules either have not been fully agreed, or have been agreed but not yet implemented or communicated sufficiently (van de Ven, 2007). JI project developers also face the risk that if and as cap-and-trade programs are expanded to the sectors and emissions sources that their projects address, their projects might no longer be eligible for generating offset credits.

Double counting

Double counting issues have been raised, for example, if the JI reduction happens in an installation under the EU ETS and no account is given for these reductions, the operator can sell the EU ETS allowances (EUAs) that were avoided through the JI project as well. As a result, the government could potentially hand out two credits (1 ERU and 1 EUA) for a reduction of just 1 tonne of CO_2. This issue is addressed in the double counting guidelines of the EU linking directive, which states that projects at installations covered by the EU ETS cannot be put forward as JI projects because the allocation of EUAs and the generation ERUs in the same installation would lead to double counting (Directive 2004/101/EC, see http://eur-lex.europa.eu). Some, however, argue that the restrictions on the eligibility of JI projects imposed by the double counting guidelines and the need to comply with other EU laws in setting the baselines restrict wind and hydropower projects, and that the double counting guidelines should be relaxed for renewable energy projects (van de Ven, 2007).

Lack of reliable data

Another barrier to JI projects is the lack of reliable data to establish project baselines, a constraint common to most offset programs. Proposed mechanisms to address these issues include: the creation of an *ex-ante* 'white list' of project types for host nation approval; making decision-making processes more transparent with the right to appeal against decisions; and taking steps to limit the sovereign risk associated with the issuance and transfer of ERUs (van de Ven, 2007).

4

Offset Features of Cap-and-Trade Programs

Cap-and-trade programs place an overall limit on emissions allowed from a specified set of covered entities, and issue tradable emission allowances (or rights to emit) that these entities can use for compliance. Allowances, which typically authorize an entity to emit a metric or a short ton of CO_2e, can be auctioned or freely distributed to covered entities or other parties. At the end of a program's compliance period, covered entities must submit an allowance for every ton of CO_2e they emitted during that period. Every greenhouse cap-and-trade program established to date has also allowed covered entities to submit offsets in lieu of allowances for compliance purposes, generally with a limit on the fraction of compliance obligations that offsets can cover. A covered entity in a cap-and-trade program, therefore, has several options for achieving compliance: using emission allowances it has received or purchased, acquiring offsets, and/or reducing its own emissions.

Cap-and-trade systems are typically implemented as government-regulated, mandatory compliance systems. The sole exception is the Chicago Climate Exchange (CCX) (www.chicagoclimateexchange.com), which has implemented a cap-and-trade system with voluntary participation and its own regulation. A voluntary cap-and-trade system can play a pioneering role in developing market rules and structures, and provide 'early movers' with the opportunity to gain experience with emission commitments and trading.

The following sections provide more detailed descriptions of the offset features of seven mandatory and one voluntary cap-and-trade systems. Mandatory systems described are: European Union Emission Trading System (EU ETS), Regional Greenhouse Gas Initiative, Western Climate Initiative, Midwest Greenhouse Gas Reduction Accord, Canada's Offset System for Greenhouse Gases, Australian Carbon Pollution Reduction Scheme and New South Wales Greenhouse Gas Abatement Scheme. The voluntary system described is the Chicago Climate Exchange.

European Union Emission Trading System (EU ETS)

http://ec.europa.eu/environment/climat/emission/

Unless referenced otherwise, the information in this section is based on the above website, personal communications and the following sources: Ellis and Tirpak (2006); Natsource (undated).

Overview

Type of standard and context

The European Union Emission Trading Scheme (EU ETS) is a mandatory cap-and-trade program that allows operators the use of compliance carbon credits from Kyoto project-based mechanisms (Clean Development Mechanism and Joint Implementation), up to a certain limit. The EU ETS began in January 2005 as the first emission trading scheme to regulate GHG emissions and continues to be the largest (European Commission, 2009a). The EU ETS is a key component of the EU climate policy commitment to the Kyoto Protocol and beyond. Emission sources regulated by the EU ETS include 11,000 downstream emission sources, accounting for half of all EU emissions, from the following industrial sectors: iron and steel; cement, glass and ceramics; pulp and paper; electric power generation; and refineries. The cap covers only CO_2 emissions, but may in the future include other GHGs, as well as air transport emissions. The implementation of the EU ETS began with Phase I (2005–2007), which – although mandatory – was primarily designed as a trial period. It is currently in Phase II (2008–2012), which coincides with the Kyoto commitment period. For Phase III of the EU ETS several revisions to the scheme will be introduced from 2013, including a single EU-wide cap to increase harmonization (Capoor and Ambrosi, 2009). On 30 September 2010 the final Phase III annual emission cap for the EU ETS is expected to be announced (Capoor and Ambrosi, 2009).

Emission sources regulated by the EU ETS may meet their compliance obligation either through surrendering emission allowances (EUAs) or they may supplement in part allowances through the purchase of offset credits available through the Kyoto Protocol project-based mechanisms, including CDM and JI credits. Regulated entities that do not meet their compliance obligation are required to pay, as of 2008, a penalty of \$157 (€100) per metric ton, and are required to make up the shortfall in subsequent calendar years, in addition to having their names published and being 'named and shamed' for non-compliance. Under the EU ETS program, the use of CDM and JI project credits is supposed to be 'supplemental' to emission reductions that take place within the EU. Limitations on the use of CDM/JI credits for compliance under the EU ETS vary by member state. Under Phase II of the EU ETS, the member state emission cap, the CO_2 emission source allowance allocations, and member state limit on the use of CDM/JI credits are based on National Allocation Plans (NAPs) submitted by each member state for approval by the European Commission. Member states specify a limit up to which individual installations will be able to use external credits to comply with the ETS. These limits vary between 0 per cent (Estonia) and 20 per cent (Germany) of allowances. The use of CERs from forestry and nuclear projects is not allowed and additional conditions apply for acceptance of credits from hydroelectric projects above 20MW. Under the third phase (2013–2020) the system of national allocation plans will be abandoned to make way for harmonized EU-wide caps and allocation rules.

Standard authority and administrative bodies

The EU ETS has been established through binding legislation proposed by the European Commission and approved by the EU member states and the European Parliament. The member states are responsible for the implementation of the emission trading system at the national level, in line with the national allocation plans approved by the Commission. They also have to submit annual reports on the implementation of the Directive to the Commission, in line with Article 21 of the ETS Directive. National administrators of the scheme manage national registries, while the Commission oversees the Community Independent Transaction Log (CITL) at the Community level, which registers changes in national registries. The proposed reform of the EU ETS envisages that from 2013 onwards the European emission trading system will be further harmonized by abolishing national allocation plans, introducing auctioning as a primary method of allocation (with 100 per cent auctioning for electricity production and a gradual increase of auctioning for other industrial processes covered by the system). The transitional free allocation will be based on benchmarking. Compliance of individual installations is attested by annual compliance reports that are verified by the accredited verifiers and monitored by member states' administrations.

Regional scope

The EU ETS focuses on emission reduction targets for the 27 member states of the EU and targets for the countries that have linked their trading system to the EU ETS. For the time being this includes Norway, Iceland and Liechtenstein.

Recognition of other standards/links with other trading systems

The EU Linking Directive, which was passed in 2004, allows operators in Phase II of the ETS to use credits from JI and the CDM to meet their targets in place of emission cuts within the EU. The EU ETS has been open to linking with other countries that have ratified the Kyoto Protocol and established compatible GHG emission trading systems, in order to enlarge the market for trading. The first expansion of the EU ETS took place on 1 January 2008, when Norway, Iceland and Liechtenstein joined the EU ETS (European Commission, 2007a). In addition preliminary discussions about future links have taken place with other programs and countries. The EU ETS has expressed interest in and encouragement for plans to set up absolute and mandatory cap-and-trade emission trading systems in Australia, New Zealand, Switzerland, California, RGGI and other US states and Canadian provinces. In October 2007, the International Carbon Action Partnership (ICAP) was created, of which the EU is a founder member, in order to help support the linking of the EU ETS with other compatible trading systems in future (European Commission, 2007a).

Market size and scope

Tradable unit and pricing information

Tradable units and pricing information for offset credits under the EU ETS are based on those used for the CDM and JI project-based mechanisms respectively. Because the EU is the largest purchaser of such credits the secondary market price for JI/CDM credits follows similar trends as the price for EUAs. In late 2008 and early 2009 the price differential between EUAs and secondary CERs narrowed and disappeared completely; the price spread for primary CERs narrowed as well (Capoor and Ambrosi, 2009). Recovering carbon prices has led again to an increasing price spread between EUAs and CERs (Capoor and Ambrosi, 2009).

Participants/buyers

Participants and buyers of CDM and JI offset credits under the EU ETS include regulated emission sources, as well as EU member states themselves. Major European banks and other financial institutions both in the private and public sector have also become active in providing finance or managing funds for prospective emission reduction projects (European Commission, 2007a).

Current project portfolio

Limits on the use of CDM and JI credits for compliance under Phase II of the EU ETS vary by member state, as shown in Table 4.1, based on national allocation plans (NAPs)

Table 4.1 *EU ETS national allocation plans summary table*

Member state	Annual cap 2008–2012 in MmtCO$_2$e	Annual JI/CDM limit in %	Annual JI/CDM limit in MmtCO$_2$e[1]
Austria	30.7	10	3.1
Belgium	58.5	8.4	4.9
Bulgaria	42.3	12.55	5.3
Cyprus	5.48	10	0.5
Czech Rep.	86.8	10	8.7
Denmark	24.5	17.01	4.2
Estonia	12.72	0	0.0
Finland	37.6	10	3.8
France	132.8	13.5	17.9
Germany	453.1	20	90.6
Greece	69.1	9	6.2
Hungary	26.9	10	2.7
Iceland	N/A	N/A	N/A
Ireland	22.3	10	2.2
Italy	195.8	14.99	29.4
Latvia	3.43	10	0.3
Liechtenstein	N/A	N/A	N/A
Lithuania	8.8	20	1.8
Luxembourg	2.5	10	0.3
Malta	2.1	tbd	tbd
Netherlands	85.8	10	8.6
Norway	N/A	N/A	N/A
Poland	208.5	10	20.9
Portugal	34.8	10	3.5
Romania	75.9	10	7.6

Table 4.1 *Contd.*

Member state	Annual cap 2008–2012 in MmtCO$_2$e	Annual JI/CDM limit in %	Annual JI/CDM limit in MmtCO$_2$e[1]
Slovakia	30.9	7	2.2
Slovenia	8.3	15.76	1.3
Spain	152.3	ca. 20	30.5
Sweden	22.8	10	2.3
UK	246.2	8	19.7
Total	2080.93	–	278.2

Note: [1]Values calculated by the author based on emission cap and JI/CDM percentage limit.
Source: European Commission, 2007b.

submitted by each member state to the European Commission for review and approval. Based on these national limits, the upper limit for the total use of JI/CDM credits under the EU ETS under Phase II is 278.2MmtCO$_2$e per year, as shown in the last column of Table 4.1.

Offset project eligibility

Project types

During Phase II all CDM and JI project types are eligible, except those from nuclear facilities and land use, land-use change and forestry activities. In the case of hydroelectric power production project activities with a generating capacity exceeding 20MW, member states shall ensure that relevant international criteria and guidelines, including those contained in the World Commission on Dams November 2000 Report 'Dams and Development: A New Framework for Decision-Making', will be respected during the development of such project activities (European Commission, 2007a).

Project locations

CDM and JI requirements apply. For projects implemented in member states in sectors falling within the scope of the trading scheme directive, the provisions on double counting apply. Credits issued to such projects have to be deducted from the allocation issued to installations in the affected sector (indirect double counting) or from allocations to the installation that implements JI/CDM project (direct double counting).

Project size

CDM and JI requirements apply.

Start date

CDM and JI requirements apply.

Crediting period

CDM and JI requirements apply.

Co-benefit objectives and requirements

CDM and JI requirements apply.

Additionality and quantification procedures

Additionality requirements

CDM and JI requirements apply.

Quantification protocols

CDM and JI requirements apply.

Project approval process

Validation and registration

CDM and JI requirements apply.

Monitoring, verification and certification

CDM and JI requirements apply.

Registries and fees

CDM and JI requirements apply.

Selected issues

Built on experience gained in sulphur oxide (SO_x) emission trading under the US Clean Air Act, the EU ETS is the first practical experiment in GHG emission trading. It has made a significant contribution to the establishment of a global carbon market by placing a clear constraint on carbon dioxide (CO_2) emissions and sending a carbon price signal to market participants where none existed before.

The EU ETS has been the primary source of demand and thus driver of growth in global offset markets through the CDM and JI. Two principal issues have been raised surrounding the EU ETS and its use of CDM and JI credits: (i) supplementarity and limits and (ii) project type eligibility.

Supplementarity and limits

Limits on the use of CDM and JI credits in Phase II of the EU ETS (2008–2012) range from 0 per cent of the annual emission allowances allocated in Estonia to 20 per cent in Germany, Lithuania and Spain (EC, 2007a). These limits are based on the principle of supplementarity, established in the Kyoto Protocol (Articles 6 and 17), which requires that the acquisition of CDM and JI credits be 'supplemental to domestic actions for the purpose of meeting quantified emission limitation and reduction commitments'. The supplementarity principle has been generally viewed as suggesting that no more than half of all required emission reductions would be met by offset purchases. However, analysis by the World Wildlife Fund suggests that the 2008–2012 limits are high enough to conceivably allow almost all (88–100 per cent) reductions to be met through CDM and JI credits in nine countries representing 80 per cent of the EU's emissions (WWF-UK, 2007). As a result, the limits may not be sufficiently strict to ensure adherence to supplementarity principles.

On the other hand, the International Emissions Trading Association (IETA) contends that EU's limits on the use of CDM and JI credits reduce the system's ability to mobilize significant capital for low-carbon technologies and increase abatement costs for industry to prohibitively high levels (IETA, undated).

A revised EU ETS directive for Phase III of the EU ETS was approved in December 2008 by the European Parliament. This new directive would limit access to international project credits from outside the EU to 50 per cent of the reductions required in the EU ETS in the 2012–2020 period.

Project type eligibility

Other issues that have been raised centre on project type eligibility and include the sustainability impact of CDM and JI projects, the need to increase participation in under-represented countries and sectors, and the varying approval processes in different member countries. Regarding sustainability, the WWF recommends that all CDM and JI credits used under the EU ETS should be certified by the Gold Standard (WWF-UK, 2007), while the IETA argues for more diverse approaches to demonstrating co-benefits to increase participation of many different actors (IETA, undated). IETA also proposes the expansion of eligible offset project types to include land use, land-use change and forestry (LULUCF) projects, which are currently exempt under the EU ETS, and the proposed harmonization of the approval process of CDM and JI projects across EU member states in Phase III (IETA, undated).

For its third phase, post-2012, the EU advocates the transition of the CDM beyond a pure project-by-project offsetting mechanism to a broader crediting approach. The EU is also considering other means of scaling up participation among developing countries using sector-based approaches such as binding sector-wide targets or 'no-lose targets', where credits are awarded for beating emission targets but no penalties are imposed for missing them.

Regional Greenhouse Gas Initiative

www.rggi.org

Unless referenced otherwise, the information in this section is based on the above website, personal communications and the following sources: Point Carbon Research (2007a); Point Carbon Research (2007b); Point Carbon Research (2007c).

Overview

Type of system/program and context

The Regional Greenhouse Gas Initiative (RGGI) is a multi-state mandatory cap-and-trade program to reduce CO_2 emission from electricity generation. It was established in 2005 by governors of seven US states in the Northeast and Mid-Atlantic regions and has since expanded to include ten states. The program applies to fossil fuel-fired electric generating units 25MW and larger.

RGGI came into effect on 1 January 2009, the first mandatory cap-and-trade program to regulate GHGs in the US. Its objective is to reduce CO_2 emissions in the electric generation sector by 10 per cent from 2009 to 2018. It will start by setting a regional cap to stabilize emissions from 2009 to 2014 at 188 million short tons of CO_2 equivalent ($MstCO_2e$) and then reduce the cap by 2.5 per cent annually until 2018. More than 85 per cent of the regional emissions budget is being allocated through auctions, with auction proceeds used by participating states to accelerate the deployment of end-use energy efficiency and clean energy technologies and provide other consumer benefits.

Offsets serve as a limited compliance flexibility mechanism for regulated facilities under the RGGI program. The program is designed to prioritize emission reductions within the capped electric generation sector of RGGI-participating states. The quantitative limit on offsets was set at a level that approximates the amount of offsets equivalent to 50 per cent of the projected avoided emissions that would need to be achieved to comply with the emissions cap (RGGI, 2006). At the start of the program, a regulated facility will be able to meet 3.3 per cent of its compliance obligation during a compliance period through the use of offsets. If the emission allowance price rises above a specified level or price trigger, a regulated facility can use a higher percentage of offsets to meet its compliance obligation. (The price trigger is evaluated on the basis of long-term price signals. These signals are determined based on a 12-month rolling average price, following a 14-month market settling period, starting from the beginning of each new compliance period.) If the price exceeds US$7 (stage-one trigger), a regulated facility can use offsets to meet up to 5 per cent of its compliance obligation; and if it exceeds US$10 (stage-two trigger), it can use offsets to meet 10 per cent of its compliance obligation. Both stage-one and stage-two price triggers are calculated based on formulas in RGGI Model Rule definitions of stage-one and stage-two 'threshold price'.

Standard authority and administrative bodies

The program authority for RGGI is distributed among the participating states with each state's environmental regulatory agency serving as the administrative authority in its state. RGGI is composed of individual CO_2 Budget Trading Programs in each of the ten participating states (RGGI, 2007b). These ten programs are implemented through state regulations, based on a RGGI Model Rule, and are linked through CO_2 allowance reciprocity. Owners and operators of regulated power plants will be able to use a CO_2 allowance issued by any of the ten participating states to demonstrate compliance with the state program governing their facilities. Taken together, the ten individual state programs function as a single regional compliance market for carbon emissions.

Each state agency is responsible for the administrative tasks related to implementation of its state CO_2 Budget Trading Program, such as monitoring compliance, tracking emissions and allowances, approving offset projects and awarding offset allowances to offset projects in its state (RGGI, 2007b). However, the participating states utilize a shared regional administrative infrastructure to help implement the program, including a single regional platform for CO_2 emissions and allowance tracking and offset project tracking, and a regional auction process that relies on a single regional auction platform. The US Environmental Protection Agency (EPA) provides administrative support to the RGGI program through the receipt and processing of quarterly CO_2 emission data reports.

Regional scope

As of July 2009, the RGGI program had ten participating US states in the Northeast and Mid-Atlantic regions: Connecticut, Delaware, Maine, Maryland, Massachusetts, New Hampshire, New Jersey, New York, Rhode Island and Vermont.

Recognition of other standards/links with other trading systems

As launched on 1 January 2009, RGGI is not linked to any other trading system. If the stage-two allowance price trigger is reached, regulated facilities will be able to utilize offsets credits or allowances generated by offset projects located outside the United States to meet a portion of their compliance obligation. This is limited to offset credits or allowances issued pursuant to a mandatory carbon constraining program outside the US that places a specific tonnage limit on GHG emissions, or GHG emission reduction credits certified pursuant to protocols adopted through the UNFCCC process (RGGI, 2007a). This provision provides the opportunity for linkage with both of the project-based mechanisms of the Kyoto Protocol, including offset credits from the CDM and JI, and potentially other mandatory programs too.

State staff members involved in the RGGI program are actively engaged in the Western Climate Initiative (WCI) and Midwestern Regional Greenhouse Gas Reduction Accord processes, supporting these efforts using the experience they have developed through the RGGI program. Links between RGGI and other mandatory programs are seen as a long-term goal, and five RGGI states are members of the International Carbon Action Partnership (ICAP), a group of countries and regions that have implemented or are actively pursuing the implementation of carbon markets through mandatory cap-and-trade systems.

Market size and scope

Tradable unit and pricing information

The tradable units generated from offset projects created under the RGGI program are referred to as 'CO_2 offset allowances' and measured in units of short tons of CO_2e. The RGGI program uses units of short tons in order to be consistent with current US EPA CO_2 emission reporting in the US for certain power plants and industrial sources.

Participants/buyers

Regulated facilities under the RGGI program include all fossil fuel-fired electric generating units with a capacity greater than 25MW within the boundaries of the ten current participating US states. There are no limitations on who may participate in the RGGI offset market. Any person may submit an offset project to a state agency for regulatory review. Such persons are referred to as offset 'project sponsors'.

Current project portfolio

RGGI's first three-year compliance period started in January 2009. The program is expected to cap CO_2 emissions at 188 million short tons to the end of 2014. Although trading of RGGI emission allowances has begun, with the first auction taking place in September 2008, no offset credits have yet been traded under the RGGI program. As the use of offsets for compliance can change with the emission allowance price triggers, it remains to be seen what future role and size the offset market will have under the RGGI program (Point Carbon, 2008b).

Offset project eligibility

Project types

The RGGI program uses a top-down model for assessing the eligibility of offset projects. Currently, only five offset project types are eligible under RGGI:

1   landfill methane capture and destruction;
2   sulphur hexafluoride (SF_6) emission reduction in the electricity transmission and distribution sector;
3   carbon sequestration through afforestation activities;
4   CO_2 emission reduction or avoidance from natural gas, oil or propane combustion due to end-use energy efficiency in the building sector;
5   avoided methane emissions from agricultural manure management operations.

Detailed requirements for the above offset project types are included in state CO_2 Budget Trading Program regulations, which are based on the RGGI Model Rule. The participating states have also indicated their intention to expand the number of eligible offset project types over time.

Project locations

Currently, eligible offset projects must be located within a RGGI participating state, or any other state or US jurisdiction where a cooperating regulatory agency has entered into a memorandum of understanding (MOU) with the appropriate regulatory agency in all ten RGGI participating states to provide oversight support for the project. However, if the stage-two trigger comes into effect, the geographic project location boundary will be expanded to allow, under certain conditions, offsets from any mandatory carbon constraining program outside the USA.

Project size

There are no project size requirements for the offset project types currently approved by RGGI participating states.

Start date

Offset projects must have commenced on or after 20 December 2005.

Crediting period

The initial crediting period for all offset projects is ten years. Once a project is approved, it can be renewed for an additional 10 years, pending project resubmission and regulatory approval. For afforestation offset projects, the initial period is 20 years and the renewal period is for an additional two 20-year periods, if approved after expiration of the previous period.

Co-benefit objectives and requirements

There are no additional co-benefit objectives or requirements for offset projects under the RGGI program. However, potential co-benefits were one criterion considered in the process of selecting eligible project types under the RGGI program (Sherry, 2008).

Additionality and quantification procedures

Additionality requirements

RGGI takes a standardized approach to evaluating additionality through benchmarks and performance standards. Additionality is evaluated through a combination of general additionality requirements for all eligible offset projects and specific requirements for each project type designed to address project-specific issues, which are specified in state regulations. The general requirements specify that CO_2 offset allowances are not awarded to offset projects that:

- commenced prior to 20 December 2005;
- are required pursuant to any local, state or federal law, regulation or administrative or judicial order;
- include an electricity generation component, unless the project sponsor transfers the legal rights to all attribute credits (other than CO_2 offset allowances) generated by the project that may be used to comply with a renewable portfolio standard or other regulatory requirement to the state regulatory agency or its agent;
- receive funding or other incentives from incentive programs funded by electricity or natural gas ratepayers, or through proceeds from the auction of CO_2 allowances;
- are awarded credits or allowances under any other mandatory or voluntary GHG program (RGGI, 2007a).

In addition, offset project applications must be submitted within six months of project commencement.

Quantification protocols

Quantification protocols for establishing emission baselines, determining emission reductions or carbon sequestration, and monitoring and verification are based on a top-down approach. Specific quantification protocols and requirements for each project type are included in state regulations, which are based on the RGGI Model Rule. The protocols provide detailed requirements and formulas for the determination of emission baselines, the calculation of emissions reduced or sequestered, and for monitoring and verification.

Leakage and permanence

There are no provisions for addressing potential project emission leakage. The protocols also require that the monitoring and verification plans of all projects be evaluated by an independent state-accredited verifier, and that offset project applications and monitoring and verification reports include a certification statement and certification report from a state-accredited independent verifier. Specific protocols have been developed to address the issue of permanence in connection with afforestation offset projects. Project developers are required to place the land developed for afforestation projects under a legally binding permanent conservation easement, which requires that the land be managed to maintain long-term carbon density in accordance with environmentally sustainable forestry practices (RGGI, 2007a). In addition, sequestered carbon is discounted by 10 per cent prior to the award of CO_2 allowances to account for potential reversals of sequestered carbon, unless the offset project sponsor holds long-term insurance, approved by the state regulatory agency, which guarantees replacement of lost sequestered carbon for which CO_2 offsets were awarded.

Project approval process

Validation and registration

Validation, referred to as 'consistency determination', is the first step of the application process for offset projects under the RGGI program. The RGGI participating states have jointly developed detailed project applications for each eligible offset project category that specify project documentation requirements to demonstrate conformity to regulatory requirements. The project's validation application, referred to as a 'consistency application', must include a certification statement and certification report from a independent verifier that is accredited by the RGGI participating state in which the offset project is located, and then must be submitted to the appropriate state regulatory agency in the state where the offset project is located. The state agency then evaluates and approves or rejects the project based on demonstrated consistency with state regulations and documentation required in the consistency application.

Monitoring, verification and certification

The submission of an annual monitoring and verification report by the offset project developer to the appropriate regulatory agency is the second step in the application process under the RGGI program. A monitoring and verification report must demonstrate the precise amount of GHG emissions reduced or sequestered during the reporting period. It must also include a certification statement and certification report from a state-accredited independent verifier demonstrating that it was reviewed by an accredited independent verifier. The monitoring and verification report is then evaluated by the state regulatory agency to determine whether and in what amount CO_2 offset allowances will be awarded.

Registries and fees

RGGI has set up an emission and allowance registry called the RGGI CO_2 Allowance Tracking System (RGGI COATS). The RGGI participating states have developed an offset module for RGGI COATS (RGGI, undated). While individual RGGI participating states may require state-specific application procedures, RGGI COATS is used for all project registration, tracking of offset project consistency application, and monitoring and verification report submissions, project regulatory status, and the state award of CO_2 offset allowances. There are no fees associated with use of the registry but each state may develop a fee structure to cover the administrative costs related to processing offset project applications.

Selected issues

As the first mandatory GHG cap-and-trade program in the USA, RGGI has set the stage and served as a laboratory for the design of other GHG cap-and-trade systems in the USA. It has already set precedents for other programs to follow, such as the collaboration between energy and environmental agencies in designing the program, and a new approach to allocating allowances through auctions (Sherry, 2008).

The RGGI cap-and-trade began in January 2009, and at the time of writing there has been little activity in the RGGI offsets market. Up until mid-2009 RGGI allowances have traded in the range of US$2–4 per ton, a relatively weak price signal for offset project development.

Since the use of offsets for compliance under the program can increase depending on the price of emission allowances, the role offsets will play over the long term remains to be seen. Some regulated facilities and investors have expressed concern that the system of price triggers adds additional uncertainty about offset eligibility and compliance requirements (Natsource, 2007). Reviews of the RGGI program design have presented what are, in some cases, conflicting concerns regarding the challenges of too small or too large an offset market. Limiting the offset project location and type has raised concern that the RGGI offset market may encounter a liquidity problem and present a missed opportunity to use the efficiency of the global markets (Capoor and Ambrosi, 2007).

Several interested parties in the region have requested that the eligible project types be expanded. For example, the Forest Guild, a forestry network, recommended that forest management projects be allowed as an offset project type (Point Carbon, 2007b), and the US Department of Agriculture recommended that avoided methane emission from aerobic treatment systems be allowed (Vanotti and Szogi, undated).

In contrast, others are concerned that the state environmental regulatory agencies lack the administrative capacity to handle the additional workload associated with expanding eligible offset project types. RGGI's administrative structure is consistent with the distributed legal structure of the program, which is based on individual state regulations in each participating state. Evaluating offset projects may become an overwhelming administrative burden for the state environmental regulatory agencies, a burden that may not be evenly distributed if some states have a greater potential for offset project development.

How the program will perform administratively remains to be seen. The participating states have coordinated to develop consistent applications and submittal materials and are using a regional registry to track project status and the state award of CO_2 offset allowances.

Western Climate Initiative

www.westernclimateinitiative.org

Unless referenced otherwise, the information in this section is based on the above website and personal communications.

Overview

Type of standard and context

The Western Climate Initiative (WCI) is a multi-jurisdictional collaboration that seeks to develop regional strategies to address climate change in North America. As of July 2008, the WCI partners included 11 jurisdictions: Arizona, California, Montana, New Mexico, Oregon, Utah and Washington in the USA; and British Columbia, Manitoba, Ontario and Quebec in Canada. Other states and provinces in Canada, Mexico and the US have joined as observers.

On 22 August 2007, consistent with previously established state and provincial goals, the WCI partners announced its regional goal to collectively reduce emissions to 15 per cent below 2005 levels by 2020.

In September 2008, Design Recommendations for the WCI Regional Cap-and-Trade Program were released. The recommended design for the WCI cap-and-trade program proposes regulating entities that exceed the emission threshold of $25,000mtCO_2e$ from electricity generation, combustion at industrial and commercial facilities, and industrial process emission sources. At the start of the second compliance period, coverage of emissions from residential, commercial and industrial fuel combustion facilities, as well as transportation fuel combustion from gasoline and diesel, is recommended. Offsets and allowances from other trading systems will be used as a limited compliance mechanism under the WCI system and may make up no more than 49 per cent of the total emission reductions from 2012 to 2020. WCI partner jurisdictions may independently further limit the use of offsets. Further development of the WCI offset program is ongoing; refer to the WCI website for the latest information.

Standard authority and administrative bodies

The WCI partners plan to create a regional administrative organization that will coordinate the regional allowance auctions, track emissions and market activity, coordinate the review and adoption of protocols for offsets, and coordinate the review and issuance of offset credits, among other tasks. WCI partner jurisdictions will serve as the regulatory and enforcement authorities.

Regional scope

The WCI partners currently include the 11 jurisdictions in the USA and Canada noted above, which encompasses approximately 20 per cent of the population of the USA and nearly 75 per cent of the population of Canada.

Recognition of other standards/links with other trading systems

The WCI partner jurisdictions will seek bilateral and multilateral links with other government-approved cap-and-trade systems in order to make allowances from all participating partner organizations fully fungible.

Regarding the WCI design and possible federal programs:

> the WCI partner jurisdictions have designed a program that can stand alone, provide a model for, be integrated into, or be implemented in conjunction with programs that might ultimately emerge from the federal governments of the United States and Canada. The WCI partner jurisdictions intend to promote and influence federal GHG emission reduction programs that are consistent with WCI cap-and-trade design principles, and ensure those programs translate into absolute GHG reductions. In the event WCI issues allowances before a federal program in Canada or the United States, WCI partner jurisdictions will work to ensure that those allowances are fully recognized and valued in the operation of a federal program (WCI, 2008).

Market size and scope

Tradable unit and pricing information

Not applicable.

Participants/buyers

Not applicable.

Current project portfolio

Not applicable.

Offset project eligibility

Project types

The WCI partners' jurisdictions have identified the following list of project types as a priority for investigation and potential participation in the offset program:

- agriculture (soil sequestration and manure management);
- forestry (afforestation/reforestation, forest management, forest preservation/ conservation, forest products);
- waste management (landfill gas and wastewater management) (WCI, 2008).

Project locations

The WCI partners' jurisdictions may approve, certify and issue offset credits for projects located throughout the United States, Canada and Mexico where such projects are subject to comparably rigorous oversight, validation, verification and enforcement as those located within the WCI jurisdictions. They will not accept offset credits for GHG reductions in developed countries (Annex-1 countries in the UNFCCC) for projects that reduce, remove or avoid emissions from sources that within WCI partner jurisdictions are covered by the cap-and-trade program. The WCI partners' jurisdictions may accept offset credits from developing countries through, for example, the CDM of the Kyoto Protocol, and they may establish additional criteria to apply similar rigour to the WCI approved/certified offset projects or other requirements appropriate to enabling the use of these offset credits in the cap-and-trade program (WCI, 2008).

Project size

To be determined.

Start date

To be determined.

Crediting period

To be determined.

Co-benefit objectives and requirements

To be determined.

Additionality and quantification procedures

Additionality requirements

To be determined.

Quantification protocols

To be determined.

Project approval process

Validation and registration

To be determined.

Monitoring, verification and certification

To be determined.

Registries and fees

Each of the WCI partners has joined the Climate Registry. It is described as 'a nonprofit organization that provides meaningful information to reduce greenhouse gas emissions. The Climate Registry establishes consistent, transparent standards throughout North America for businesses and governments to calculate, verify and publicly report their carbon footprints in a single, unified registry' (The Climate Registry, 2009). The Climate Registry will play an important role in establishing an accurate reporting mechanism and an accounting infrastructure on which the WCI cap-and-trade program could be based.

Selected issues

The WCI offset program is still under development. Therefore, there are a limited number of specific issues to date.

By restricting offsets to 49 per cent of emissions reductions relative to 2012 levels, the WCI offset limit is perhaps the most stringent among cap-and-trade programs. This has raised concerns among some stakeholders that access to offsets may be too limited, while other stakeholders remain concerned that this amount of offsets is still too high.

The WCI is currently exploring the adaptation of currently available project protocols or the development of the new ones. The WCI offsets program will be concentrated on agriculture and forestry mitigation options; for many of the project types with considerable offset potential, such as forest management, experience with offsets and offset protocols is thus far relatively limited.

Midwestern Greenhouse Gas Reduction Accord

www.midwesternaccord.org

Unless referenced otherwise, the information in this section is based on the above website and personal communications.

Overview

Type of standard and context

The Midwestern Greenhouse Gas Reduction Accord (MGGRA) calls for the establishment of GHG emission reduction targets and the development of a regional cap-and-trade program. It was established in 2007 by governors of six US states in the Midwest and one Canadian province. The MGGRA cap-and-trade program aims to begin the first compliance period on 1 January 2012.

The MGGRA Advisory Group was convened in 2008 to develop draft recommendations for the establishment of GHG emission reduction targets and for the design of a regional cap-and-trade system. These draft recommendations were released on 8 June 2009. The final design recommendations are expected later in 2009. The recommendations include an emission reduction target of 20 per cent below 2005 levels by 2020 and 80 per cent below 2005 levels by 2050 (MGGRA Advisory Group, 2009). Offsets are recommended as part of the proposed cap-and-trade program and are required to be real, additional, verifiable, permanent and enforceable. The use of offsets is recommended to be limited to 20 per cent of each regulated facility's compliance obligation (MGGRA Advisory Group, 2009). The Advisory Group recommends that this limit on the use of offsets be subject to review and adjustment based on experience with the offset program, including the 'jurisdictions' comfort level with offsets and the availability of offsets that meet the protocol requirements and cost containment needs of the program' (MGGRA Advisory Group, 2009).

Standard authority and administrative bodies

The MGGRA Advisory Group recommends the establishment of a Regional Administrative Organization (RAO), which would include a board staffed by representatives from each participating jurisdiction and additional staff employed directly by the RAO. The RAO would serve as a technical assistance organization and would have no regulatory or enforcement authority itself (MGGRA Advisory Group, 2009). Accord partner jurisdictions would continue to serve as the regulatory and enforcement authorities.

The MGGRA Advisory Group recommends the establishment of a technical committee, tasked with drafting offset project protocols and reporting findings to the scientific committee, a standing body comprising scientists and experts with 'in-depth understanding of climate science and offset program principles and implementation challenges' (MGGRA Advisory Group, 2009). The scientific committee would 'accept, reject, or suggest modifications to the technical committees' (MGGRA Advisory Group, 2009).

Regional scope

As of June 2009, the MGGRA had six participating US states in the Midwest and one Canadian province: Iowa, Illinois, Kansas, Manitoba, Michigan, Minnesota and Wisconsin. Additionally, Indiana, Ohio, Ontario and South Dakota are serving as observers in the process and considering participation.

Recognition of other standards/links with other trading systems

The Advisory Group recommends that the MGGRA link to the Regional Greenhouse Gas Initiative (RGGI), the Western Climate Initiative (WCI), the European Union Emission Trading System (EU ETS) and other mandatory GHG reduction programs as appropriate (MGGRA Advisory Group, 2009). Further consideration of offset credits generated under the CDM and JI programs was also recommended based on the extent to which MGGRA offset requirements are met by these programs and whether or not other programs accept these credits.

The MGGRA Advisory Group recommends that the proposed program enable a transition to a federal program in the USA and Canada.

Market size and scope

Tradable unit and pricing information

To be determined.

Participants/buyers

Regulated facilities under the Midwestern Accord are recommended to include all facilities in participating states and provinces with annual emissions of greater than 25,000 metric tons that are in the following sectors and use the following fuels: electricity generation and imports; industrial combustion and process sources; residential, commercial and industrial fuels; and transportation fuels. Manitoba will include the latter two fuel categories beginning in the second compliance period (MGGRA Advisory Group, 2009).

Current project portfolio

Not applicable.

Offset project eligibility

Project types

To be determined.

Project locations

Initially, the MGGRA Advisory Group recommends that offset projects be limited to MGGRA participating jurisdictions and those states and provinces that have signed a memorandum of understanding (MOU) with the MGGRA. States and provinces not part of the MGGRA may be required to have a GHG regulatory program comparable to the MGGRA. Participation of international offsets beyond the USA and Canada is to be determined.

Project size

To be determined.

Start date

To be determined.

Crediting period

To be determined.

Co-benefit objectives and requirements

To be determined.

Additionality and quantification procedures

Additionality requirements

The MGGRA requires that offsets be additional. The MGGRA Advisory Group recommends that additionality of offsets be defined as:

> *The reductions resulting from offset projects must be shown to be 'in addition to' reductions that would have occurred without the incentive provided by offset credit. To be eligible for offsets, offset projects cannot be required by law or regulations, and must exceed baseline criteria. The baseline should use standardized criteria (including but not limited to, performance standards, financial feasibility criteria, market penetration, and project start date) that serve to exclude 'business as usual' projects from eligibility. (MGGRA Advisory Group, 2009)*

Quantification protocols

The MGGRA Advisory Group recommends the use of standards-based protocols. Prior to program launch, the Advisory Group recommends selecting initial offset project types and protocols through the use of the technical and scientific committees.

Permanence

Specific requirements to ensure that offsets are permanent have been recommended by the MGGRA Advisory Group:

> *Emission reductions or removals must be backed by guarantees if they can be reversed, i.e. re-emitted to the atmosphere. For emission reductions or sequestration activities that can be reversed, adequate safeguards should be established to minimize the risk of reversal, or a mechanism should be provided for the replacement of those tons. (MGGRA Advisory Group, 2009)*

Project approval process

Validation and registration

The MGGRA Advisory Group recommends a two-step review process for individual offset projects. Validation, referred to as a 'consistency determination', a preliminary review prior to the project commencement would serve as the first step (MGGRA Advisory Group, 2009).

Monitoring, verification and certification

The second recommended step in the review process, monitoring and verification, would include the application for offset credits equal to the actual emission reductions or sequestrations demonstrated by the offset project. The Advisory Group recommends that all applications be verified by an accredited, independent third-party verifier, and that these verified applications be reviewed by states or provinces. Additionally, the Advisory Group recommends periodic auditing of projects. Certification requirements are to be determined.

Registries and fees

To be determined.

Selected issues

The MGGRA offset program is still under development.

Canada's Offset System for Greenhouse Gases

www.ec.gc.ca/creditscompensatoires-offsets/

Unless referenced otherwise, the information in this section is based on the above website, personal communications and these sources: Environment Canada (2008a); Environment Canada (2009c).

Overview

Type of standard and context

Canada has committed to an overall emission reduction target of 20 per cent below 2006 levels by 2020. Canada's Offset System for Greenhouse Gases will serve as a compliance mechanism for facilities that will be regulated under the Government of Canada's planned GHG regulations. The Government has stated that it will announce a full suite of specific policies covering all major sources of Canadian GHG emissions in autumn 2009, and complete the detailed regulatory development work in 2010. Details of other compliance mechanisms available to regulated facilities may be announced as part of the full suite of specific policies covering all major sources of Canadian GHG emissions in autumn 2009.

In June 2009, Environment Canada released an overview of the Offset System and two draft guides for public comment: 'Program Rules and Guidance for Project Proponents' and 'Program Rules for Verification and Guidance for Verification Bodies'. The draft 'Guide for Protocol Developers' was previously published in August 2008. Final versions of the three Program Rules and Guidance documents are expected in the autumn of 2009. The following information is based on the draft documents and should therefore not be considered final.

Standard authority and administrative bodies

The Minister of the Environment will have overall authority over the design and operation of the offset system, which will be administered as a voluntary program under the Canadian Environmental Protection Act, 1999, section 322 (Environment Canada, 2009a).

Regional scope

Only GHG reductions or removals achieved in Canada are eligible for generating offsets under Canada's Offset System for Greenhouse Gases (Environment Canada, 2009a).

Recognition of other standards/links with other trading systems

The offset system overview states that if formal linkages are established with other regulatory-based systems in North America or abroad, including offset systems, consideration will be given to the mutual recognition of credits among systems.

Market size and scope

Tradable unit and pricing information

The tradable units will be referred to as an 'offset credit', which is equivalent to 1 metric ton of CO_2e emissions reduced or removed (Environment Canada, 2008b). No pricing information is currently available as the program is not yet in force.

Participants/buyers

Sellers in the offset system can be any legal entity developing an eligible offset project. Buyers may include facilities complying with their reduction targets under the regulations, or any other entities purchasing the credits voluntarily for trading or for compliance under other regulatory systems. Other participants in the offset system may include technical service providers, third-party verifiers, aggregators and traders.

Current project portfolio

There are currently no offset projects as the scheme is not yet in force.

Offset project eligibility

Project types

A draft schedule for reviewing protocols for different project types has been made available for public comment (Environment Canada, 2009a). The final approved schedule is expected to be released with the program rules and guidance for protocol developers in the autumn of 2009. The draft schedule references external protocols from other programs that may be adapted under the Canadian program. These are as follows:

- afforestation;
- landfill gas capture and combustion;
- reduced or no tillage;
- wind;

- forest management;
- wastewater management;
- anaerobic biodigesters.

The draft schedule indicates that, tentatively, the review of the first four of the project types listed above will begin in November 2009, and the review of the last three project types will begin in February 2010. The schedule will be updated with new project types on a quarterly basis.

As the system matures and resources become available, it is anticipated that one-of-a-kind projects and quantification methodologies will be reviewed to determine whether they meet the requirements of the offset system.

Project locations

Offset projects must result in GHG emission reductions or removals in Canada (Environment Canada, 2009a).

Project size

There are no limitations on project size. Similar smaller projects may be aggregated or bundled to reduce project application costs (Environment Canada, 2009a).

Start date

Projects must have started on or after 1 January 2006 (Environment Canada, 2009a). For projects susceptible to easy reversal (such as no- or reduced-tillage projects in agriculture), a normalized baseline may be specified that projects can use regardless of start date (Environment Canada, 2009a). Reductions occurring on or after 1 January 2011 are eligible for offset credits (Environment Canada, 2009a).

Crediting period

The crediting period for an offset project is equal to or less than the length of the registration period (Environment Canada, 2009b). The registration period lasts for eight years and typically begins on the registration date, either the date of acceptance of the project application or any date up to one year after this acceptance if requested (Environment Canada, 2009b). In the case where a project has started to achieve reductions before a quantification protocol is approved for the project type, and the application form is submitted within six months of the publication of an approved protocol, the project proponent may select a registration period starting in the year that the project began reducing emissions.

Registration periods may be renewed once after the first period of eight years with the following restrictions: the registration periods must be contiguous, agricultural sink projects may register for up to three registration periods, and forestry sink projects (excluding avoided or reduced deforestation) may register for up to five registration periods (Environment Canada, 2009a).

Co-benefit objectives and requirements

Offset projects have to comply with existing environmental regulations but do not have to achieve additional co-benefits. In the future, projects may be required to identify and address broader environmental impacts.

Additionality and quantification procedures

Additionality requirements

The project's emission reductions/removals must go beyond the baseline scenario identified in the project quantification protocol (Environment Canada, 2009a). Emission reductions or removals from an offset project must be surplus to all federal, provincial/territorial and regional legal requirements and other climate change incentives (Environment Canada, 2009a). Exceptions to this regulatory surplus requirement include cases where: the project reductions are surplus to the performance standard or emission reduction benchmark legally required; a normalized baseline has been prescribed in the quantification protocol; or where the project developer can demonstrate an alternate cost-effective way to stay in compliance with the legal requirement without undertaking the project (Environment Canada, 2009a). If legal requirements vary significantly across the country, the quantification protocol may specify the use of a normalized baseline to ensure jurisdictions with GHG regulations are not disadvantaged (Environment Canada, 2009a). Projects are eligible to receive credits up until the date that a legal requirement comes into force. In order to receive credits beyond that date, reductions must be surplus to legal requirements (Environment Canada, 2009a). Climate change incentive programs will not affect eligibility if an agreement to receive funding from the incentive program is entered into prior to 1 January 2011, or a tax incentive is claimed under terms that are in effect as of 15 June 2009, unless otherwise specified (Environment Canada, 2009b).

Quantification protocols

The quantification requirements presented in the draft guide for protocol developers, from August 2008, are based on the framework and principles of International Organization for Standardization (ISO) standard ISO 14064–2: specification with guidance at the project level for quantification, monitoring and reporting of greenhouse gas emission reductions or removal enhancements (Environment Canada, 2008b). Following a period of public comment and review, the final version of the program rules and guidance for protocol developers will be published in the autumn of 2009 (Environment Canada, 2009a). A top-down approach is outlined in the draft guide, which requires that all projects are quantified using protocols that have been pre-approved by Environment Canada. Offset System Quantification Protocols (OSQPs) are developed by protocol developers external to the federal government. OSQPs set out the quantification approach, and the monitoring and data management requirements that must be followed by a project proponent when implementing and reporting on an offset project. Protocol developers may choose from a range of approaches for baseline quantification development, including a historic benchmark, a performance standard, and comparison-based, projection-based, pre-registered and normalized baselines; or they may propose another approach. Protocol developers must provide justification for the baseline approach proposed in the Base Protocol Plan they submit for review to Environment Canada. Review and development of quantification protocols will be in accordance with the protocol submission schedule posted on the offset system website.

Permanence

Permanence of carbon sequestration projects is addressed through a 25-year liability period (Environment Canada, 2009b). Project proponents must submit evidence and a certification statement to confirm that carbon storage is maintained for 25 years after the last offset credit is issued (Environment Canada, 2009b). Certification statements must attest that no reversal has occurred and provide evidence that quantification protocol requirements are maintained; however, verification of the certification statement is not required (Environment Canada, 2009b). If there is a reversal during the liability period or if a certification statement is not submitted, then the project proponent must replace all previously issued credits with an equivalent number of credits that are accepted for compliance by the federal GHG regulations, to ensure that the environmental integrity of the offset system is maintained (Environment Canada, 2009b). To address the risk that a project proponent may not be able to replace the credits when a reversal occurs, a discount factor, specified in the quantification protocol, will be applied to all offset credits from carbon sequestration projects (Environment Canada, 2009b).

Project approval process

Validation and registration

The first step in the offset credit creation process is project registration. To register a project, the project proponent must make an assessment of the project's eligibility to generate offset credits, and ensure that there is an approved applicable Offset System Quantification Protocol. If no Offset System Quantification Protocol has been approved for the project type, the project proponent can work to develop a new one. Once the project proponent has made this initial assessment, they must prepare the project application form provided in the *Program Rules and Guidance for Project Proponents*, demonstrating that the project will satisfy the offset system eligibility criteria. The completed application must be submitted for review. Environment Canada will review the application to ensure that the documentation is complete and to make a preliminary assessment that all eligibility criteria are likely to be satisfied if the project proceeds as per the application. The project application form will be posted on the offset system website for public review and comment. Once the application has been accepted, the project will be registered as an offset project.

Monitoring, verification and certification

Monitoring, data quality assurance, quality control and record keeping requirements for offset projects will be specified in the quantification protocol for each project type (Environment Canada, 2009b). Offset credits generated must be verified by an accredited third-party verifier, referred to as a 'Verification Body', as defined by the 'Program Rules for Verification and Guidance for Verification Bodies' (Environment Canada, 2009b). Environment Canada will certify the issuance of offset credits from an offset project by issuing a certification report and depositing the designated number of offset credits in the project proponent's account in the tracking system once all certification conditions have been met (Environment Canada, 2009b).

Registries and fees

Each verified offset credit will be assigned a unique serial number (Environment Canada, 2009a). The offset credits will be managed by an online tracking system that is currently under development (Environment Canada, 2009b).

The Offset System is expected to operate on a cost-recovery basis. Fees may be charged for registration and certification, and to cover the cost of operating the unit tracking system. Fees will not be charged at the outset of the program to facilitate a quicker start to the Offset System. The fee structure is currently under development.

Selected issues

Canada's Offset System for GHG is still under development. All program rules are drafts and have been published for public comment. Final program rules are expected to be published in autumn 2009.

Australian Carbon Pollution Reduction Scheme

www.climatechange.gov.au

Unless referenced otherwise, the information in this section is based on the above website and personal communications.

Overview

Type of standard and context

The Australian Government plans to establish a Carbon Pollution Reduction Scheme outlined in the December 2008 release of the Australia's Low Pollution Future White Paper (Australian Government, 2008b). The Carbon Pollution Reduction Scheme Bill 2009 legislation was introduced to the Australian Parliament in early May 2009 (Point Carbon, 2009). This scheme would establish the long-term target of a 60 per cent reduction in GHG emissions from 2000 levels by 2050 and a medium-term target to reduce emissions by a minimum of 5 and maximum of 15 per cent below 2000 levels by 2020, in the context of a global commitment to reduce emissions,. The Australian Government intends to have the Carbon Pollution Reduction Scheme commence on 1 July 2010, though this is looking increasingly unlikely (Point Carbon, 2009). The cap-and-trade scheme will initially cover the stationary energy, transport, fugitive, industrial processes, waste and forestry sectors. The Australian Government plans to consider allowing domestic offsets in 2013, while concurrently considering the inclusion of the agricultural sector in the scheme. Until then, regulated entities are eligible to use CER and ERU credits generated from CDM and JI projects as an unlimited compliance mechanism (Australian Government, 2008b). Both the 'Report of the Task Group on Emissions Trading' and the 'Garnaut Climate Change Review Interim Report' have explicitly recommended the use of domestic and international offsets as a cost-efficient compliance mechanism under the proposed emission trading scheme (Australian Government, 2007; Garnaut, 2008a).

Standard authority and administrative bodies

The Carbon Pollution Reduction Scheme will need to be established by legislation and associated regulations. A single independent regulator will administer the Carbon Pollution Reduction Scheme, along with the National Greenhouse and Energy Reporting System and the Renewable Energy Trust. Functions of the regulator will include enforcing compliance, maintaining the registry of domestic and international units, auctioning permits and administering permit allocation rules (Australian Government, 2008a). An independent expert advisory committee will be convened to conduct strategic reviews of the scheme; the first review is expected in 2014 (Australian Government, 2008b).

Regional scope

The scheme outlined in December 2008 is focused on developing a domestic emission trading scheme limited to Australia. However, in February 2008, Australia and New Zealand announced that they were examining ways to develop a linked scheme (Point Carbon, 2008a). (New Zealand introduced its domestic cap-and-trade scheme on 1 January 2008. Forestry was the only sector covered in the first year (Point Carbon, 2008a).)

Recognition of other standards/links with other trading systems

The scheme has been designed to be able to link with international carbon markets. Entities are permitted to use credits generated from the CDM (CERs) and JI (ERUs). No exports of allowance credits under the Australian Scheme will be permitted, unless bilateral agreements with one other country are established following a five-year notice period (Australian Government, 2008b). NSW legislation states that the NSW GGAS will cease to operate upon the commencement of a Australian national emissions trading scheme (NSW DWE, 2008).

Market size and scope

Tradable unit and pricing information

Offset credits will be measured in units of metric tons of CO_2e. Pricing information is not available as yet.

Participants/buyers

Under the proposed cap-and-trade scheme, regulated facilities will include direct emissions from large facilities and upstream fuel suppliers (Australian Government, 2007). Offset credits from CDM and JI have been recommended as an unlimited compliance mechanism for the facilities regulated under the cap-and-trade system (Australian Government, 2008a).

Current project portfolio

Not applicable.

Offset project eligibility

Project types

Offset credits generated from land use, forestry, wood production, avoided deforestation and carbon geosequestration projects have been identified as priorities under the proposed national emission trading scheme (Australian Government, 2007). Unlimited offset credits for carbon sequestration projects from forestry and possibly soil management practices have been recommended in 'The Garnaut Climate Change Review Final Report' (Garnaut, 2008b).

Project locations

International offsets generated through CDM and JI projects are proposed as eligible for compliance under the scheme (Australian Government, 2008b). The use of domestic offsets is proposed for 2013 and has yet to be defined (Australian Government, 2008a).

Project size

Under development.

Start date

Under development.

Crediting period

Under development.

Co-benefit objectives and requirements

Under development.

Additionality and quantification procedures

Additionality requirements

Under development.

Quantification protocols

Under development.

Project approval process

Validation and registration

Under development.

Monitoring, verification and certification

Under development.

Registries and fees

Under development.

Selected issues

Because Australia's Program is still in the process of being developed, there are few lessons to be learned to date. With the commencement of an Australian national emission trading scheme, the currently operating NSW GGAS would cease to operate. Several issues for consideration raised in 'The Garnaut Climate Change Review Final Report' address the transition from the regional to the national emission trading scheme and may also be relevant for other nations where regional programs have been established prior to a federal system. The issues raised include (Garnaut, 2008a):

- Treatment of accredited abatement providers: project income could be reduced if projects eligible under GGAS are not eligible or to a lesser degree under the national scheme.
- Forestry carbon sequestration projects may be inconsistent with the intention to include the forestry sector under the cap of a national scheme.
- Mechanisms are needed to prevent hoarding of GGAS certificates in expectation of a higher price under the national emission trading scheme.

New South Wales Greenhouse Gas Reduction Scheme

www.greenhousegas.nsw.gov.au

Unless referenced otherwise, the information in this section is based on the above website, personal communications and these sources: NSW GGAS (2004a); NSW GGAS (2004b); Crossley (2005); Tradition Financial Services (2007); GGAS (2007a); GGAS (2007b).

Overview

Type of standard and context

The New South Wales Greenhouse Gas Reduction Scheme (NSW GGAS, formerly the New South Wales Greenhouse Gas Abatement Scheme) is a mandatory emission trading scheme for the state's electricity sector. It was established initially as a voluntary scheme, which commenced in 1997, via amendments to the Electricity Supply Act 1995. The scheme became mandatory on 1 January 2003. On 1 January 2005 the Australian Capital Territory (ACT), a separate jurisdiction physically located inside New South Wales, also introduced legislation to become part of the NSW GGAS.

The NSW GGAS establishes an annual state-wide per capita GHG emission target, a 'benchmark', for the electricity sector, based on the reductions necessary to achieve the global target set in the Kyoto Protocol of reducing overall GHG emissions to 5 per cent below the baseline year (1990) emissions (NSW GGAS, undated). The scheme's initial benchmark target of $8.65mtCO_2e$ per capita in 2003 was reduced steadily each year to $7.27tCO_2e$ per capita in 2007.

An obligation to achieve the reductions is placed on regulated entities (called 'benchmark participants'), which are predominantly electricity retailers, but also include some generators who sell electricity directly to customers, as well as some large energy-using customers who opt voluntarily to manage their own emission targets (the latter are referred to as 'elective benchmark participants'). For each benchmark participant, targets are based on the entity's share of electricity sales (or use, in the case of large users) multiplied by the overall regional electricity emission benchmark, i.e. the per capita emission benchmark described above multiplied by the region's population for that year (IPART, 2007).

The regulated entities can meet their emission reduction targets either by directly reducing the average emission intensity of the electricity they sell (or use) or by purchasing accredited offsets and surrendering these to the scheme's compliance regulator. Two forms of offset can be used. The first, and most widely used, are tradable abatement certificates called NSW GHG Abatement Certificates (NGACs), while Renewable Energy Credits (RECs) created under a separate national scheme aimed at stimulating renewable energy projects (the Mandatory Renewable Energy Target, MRET) can also be used.

To encourage compliance, a penalty is imposed if participants fail to meet their targets. The current rate is AU$12 per tCO_2e (note that the tax-effective rate is considerably higher). The choice of penalty level was set initially to allay concerns by some parties that compliance costs for regulated entities could become too high, and effectively caps compliance cost for participants.

Standard authority and administrative bodies

The Independent Pricing and Regulatory Tribunal of New South Wales (IPART) serves as both the scheme administrator and the compliance regulator, although the two functions are managed separately. (In the ACT GGAS, IPART has been appointed as the scheme administrator, but the compliance regulation function is performed by the ACT's Independent Competition and Regulatory Commission (ICRC).) As the scheme administrator, IPART's role includes the management of applications for project accreditation and the approval of Abatement Certificate Providers (ACP). ACPs are the offset project developers. As compliance regulators, they also have the authority to enforce the obligations of the scheme's participants. All audits under the GGAS are required to be performed by specialized auditors appointed to the Audit and Technical Services Panel.

Regional scope

NSW GGAS and ACT GGAS regulate the emissions of the electricity sector within the jurisdictions of New South Wales and the ACT, respectively. The obligations are imposed by and large on retailers, and the costs for reducing emissions are ultimately borne by residents in these jurisdictions.

NSW and the ACT are part of a regional electricity grid, the National Electricity Market (NEM), which connects the States along Australia's eastern seaboard (Queensland, New South Wales, Victoria, the ACT, South Australia and Tasmania). Projects that achieve abatement at the point of electricity generation in any part of the NEM are eligible to create NGACs; however, projects that create NGACs via measures to reduce electricity demand, sequester carbon and/or reduce industrial process emissions must be physically located in NSW or the ACT.

Recognition of other standards/linkage with other trading systems

The experiences gained in establishing and administering the NSW GGAS have been used in the development of the proposed Australian Carbon Pollution Reduction Scheme. If implemented, this scheme will expand the emission trading framework beyond NSW and the ACT to include all other Australia States and Territories. Legislation to implement the scheme was introduced to the Australian Parliament in May of 2009.

To avoid having two schemes operating simultaneously, in 2005 the NSW Government passed legislation extending the GGAS scheme to 2020 or until a national trading scheme is introduced. That is, NSW GGAS will cease to operate upon the commencement of an Australian national emission trading scheme (NSW DWE, 2008).

In order to maintain a strong incentive for demand-side activities (which will not be part of the national scheme), in April 2009 the NSW GGAS released a plan proposing a new Energy Savings Scheme (ESS). The ESS aims to build on the Demand Side Abatement rule of the NSW GGAS by setting an energy savings target for energy retailers. Retailers meet their target by obtaining and surrendering energy-saving certificates (ESCs), which represent delivered energy efficiencies (NSW, 2009). Legislation to implement the ESS is expected to be introduced by the NSW Government in 2009.

The Mandatory Renewable Energy Target (MRET), established by the Renewable Energy (Electricity) Act 2000, commenced on 1 April 2001. The MRET requires the generation of 9000GW of renewable energy production per year by 2010. Regulated entities under the NSW GGAS can meet their compliance mechanism by purchasing RECs generated under the MRET.

Market size and scope

Tradable unit and pricing information

NSW GHG Abatement Certificates (NGACs) are the tradable units in the NSW and ACT GGAS and represent the abatement of 1 metric ton of CO_2e emissions (tCO_2e).

The maximum price for NGACs on the open market is effectively constrained by the cost of non-compliance (i.e. the penalty set by the scheme administrator) set at AU\$12 per tCO_2e (NSW GGAS, 2007). In 2008, NGACs traded for about US\$5 (Hamilton et al, 2009).

Demand for NGACs is expected to rise throughout 2009 as a result of the lowering of the State's GHG benchmark and an expected increase in the average emission intensity of electricity production. However, the transition to a national emission trading scheme, and in particular uncertainty around the treatment of NGACs and the future of compliance obligations, is likely to remain a source of uncertainty in the NGAC market until transitional arrangements are fully clarified.

Participants/buyers

The NSW GGAS and the ACT GGAS have both mandatory and voluntary participants. Mandatory participants are predominantly electricity retailers, but also include a small number of electricity generators that supply directly to retail customers and market customers with a market load supplied directly from the National Electricity Market (NEM). Voluntary participants can include large electricity customers and State Development projects designated by the Minister of Planning to manage their own GHG targets. To be eligible as 'elective benchmark participants', large energy users must have annual electricity loads greater than 100GWh, with at least one site that consumes 50GWh annually. As of June 2008, there were 13 voluntary benchmark participants. No State Development projects participate in the scheme.

Current project portfolio

A total of 224 offset projects have been accredited under the NSW GGAS, as of 31 May 2009 (NSW GGAS, 2009). The scheme administrator reports that since the scheme began in 2003, the offset credits generated to 31 May 2009 have amounted to over 90MmtCO$_2$e (NSW GGAS, 2009). (Information on the current project portfolio changes rapidly. For the latest Scheme Newsletter and project portfolio information, see www.greenhousegas.nsw.gov.au/Documents/syn96.asp.) Table 4.2 provides information on offset credits generated by project type.

Table 4.2 *Offset credits created in the NSW GGAS as of 31 May 2009, by project type*

Offset project type	Cumulative offset credits (NGACs) created since 2003 (each equivalent to 1mtCO$_2$e)
Generation	55.6 million
Demand-side abatement	29.2 million
Large-user abatement	3.4 million (including RECs)
Carbon sequestration	2 million

Source: NSW GGAS, 2009.

Offset project eligibility

Project types

The GGAS allows for the creation of offset credits by Abatement Certificate Providers (ACPs) for activities in one or more of the four offset project types outlined in the Greenhouse Gas Abatement Rules (IPART, 2007):

1   Electricity generation: Covers low-emission generation of electricity including co-generation and renewable energy production, or improvements in the emission intensity of existing generation activities.
2   Demand-side abatement: Covers activities that result in reduced consumption of electricity in residential, commercial or industrial settings.
3   Large-user abatement: Covers activities carried out by elective participants to reduce on-site emissions not directly related to electricity consumption. Project examples include increasing the efficiency of on-site fuel use; switching to lower emission intensity fuels; the abatement of on-site GHG emissions from industrial processes; and the abatement of on-site fugitive GHG emissions.
4   Carbon sequestration: To be eligible, sequestration projects must:
    • qualify as either an afforestation or reforestation project as defined by the United Nations Framework Convention on Climate Change (UNFCCC);
    • take place in NSW;
    • own or control the Carbon Sequestration Rights for the land;
    • demonstrate that the carbon sequestration achieved will be maintained for at least 100 years;
    • provide documentation that appropriate procedures are in place to manage risks of carbon loss, such as fire, disease or climate variability; and
    • maintain adequate records of carbon storage.

Project locations

For the certification of offset projects, activities must meet the location criteria outlined in the Greenhouse Gas Abatement Rules. Generation offset projects can be located in any part of the NEM. Demand-side abatement, large-user abatement and carbon sequestration offset projects are only eligible if implemented within NSW.

Project size

There are no project size restrictions for demand-side management, large-user on-site reduction or electricity generation projects. Carbon sequestration projects are required to meet the size requirements established by the definition of a forest in Australia and to be consistent with Kyoto Protocol guidelines: forests must be at least 0.2ha, have 20 per cent crown cover and contain tree species whose height attains 2m.

Start date

Electricity generation projects implemented after 1 January 2003 are eligible to create NGACs. However, a number of projects that pre-date the start of the scheme are also eligible. The NSW Government's rationale for this was that it provided 'credit for early action'; however, this has been one of the main sources of contention around the NSW GGAS (see Selected issues, below).

Demand-side projects must have been implemented after 1 January 2002 in NSW or after 1 January 2004 in the ACT. Carbon sequestration projects are required to take place on land that was predominantly non-forest prior to 1 January 1990. In addition, the increases in carbon stocks are only recognized after 1 January 2003 and the projects must provide continued carbon storage for at least 100 years.

Crediting period

No explicit crediting period was established under the NSW GGAS as it was always intended to be a transitional mechanism.

Co-benefit objectives and requirements

There are no co-benefit requirements for offset project eligibility.

Additionality and quantification procedures

Additionality requirements

The NSW GGAS addresses additionality by using a performance standard approach through the development of a positive technology project list and by establishing baseline scenarios for each project and technology type.

Quantification protocols

The NSW GGAS uses a top-down approach for baseline quantification. The Greenhouse Gas Benchmark Rules provide rules for calculating baseline emission rates for each type of eligible offset project.

For electricity generation abatement activities, the baseline is calculated using a variety of methods that depend on whether the generator is new or existing, fossil fuel based, and/or covered by a prior NSW voluntary benchmark system. In general, the baseline is set either relative to the regional benchmark intensity indicated above or to the facility's prior emission rate.

To accommodate the variability among projects, four different methods are used to calculate the baselines for demand-side abatement activities.

For large-user abatement activities, the baseline is expressed in tCO_2e per unit of industrial output.

Permanence

For carbon sequestration activities, the credits generated are calculated based on the change in carbon stocks over a defined time period. NSW GGAS outlines specific criteria and procedures to ensure the permanence of offset credits generated from carbon sequestration projects. Forest managers are required to conduct an uncertainty analysis and demonstrate that a 70 per cent probability exists that the actual net increase in the carbon stocks is greater than the number of offset credits created. They are also required to conduct periodic monitoring of the forest to verify carbon storage. If carbon stocks fall below the number of offset credits granted, then forest managers are required to inform the scheme administrator (IPART) and to discontinue registration of additional offset credits. IPART can also decide that the project developer (the ACP) needs to purchase offset credits from the open market to account for the shortfall in carbon stocks.

Project approval process

Validation and registration

The regulations governing the NSW GGAS do not prescribe a specific validation approach. The scheme administrator (IPART) has established a risk-based approach to determining whether the eligibility of or the abatement from an offset project must be audited by a third party. The higher the risk is determined to be, the more likely it is that IPART will require a third-party audit. IPART also decides the frequency and scope of such an audit. The risk assessment is based on the participant's compliance history, the complexity of the offset project, the number of projects that share a common process and additional relevant factors. In some cases, where the risk is considered to be very low, the scheme administrator may not require an audit prior to accreditation of the project.

Monitoring, verification and certification

Projects are required to report their status and the emissions abated every year. The offset credits generated are required to be verified to demonstrate ongoing compliance with the NSW GGAS, and the frequency of the verification is determined by the scheme's administrator. The reporting requirements for monitoring the compliance of offset credits are outlined in the Guide to Record Keeping for Abatement Certificate Providers, available at www.greenhousegas.nsw.gov.au/documents/GtRK-ACP.pdf.

Qualifying reductions from electricity generation, demand-side abatement and large-user offset projects are calculated on an annual basis and credited as offset credits for the duration of the project.

Registries and fees

The NSW GGAS Registry was commissioned by IPART, and is operated and maintained by LogicaCMG, an IT and business services company. Offset credits are registered on the online registry for a fee of US$0.13 (AU$0.15) per certificate. Change in ownership is recorded in the registry, but the registry does not serve as a platform for offset credit trading. The buying and selling of offset credits is done on the open market.

Selected issues

The NSW GGAS was not originally set up as an offsets scheme. The primary objectives were to provide incentives for abatement (across power generation, energy efficiency, forests and industrial processes), rather than provide an avenue for entities to offset their emissions. There was no direct link established between actual emissions and the surrender of GGAS credits to offset those emissions. Rather, the scheme created a mandatory requirement to surrender a certain number of GGAS credits based on share of power sales in a year. This is more akin to a renewable portfolio standard than a cap-and-trade system with offsets.

The approaches used by the NSW GGAS to address forest permanence and forest carbon accounting have been used as a platform for the development of other forest schemes, including the Australian national emission trading scheme, and the New Zealand Permanent Forest Sinks Initiative.

Several examples of best practice in the NSW GGAS offset program scheme design were identified in a 2007 report by Abatement Solutions – Asia Pacific (AS-AP, 2007). They include the following:

- The NSW GGAS has a strong legal basis, which allows the scheme's administrator (IPART) to use enforcement mechanisms to create a strong culture of compliance among the program participants. This is possible because Australia already has a very strong regulatory culture.
- The NSW GGAS reduces the administrative burden for smaller projects by using a risk-based approach to determining auditing frequency and flexibility of unit creation, as well as using a tiered approach for compliance and performance monitoring requirements.
- The NSW GGAS has enhanced the consistency and ease of project assessment and project applications by developing a set of document templates for project assessment and user-friendly application guidelines for each project type.

Concerns about the effectiveness, efficiency and equity of the NSW GGAS were raised in a report prepared by the Center for Energy and Environmental Markets (CEEM) in 2007 (Passey et al, 2007):

- The lack of any required assessment of additionality in the validation process of offset credits is a primary criticism. The report cites several examples of the generation of offset credits from pre-existing power generation facilities, one of which pre-dates even the voluntary scheme and creates a large portion of total NGACs. This claim is corroborated by the Australian Government's estimate that the additional abatement driven by the NSW GGAS in 2010 will be only $5MtCO_2e$ and not the $20MtCO_2e$ claimed by IPART.
- Given concerns about additionality, CEEM's overall concern is that NSW GGAS may actually delay more significant action to reduce GHGs at the state and national levels by creating a perception that emissions are already being reduced.
- A conflict of interest exists by having both the scheme administrator and compliance regulator responsibilities managed by IPART.
- There is concern about the transparency of the reporting process due to the lack of publicly available data and information on the methodology or the equation used, on how the baselines were calculated and on how compliance is achieved.

- The diversity of project types and providers in the early years of the scheme is low. Most of the offset credits from 2003 to 2005 came from only a few project types. Since then, there has been a greater level of diversity in the types of projects registered under the scheme, including forests, industrial energy efficiency, commercial energy efficiency and industrial process emissions.

With the commencement of an Australian national emission trading scheme, the currently operating NSW GGAS will cease to operate. However, the NSW Government has taken the energy efficiency aspects of the scheme and created a state-based energy efficiency target scheme that will continue to operate in parallel with a national emission trading scheme. The other parts of the NSW GGAS will transition to the national scheme but details of the transition are yet to be released. See the selected issues in the earlier section above on the 'Australian Carbon Pollution Reduction Scheme' for further comments.

Chicago Climate Exchange

www.chicagoclimateexchange.com

Unless referenced otherwise, the information in this section is based on the above website, personal communications and these sources: Goodell (2006); Chicago Climate Exchange (CCX) (2007); Point Carbon Research (2007b).

Overview

Type of standard and context

The Chicago Climate Exchange was launched in 2003 as a voluntary greenhouse gas (GHG) emission cap-and-trade scheme located in North America. This section gives a short overview of the CCX cap-and-trade program, but primarily focuses on its offset program.

Participation in the CCX cap-and-trade scheme is voluntary, but once entities elect to participate and commit to emission reduction targets, compliance is legally binding. Members can comply by either cutting their emissions internally, trading emission allowances with other CCX members, or purchasing offsets generated under the CCX offset program. There is a 50 per cent limit on the use of offsets to meet compliance standards. Offsets currently account for approximately 15 per cent of all emission reductions achieved under the CCX program.

In the first phase of the scheme, from 2003 to 2006, CCX members agreed to cut their emissions by 1 per cent each year below their annual average emissions for the period 1998–2001, thereby achieving a reduction of 4 per cent by the end of the fourth year. For the second phase from 2007 to 2010, the original members agreed to cut their emissions by an additional 0.5 per cent each year to achieve an overall target of 6 per cent below 1998–2001 levels by 2010. New members participating in the second phase must achieve a similar overall reduction target by 2010 by reducing their emissions by 1.5 per cent each year.

Standard authority and administrative bodies

The CCX has a well-developed administrative structure, which includes:

- senior management and staff responsible for the day-to-day administration of the CCX and its operations;
- reviewing and approving offset projects that follow standardized protocols;
- a 12-member Committee on Offsets comprising CCX members responsible for reviewing and approving proposed offset projects that use non-standardized protocols. Each member is appointed by the CCX Executive Committee for one year with the possibility of renewal;
- a Committee on Forestry comprised of CCX members responsible for the review of proposed forestry projects;
- a Regulatory Services Provider who is responsible for auditing the baseline and annual emission reports of CCX members, monitoring trading activity and reviewing verifiers' reports for offset projects;
- independent auditors called CCX Verifiers responsible for verifying a project's annual GHG sequestration or destruction; there are currently 29 approved auditors;
- Technical Advisory Committees comprised of external experts, established at the request of the Committee on Offsets or on an ad hoc basis by CCX administrators to assist in the development of rules for each offset type.

Regional scope

Initially, CCX membership was limited to the USA but it is now open to participants from other countries. Similarly, offset projects were mostly implemented in the USA but offsets generated by projects outside the USA are now also sold on the CCX.

Recognition of other standards/links with other trading systems

The CCX allows trading of CDM Certified Emission Reductions (CDM CERs) once the project has been approved by the CCX Committee on Offsets. The CERs must be retired in exchange for receiving the CCX's tradable unit, the Carbon Financial Instrument (CFI).

Market size and scope

Tradable unit and pricing information

Carbon Financial Instruments (CFIs) are the tradable units of voluntary carbon dioxide equivalent (CO_2e) reductions under the CCX. One CFI is equivalent to 100 metric tons of CO_2e. CFIs have been traded at an average price of US$2–7.5 per metric ton of CO_2e.

Participants/buyers

The CCX distinguishes between members, associate members and participant members. Members are organizations, companies, institutions and municipalities that produce significant direct GHG emissions and are committed to reducing their emissions. In 2008, the CCX had nearly 400 members, including companies such as the Ford Motor Company, American Electric Power, Sony Electronics and Bank of America; US state governments such as the State of New Mexico; and educational institutions such as Michigan State University.

Associate members are entities that produce negligible direct GHG emissions but are committed to offsetting 100 per cent of their indirect emissions associated with energy purchases and business travel.

Participant members include Offset Providers, owners of title rights to credits generated by offset projects and Offset Aggregators, which are entities that serve as the administrative representative of multiple offset projects, in particular projects generating less than $10,000mtCO_2e$ in emission reductions per year.

Current project portfolio

As of March 2009, the CCX had registered approximately $60MmtCO_2e$ in offsets from over 137 projects. (The latest information is available at www.chicagoclimateexchange.com/offsets/projectReport.jsf.)

Offset project eligibility

Project types

Project types eligible to register and sell offsets on the CCX include:

- energy efficiency projects;
- fuel-switching projects;
- renewable energy projects;
- methane capture coal mines, livestock operations and landfills;
- biosequestration through forestry and agricultural management practices; and
- destruction of ozone depleting substances.

Project locations

Projects cannot be located in EU-ETS (http://ec.europa.eu/environment/climat/emission/index_en.htm) member states or in other Annex B countries that have ratified the Kyoto Protocol (see http://unfccc.int/kyoto_protocol/items/2830.php).

Project size

There is no limit on project size.

Start date

Projects that sell offsets on the CCX should not have started before 1 January 1999. However, the earliest start date for forestry projects is 1 January 1990 and for HFC destruction projects is 1 January 2007.

Crediting period

Most of the eligible project types can earn offsets for the eight-year period 2003–2010. The exceptions include renewable energy projects, which can earn offsets from 2005 to 2010 (six years), HFC destruction projects, which can earn offsets from 2007 to 2010 (four years) and rangeland soil carbon projects, which can earn offsets from 2006 to 2010 (five years).

Co-benefit objectives and requirements

Offset projects must comply with the rules and regulations of the host country. Beyond this legal prerequisite, the CCX does not have requirements to ensure stakeholder involvement and other secondary benefits.

Additionality and quantification procedures

Additionality requirements

The CCX requires that offset projects are 'recently implemented', 'beyond regulation', and involve 'rare/best in class' practices. Some project types are required to fulfil specific rules:

- Commit to five years of continuous no till or strip till on enrolled acres for agricultural soil carbon sequestration projects.
- Be located within designated land resource regions or other specified locations for rangeland soil carbon sequestration projects.
- Be located on deforested or degraded land for forestation and forest enrichment projects, or in specified locations for forest conservation projects if they are undertaken in conjunction with forestation on a contiguous site.
- Only destroy ozone-depleting chemicals that can no longer be produced (e.g. CFCs that can no longer be manufactured in the USA but are still present in refrigerators and air conditioning units); ensure that electricity generated from renewable energy projects is not also sold as 'green'; and that if Renewable Energy Credits (RECs) are applicable to the project, they must be surrendered and retired by the CCX to avoid double-counting.

Quantification protocols

The baselines and methodologies for calculating emission reductions are predefined for each eligible project activity. Some baselines are project-specific, including large reforestation projects that are credited relative to measured, site-specific carbon levels prior to the start of the project. Other baselines are quantified using performance standards, such as avoided deforestation projects in Brazil that use predetermined annual deforestation rates for specific Brazilian states.

Permanence

CCX rules address the permanence issues around forestry projects by deducting 10–20 per cent from the recommended crediting rate. This deduction is intended to account for reversals in carbon storage that take place *after* the crediting period. This 10–20 per cent is never given back to the project owner.

Furthermore, CCX deducts an additional 20 per cent of the issued offsets and places them in a reserve pool. This reserve pool is intended to account for reversals that take place *during* the crediting period. These credits are given back to the project owner at the end of the five-year crediting period as long as no reversals in carbon storage have occurred during the crediting period.

Project approval process

Validation and registration

The CCX does not distinguish between validation and verification. Both steps are usually done at the same time and are called 'project verification and enrolment'. The initial validation of projects is optional.

Monitoring, verification and certification

Verification of emission reductions is done annually and projects are subject to on-site inspections at any time for the duration of the project's enrolment with CCX. A CCX-approved third-party auditor verifies an eligible project's actual annual GHG emission reductions, sequestration or destruction, and submits a Verification Statement to the CCX. Following a successful review by CCX staff and by third-party providers of regulatory services, the CCX issues the offset provider or aggregator with Carbon Financial Instrument (CFI) contracts equivalent to the quantity of emissions reduced, sequestered or destroyed.

Registries and fees

The CCX Registry (www.chicagoclimatex.com/content.jsf?id=501) is the electronic database that serves as the official record holder and transfer mechanism for CFI contracts. All CCX members have CCX Registry Accounts.

Fees for CCX membership are US$1000–60,000 per year, depending on the size and type of member. Offset registration fees are US$0.12 per metric ton from non-Annex-I countries and US$0.15 per metric ton from Annex-I countries. The trading fee is US$0.05 per metric ton. Trading and offset registration fees are posted on the CCX website and are subject to change.

Selected issues

The CCX has been a pioneer in establishing a cap-and-trade system. It was the first such system established in North America and it has given companies the opportunity to learn from and gain experience with emission reduction commitments and carbon trading.

Additionality

The CCX has been criticized for the lack of additionality of some of its offsets, in particular those issued to no-till or reduced-tillage projects (Bryk, 2006). Under CCX rules, farmers can receive CCX offset credits for practising reduced-till agriculture, even if they have been practising it for many years prior to joining the program. If such credits do not represent a change from 'business-as-usual' practices for these farmers, then no 'additional' soil carbon sequestration will occur; the buyer of these credits will be allowed to emit more GHGs without the achievement of corresponding reductions through the offsets.

CCX administrators recognize this concern, but argue that investments in no-till agriculture by proactive farmers should be rewarded. The argument is that it would unfair to the proactive farmer if only farmers who had just started practising no tillage were allowed to earn the credits. CCX administrators further argue that if they did not provide offset credits to farmers already practising no till it could introduce a perverse incentive to cease no-till practices now in order to take them up again at a later point and earn offset revenue.

Permanence

CCX deducts 10–20 per cent from the recommended crediting rate to account for reversals in carbon storage that take place after the crediting period. In addition, CCX requires a carbon reserve pool equal to 20 per cent of all offset credits issued for the project, and cancellation of reserve pool offsets in case of sequestration reversal. Offsets held in this reserve pool are returned to the project developer after five years of compliance. CCX notes that to date the need to address reversal or non-performance has been significantly less than the reserved offsets. While the latter mechanism addresses short-term reversals (within the five-year crediting period), the first mechanism seems insufficient to address the risk of long-term reversals (e.g. the release of stored carbon due to a return to full tillage agriculture).

5

Offset Features of Other GHG Reduction Programs

In addition to cap-and-trade systems, there are other mandatory systems that establish GHG emission reduction targets for regulated or government entities and allow offsets to serve as a compliance mechanism to meet emission reduction requirements.

The following sections describe in more detail the offset features of three mandatory systems:

Alberta-Based Offset Credit System
State Power Plant Rules in Oregon, Washington and Massachusetts
British Columbia Emission Offsets Regulations

Voluntary GHG reduction programs enlist entities to voluntarily reduce emissions through internal actions or through the purchase of offsets or allowances. While neither strictly offset programs nor cap-and-trade systems, they provide frameworks for the development of offset markets and methodologies. Later in this chapter we review the US Environmental Protection Agency's Climate Leaders program. Other examples of voluntary GHG reduction programs not further described in this book include:

Japan's Keidanren Voluntary Action Plan on the Environment: Sixty-one different Japanese business associations and corporations have committed to reducing their average emissions from 2008 to 2012 to below 1990 levels. CDM and JI offsets generated through Ministry of Economy Trade and Industry Domestic Credit Program can be purchased to achieve this goal. More information can be found at: www.keidanren.or.jp/english/policy/pol058/index.html.

Australia's Greenhouse Challenge Plus program: Similar to the US EPA Climate Leaders program, Challenge Plus provides emission reduction reporting and technical assistance. Challenge Plus members can purchase offsets through the 'Greenhouse Friendly Initiative', which certifies offsets from Australian projects as well as from 'carbon neutral' products. More information can be found at: www.environment.gov.au/settlements/challenge and www.climatechange.gov.au/greenhousefriendly.

Canada's GHG Clean Start Registry: Based on ISO 14064 standards, the Clean Start Registry provides participating Canadian businesses with the opportunity to post their carbon footprint and to claim carbon neutrality by purchasing carbon offsets. More information can be found at: www.ghgregistries.ca/cleanstart/index_e.cfm (Hamilton et al, 2009).

Alberta-Based Offset Credit System

www.environment.alberta.ca/1238.html

Unless referenced otherwise, the information in this section is based on the above website and personal communications.

Overview

Type of standard and context

Alberta's offset credit system is a compliance mechanism for entities regulated under the province's mandatory GHG emission intensity-based regulatory system. As part of the 2002 Climate Change and Emissions Management Act (CCEMA) (www.canlii.ca/ab/laws/sta/c-16.7/index.html) and the 2007 Specified Gas Emitters Regulation (www.canlii.org/ab/laws/regu/2007r.139/20070717/whole.html) passed by the Alberta legislature, large final emitters (any facility in the province that emits more than 100,000mtCO$_2$e of GHGs per year) are required to reduce their GHG intensity by 12 per cent per year. The Regulation, which took effect on 1 July 2007, represents the first GHG emission legislation in Canada.

Emission intensity, under the Alberta CCEMA regulation, is defined as the quantity of GHGs released by a facility per unit of production. The CCEMA regulation has set different emission intensity reduction targets for established and new emission sources. For 'established' emitters (facilities that started commercial operations on or before 1 January 2000), emissions must be reduced by 12 per cent below their approved baseline emission intensity (based on the average of the facilities' emissions for the years 2003–2005). For 'new' emitters, (facilities that began commercial operation after 1 January 2000 and have completed less than eight years of commercial operation) the regulation has established reductions at an incremental level of 2 per cent per year beginning in the fourth year of operation (until the full 12 per cent annual reduction level is achieved).

Regulated facilities that are not able to meet their reduction obligation through direct facility improvements can meet the emission intensity reduction target through three compliance mechanisms:

- purchase or use Emission Performance Credits[a];
- contributions to the Climate Change and Emissions Management Fund at a price of CA$15 per metric ton of CO$_2$e; or
- purchase of Alberta-based offset credits.

[a]Regulated entities that are able to do better than their emission reduction target can generate Emission Performance Credits (EPC), which are serialized by Alberta Environment. These credits can be banked for use in future years or sold to other regulated facilities that have not met their emission reduction obligation.

Standard authority and administrative bodies

The Alberta provincial government has the overall program authority for the Alberta-based offset credit system. Third-party verifiers serve to verify baselines, annual compliance reports and offset credits being registered on the Alberta Emissions Offset Registry. Third-party verifiers must be professional engineers or chartered accountants with appropriate experience. Third-party verifiers must complete and submit a Statement of Qualification that states that the review team has adequate areas of knowledge and expertise as part of the required verification documentation (Alberta Environment, 2007b).

Regional scope

The regional scope of the Alberta offset system is the Canadian province of Alberta.

Recognition of other standards/links with other trading systems

Alberta has emphasized that they work with other jurisdictions and the federal government to identify how Alberta's offset system will be linked to or incorporated into Canada's GHG offset program (see Canada's Offset System for Greenhouse Gases) or other programs as they come on line.

Market size and scope

Tradable unit and pricing information

The tradable units in the Alberta offset system are referred to as 'Alberta-based offset credits' or Verified Emission Reductions or Removals (VERRs) and are measured in units of metric tons of CO_2e.

Participants/buyers

Offset projects can be developed in unregulated sectors such as small industrial facilities emitting under $100,000tCO_2e$ per year, and agricultural sectors. Market participants include project developers, aggregators, brokers and end buyers. End buyers are the regulated facilities that intend to submit offset credits for compliance (as of June 2008, regulated facilities comprised close to 100 large emitters accounting for approximately $100MmtCO_2e$ per year, nearly one half of total provincial emissions).

Current project portfolio

For the first six-month compliance cycle (July–December 2007), there were 1.5 million verified Alberta-based offset credits created and 1 million of these credits had been retired for compliance by regulated facilities (Rund et al, 2008). Approximately 2.75 million metric tons of offsets were retired for compliance in the 2008 round. As of March 2009, 36 projects were approved/created, including 15 no till/reduced tillage, 7 wind energy, 4 biomass energy, 2 enhanced oil recovery, 2 composting, 2 acid gas injection, 1 landfill, 1 energy efficiency, 1 wastewater project and 1 hydropower project. These projects are estimated to generate over 25 million offset credits through the project lifetimes (Carbon Offset Solutions, 2008).

Offset project eligibility

Project types

The Alberta offset system takes a top-down approach to approving eligible project types. Offset projects must meet the requirements for an offset project stated in section 7 of the Specified Gas Emitters Regulation. Projects must also be generated in accordance with a government-approved protocol that articulates minimum requirements for specific offset reduction activities in the province. As of July 2008, Alberta Environment, the provincial environmental regulatory agency, has 24 government-approved offset project quantification protocols.

As of March 2009, quantification protocols are available for the following projects types: acid gas injection, anaerobic wastewater treatment, beef feeding, beef-feed days, beef lifecycle, biofuel, biogas, biomass, compost, energy efficiency, enhanced oil recovery, streamlined enhanced oil recovery, landfill bioreactor, landfill gas, modal freight, non-incineration of thermal waste, pork, road rehabilitation, run-of-the-river electricity systems, solar electricity systems, tillage, waste heat recovery, streamlined waste heat recovery and wind-powered electricity systems. (The latest approved protocols are available at: www.environment.alberta.ca/1238.html.)

Project locations

All projects are required to be based in the Canadian province of Alberta.

Project size

There are no general restrictions on project size. Specific project size requirements, if any, are included in project protocols.

Small reduction projects may be aggregated into larger volume bundles for cost-efficiency of verification and transaction costs.

Start date

Project-based emission reductions or removals under the Alberta offset system are required to have resulted from actions taken on or after 1 January 2002.

Crediting period

All projects, except reduced/no-till and afforestation projects, have an initial crediting period of eight years with the possibility of extension for an additional five years from the project start date. The crediting period is 20 years for sequestration resulting from tillage management projects. Afforestation projects will be eligible for three 20-year crediting periods for a total project crediting period of 60 years.

Co-benefit objectives and requirements

There are no specific co-benefit requirements for project eligibility. Other environmental benefits may be considered when determining the eligibility of an offset project (Alberta Environment, 2008).

Additionality and quantification procedures

Additionality requirements

Additionality requirements under the Alberta offset system are defined in generic terms. Projects are required to be real, demonstrable and quantifiable, and not required by law (Alberta Environment, 2007b). Issues concerning additionality are addressed during the multi-stakeholder technical review process and during the public posting period. Project developers must demonstrate that the project meets start date and regulatory surplus requirements. No additional additionality screening tests are required.

Quantification protocols

A bottom-up approach is used to develop baseline quantification protocols under the Alberta offset system. Offset project developers propose baseline quantification methodologies that are then reviewed and approved by Alberta Environment. Monitoring requirements are not specified in the quantification protocols.

Permanence

In order to address the issue of permanence in conservation projects, the Alberta offset system has developed an 'assurance factor approach' based on consultations with the industry, Canadian Government agencies and experts. Assurance factors are used to discount the offset credits generated from carbon sequestration projects in any one year to the volume of offset credits that would be considered permanently sequestered. Once discounted, the liability is transferred from the project proponent to the Government of Alberta and the offsets achieved are valued as permanent. The Government of Alberta intends to continue to monitor the effectiveness of assurance factors in managing risk and maintaining environmental integrity.

Project approval process

Validation and registration

Validation is optional under the Alberta offset system. The Alberta Government's position is that validation is considered a business risk management tool. Validation, where undertaken, is contracted by the project developer in the private sector to perform this task (Alberta Environment, 2007b). All offset credits must be registered on the Alberta Emissions Offset Registry to be considered for compliance under the Specified Gas Emitters Regulation.

Monitoring, verification and certification

Verification and monitoring of the offsets used to achieve compliance are required under the Alberta Offset System. Offset project developers are required to prepare a monitoring plan, which includes details of the monitoring equipment to be used, the locations of the sampling points, the frequency of the sampling events and the data collection methodology. The plan must be presented to the third-party verifier as part of the verification process, and may be requested by Alberta Environment during its offset credit review.

A verification report must be submitted to the Alberta Emissions Offset Registry with the request for serialization of Offset Credits. The verification report must also be submitted to Alberta Environment by all regulated entities using offset credits to achieve compliance as part of the facility's compliance submission. All verification reports must have the endorsement of a third-party verifier who is either a professional engineer or a chartered accountant with a background in both auditing and gas emissions. The regulator tracks all verified emission offsets from projects that are used for compliance and may randomly audit offset credits submitted for compliance to ensure the credits meet government requirements.

Registries and fees

Each offset project developer is required to develop an Offset Project Plan, which includes a description of the project and the baseline used, and a monitoring and quantification plan. This information is included in the Alberta Emissions Offset Registry, a registry supported by the GHG Clean Projects Registry for Alberta's emission offset project participants only. The purpose of the registry is not to provide assurance of the validity of credits or to serve as an offset credit trading platform, but only to serve as a means of recording project and credit information, including assigning serial numbers, which are used to track offset credits.

The registry fee for activating a project account and filing a completed application is US$193 (CA$200). A fee of US$241 (CA$250) is charged for displaying preliminary project information, the GHG Project Report, GHG Project Plan, Verification Report, Statement of Verification, GHG Assertion and, where applicable, the Validation Report. To allocate a serial number to and display VERRs from a project, there is a fee of US$0.05 (CA$0.05) per VERR. No additional fees are charged to delist or retire VERRs (Canadian Standards Association, undated).

Selected issues

Following the completion of the first compliance period in March 2008, Alberta Environment collected stakeholder feedback on successes and areas for improvement in the system. The resulting report identified several issues with the Alberta offset system, including:

- a lack of market liquidity due to long transaction times and high transaction costs, although these are expected to decline with increased learning by participants;
- a lack of pricing transparency, with the news media being the only reporting source;
- a lack of general understanding among offset suppliers of the offset protocol calculation methodologies for generating carbon credits;
- market uncertainty over the future regulatory environment in Canada (Ruud et al, 2008).

The report also included several suggestions for future improvements, including:

- allowing non-Alberta offsets for compliance;
- creating an Alberta-based public exchange for credits that would facilitate more trading and provide more communication on where and how to purchase offsets;

- streamlining the protocol review and approval process;
- developing more protocols for different offset project types (Ruud et al, 2008).

Additionality concerns have been raised about the 1 January 2002 start date for determining the eligibility of offset projects. Critics argue that it is ten months before the release of Alberta's first climate change plan (in October 2002) and that commercial projects that became operational in 2002 and 2003 were highly likely to have already been in the planning and construction phases before the plan was published (Whitmore and Shariff, 2007).

State Power Plant Rules of Oregon, Washington and Massachusetts

Oregon: www.oregon.gov/ENERGY/SITING/docs/ccnewst.pdf
Washington: www.leg.wa.gov/pub/BillInfo/2003–04/Pdf/Billpercent20Reports/House/ 3141.HBR.pdf
Massachusetts: www.mass.gov/dep/air/laws/ghgappb.pdf

Unless referenced otherwise, the information in this section is based on the above website, personal communications and these sources: Trinity Consultants (2006); MassDEP (undated b).

Overview

Type of standard and context

Three US states, Oregon, Washington and Massachusetts, have set mandatory CO_2 emission standards for their state's energy facilities. Although the specific programs vary by state, regulated facilities in all states have the option of meeting their emission reduction obligations either through on-site emission reductions or the purchase of eligible offset credits.

In 1997, HB 3283 legislation established Oregon as the first US state to regulate greenhouse gas (GHG) emissions from energy facilities. The regulations were updated in 2003, requiring energy facilities to meet an emission standard that is 17 per cent better than the most efficient base-load gas plant currently operating in the USA. This translates to a standard of 0.675 pounds (lbs) of CO_2/kWh of net electricity output (Oregon Energy Facility Siting Council, undated). See www.oregon.gov/ENERGY/ SITING/docs/ccnewst.pdf for the most recent standard.

In Washington, HB 3141 legislation governing GHG emissions from energy facilities was passed in 2003 and updated in 2004. It establishes a CO_2 mitigation plan requiring energy facilities to offset 20 per cent of CO_2e emissions over a 30-year period.

In Massachusetts, 310 CMR 7.29 capped emissions from six energy facilities at historical emission levels for 2006–2008, and also capped emission rates at the same facilities to 1800lbs CO_2/MWh for 2008. Compliance may be achieved through the use of offsets. These regulations were phased out at the end of 2008 because the RGGI program regulated emissions from these facilities beginning 1 January 2009.

Facilities in all three states may meet their emission standards through on-site emission reductions. In Oregon and Washington, facilities can sponsor their own offset projects or pay a fee to a qualified organization to manage and purchase offsets on their behalf at a cost that is below the market value for offsets.

In Massachusetts, the use of offsets called GHG credits was the only alternative mechanism for compliance in the original regulation. However, on 24 December 2007, the Massachusetts Department of Environmental Protection (MassDEP) determined that insufficient GHG credits were available for affected facilities to demonstrate compliance and they allowed payments into the GHG Expendable Trust at the trust trigger price set by regulation, as an alternative means of compliance (MassDEP, undated a). After another regulation change in May 2008, facilities are now allowed to comply using certain offsets generated under the CDM and the EU ETS (MassDEP, 2008).

Standard authority and administrative bodies

All three states have a program authority to administer, verify, validate, approve and register offset projects used for compliance with state regulations. These are:

Oregon: The Energy Facility Siting Council
Washington: For energy facilities 350MW and larger, the Energy Facility Site Evaluation Council; for energy facilities 25MW–350MW, the Department of Ecology
Massachusetts: The Department of Environmental Protection

In addition, the Climate Trust was established as the only qualified organization to manage and purchase offset credits using the funds generated from Oregon's compliance fees. The Climate Trust is an offset project developer as well as an offset retailer.

Regional scope

Each state program regulates GHG emission from energy facilities within its state jurisdiction only.

Recognition of other standards/links with other trading systems

In 2007 and 2008, the Washington Legislature passed laws related to GHG emissions. The 2007 law establishes a GHG intensity requirement for new and existing power plants, which is set at 1100lbs of CO_2e/MWh. The 2008 law establishes a GHG emission reporting program in support of the anticipated Western Climate Initiative (WCI) cap-and-trade program.

In Massachusetts, 2007–2008 was the first and only compliance period for the state emission cap on energy facilities. Once the Regional Greenhouse Gas Initiative (RGGI) began in 2009, the Massachusetts program was phased out. Based on the June 2008 determination of the availability of GHG credits, regulated facilities were able to apply to verify and use European Union Emission Trading System (EU ETS) Phase II Allowances and Clean Development Mechanism (CDM) Certified Emission Reductions (CERs) that are eligible for use under Phase II of the EU ETS for compliance purposes (MassDEP, 2008).

Market size and scope

Tradable unit and pricing information

All tradable units for each of the state power plant programs are measured in short tons of CO_2e.

Oregon term: *CO_2 offset*. All facilities to date have chosen to pay a fee of US$1.27 per short ton CO_2e (US$1.40 per metric ton CO_2e) using a qualified organization (the Climate Trust) to purchase/manage offsets at below the market price of offsets. No facilities have successfully directly implemented their own offset projects and no pricing information is available for this approach.

Washington term: *carbon credit*. Facilities can pay a fee of US$1.60 per metric ton CO_2e using a qualified organization to purchase/manage offsets at below the market price of offsets. No pricing information is available for facilities that may choose in the future to directly implement their own offset projects.

Massachusetts term: *GHG credit*. The first compliance period for regulated sources was from 2007 to 2008, and several GHG Credit applications have indicated that project developers expect GHG credit prices to be approximately US$5.00 per short ton. Payments into the GHG Expendable Trust, a recent supplemental compliance mechanism, are expected to be set at a price of US$11.04 per short ton of CO_2e.

Participants/buyers

Energy facilities serve as both the program participants and the offset buyers in each of the state power plant programs.

Oregon: Regulation applies to all new energy facilities.

Washington: Regulation applies to all new energy facilities greater than 25MW in size and existing facilities that increase their energy output by 25MW or CO_2e emissions by 15 per cent or more.

Massachusetts: Regulation applies to six currently existing power generation facilities.

Current project portfolio

Oregon: Oregon was the first state with offset transactions for offsets from regulated facilities for compliance. The monetary offset rate payments have remained below the market price for offsets; all six of the new energy facilities regulated under the state power plant rule in 1997 have achieved compliance with the emission standard through payments to the Climate Trust. The Climate Trust reports that payments through the OR program have offset 1.5MmtCO$_2$e (Climate Trust, undated a) through a range of project types in the Climate Trust's offset portfolio.

Washington: None of the new qualifying energy facilities has chosen to purchase offsets for compliance since this legislation came into effect and, as a result, no transactions have occurred. The only new facilities subject to the law and regulation are a few small co-generation or biomass fuelled facilities. The co-generation facilities had to demonstrate that their CO_2 emissions were not subject to the law's provisions and the biomass facilities have undertaken small self-directed mitigation projects.

Massachusetts: Massachusetts has approved (or proposed to approve) eight offset projects. The deadline to submit applications was 31 March 2009. Massachusetts expects to create approximately 800,000 verified credits that can be used by facilities to comply with the 310 CMR 7.29. All the verified GHG credits have been transferred into compliance accounts and held by facilities; no GHG credits have been retired. Two projects may continue to generate GHG credits until 2012. These GHG credits may be exchanged for RGGI allowances from a Massachusetts set-aside account at a 2:1 discount.

Offset project eligibility

Project types

Oregon: Any project that avoids, sequesters or displaces CO_2 emissions.
Washington: Any project that avoids, sequesters or displaces CO_2 emissions and is approved by the Energy Facility Site Evaluation Council or the Department of Ecology, as applicable.
Massachusetts: Any project that reduces, avoids or sequesters emissions, except for nuclear power generation and underwater or underground sequestration activities.

Project locations

Oregon: Any location.
Washington: Not specified.
Massachusetts: Anywhere in the United States or the coastal waters thereof. Approved European Unit Allowances (EUAs) and CERs have no project location restrictions (MassDEP, 2008).

Project size

Oregon and Washington: There are no project size limitations for the Oregon or Washington programs.
Massachusetts: Offset projects must generate an average of at least 5000 short tons of CO_2e per year over the period applied for. For projects not located in Connecticut, Delaware, Maine, Massachusetts, Maryland, New Hampshire, New Jersey, New York, Rhode Island and Vermont or the coastal waters thereof, the minimum is 20,000 short tons of CO_2e.

Start date

Oregon: For compliance under the monetary path, a site certificate holder must provide the funds to the Climate Trust prior to start of construction of the energy facility. The Climate Trust has two years to fund the offset projects for that energy facility.
Washington: Mitigation projects directly managed by the facility owner must have started after 1 July 2004.
Massachusetts: The start date for offset projects is 1 January 2006.

Crediting period

There are no crediting period specifications for any of the state programs.

Co-benefit objectives and requirements

Oregon and Washington: No co-benefit requirements.

Massachusetts: No explicit rules, but the program administrators may consider 'the extent to which a project may be harmful to the environment or public health when certifying or verifying GHG credits' (MassDEP, undated b).

Additionality and quantification procedures

Additionality requirements

Additionality requirements in all three programs are very general.

Oregon: Offsets must be regulatory surplus and will be evaluated based on the 'extent to which the CO_2 reductions would have occurred in the absence of the offset project' (Oregon Energy Facility Siting Council, undated).

Washington: Offsets must 'accomplish CO_2 reductions that would not otherwise take place' (Washington State Legislature, 2004).

Massachusetts: Offsets must be regulatory surplus, 'real and additional' and applicants may be required to 'specify the best management practice used to determine an emission baseline' (MassDEP, undated b).

Quantification protocols

Oregon: No specific quantification protocols are provided. The Oregon regulation simply states that sufficient documentation must be provided to the program administrator in order 'to determine what reductions resulted from the projects, based on the monitoring and evaluation the applicant proposes' (Oregon Energy Facility Siting Council, undated).

Washington: No specific quantification protocols provided.

Massachusetts: Offset project developers must specify the best management practice used to determine the emission baseline and the quantification protocol used for calculating offset credits, as well as a proposed method for determining, monitoring and assuring compliance. All offset project applications must contain a description of potential project leakage, and describe how such leakage was or will be monitored and avoided. Offset credits will be voided to the extent of any leakage that is identified. To address permanence concerns of carbon sequestration projects the landowner must, at a minimum, 'place the land within the sequestration project boundary under a legally binding instrument, acceptable to the Department, that the sequestered emissions remain captured and securely stored in perpetuity' (MassDEP, undated b).

Project approval process

Validation and registration

Oregon: The program administrator reviews the project additionality and baseline quantification materials submitted for an offset project sponsored by a regulated entity. Validation of offset projects is carried out by the program administrator based on the review of submitted materials.

Washington: Offset projects must be approved by either the program administrator, the Washington State Energy Facility Site Evaluation Council or Department of Ecology, or a local administrator, and must be included in the regulated entities' site certificates or order of approvals.

Massachusetts: There are no offset project validation or registration requirements. All offset projects are reviewed and approved through either the prospective or the retrospective certification process discussed in the section below.

Monitoring, verification and certification

Oregon: Offset project monitoring, verification and certification are carried out by the program administrator. The program administrator ensures that the proposed project is implemented by including restrictions in the site certificate for regulated facilities, but may not require of 'the applicant guarantee that it will achieve the predicted CO_2 offsets from these projects' (Oregon Energy Facility Siting Council, undated).

Washington: There are no explicit verification or certification requirements, but the legislation states that 'implementation will be monitored by an independent entity' (Washington State Legislature, 2004).

Massachusetts: Certification and verification of offset projects are based on approval by the Massachusetts Department of Environmental Protection. Certification can take place either prior to project implementation (prospective certification) or after implementation (retrospective certification). Verification of offset credits must occur within two years of project activity. Applications for project certification and verification must contain a complete project description, a quantification protocol, an estimate of the offset credits generated, a monitoring methodology and the expected offset sale price.

Registries and fees

Oregon: No registry exists for tracking offset projects, but the program administrator holds 'in trust the CO_2 offsets that the certificate holder provides in order to meet the CO_2 standard' (Oregon Energy Facility Siting Council, undated).

Washington: No registry requirements exist for tracking offset projects or credits generated.

Massachusetts: The GHG Registry serves as the Massachusetts state registry to track offset credits used for compliance under the state program.

Selected issues

The power plant offset rules are among the earliest GHG policy initiatives in the USA. As such, the current development of more comprehensive regional and national climate policy initiatives in the USA could bring significant changes to these rules in the near future.

For example, Massachusetts, as a partner to RGGI, phased out its state CO_2 emission standard at the end of 2008. Compliance with RGGI expands the number of regulated facilities in Massachusetts from 6 under the state regulation to 32. The GHG offset credits generated under the power plant emission standard may be applied towards the 2007–2008 state compliance period. However, if they were not from one of the five offset categories allowed under RGGI, and if applications were received by 25 January 2008, credits generated until 2012 can be exchanged for RGGI allowances at a ratio of 2:1 short tons of CO_2e to one RGGI allowance.

Development of state-level emission standards has provided valuable experience and lessons have been learned for state involvement in RGGI and Western Climate Initative processes. In Massachusetts, the Department of Environmental Protection has served as the program authority for the state emission standard, developing and revising regulation and participating in the development of the RGGI Model Rules. Although few offset projects have been developed and reviewed under the state standards, the development of the state emission standards is believed to have increased staff understanding and capacity related to GHG offset credits, and overall has increased readiness for the state's participation in RGGI.

Washington and Oregon are both members of the WCI. The WCI design process is ongoing and it is yet to be determined how the development of WCI may influence the state emission standards in Washington and Oregon.

In Oregon, where emission standards have been in place the longest, since 1997, experience has provided several lessons learned for the states participating in the WCI process. Regulation in Oregon resulted in the establishment of the Climate Trust, which has demonstrated an effective business model for offset providers and has provided valuable lessons for the developing carbon offset market.

Although regulated entities have the option to acquire their own offset credits to achieve compliance, Oregon Department of Energy has found that the failed attempt of the Klamath Cogeneration Plant to do so has strongly increased support from utilities for a fixed price compliance option. The Klamath Cogeneration Plant, constructed prior to the establishment of the Oregon state emission standard, won the bid to build a new energy facility by agreeing to acquire GHG offsets. When the international offset projects developed by the plant's third-party contractor failed to be verifiable, the plant was required instead to pay the monetary offset fee to the Climate Trust. Since then, other investor-owned utilities in the state have expressed increased concern about independently developing offset credits for compliance.

Although state emission standards appear to have provided valuable lessons for regional initiatives, concerns have been raised regarding the effectiveness of the emission reductions in the Washington and Oregon state regulations. Monetary offset fees have been set at levels well below the market price: facilities in Oregon pay a fixed price to the Climate Trust, currently set at US$1.67 per short ton of CO_2e, a price significantly lower than the retail offset price of US$12 per short ton that the Climate Trust offers. There is obvious concern that the contributions made by regulated facilities have not effectively offset actual emissions. It is suggested by staff members that the starting price for the monetary offset fees was expected not to cover the full cost of equivalent offset credits, but to serve as a starting point from which to raise fees over time, providing incentives for emission reductions.

British Columbia: Emission Offsets Regulation

www.env.gov.bc.ca/epd/codes/ggrta/offsets_reg.htm

Unless referenced otherwise, the information in this section is based on the above website and personal communications.

Overview

Type of standard and context

British Columbia's Greenhouse Gas Reduction Targets Act (GGRTA) was passed in November 2007 and came into force on 1 January 2008. The GGRTA established targets for reducing GHG emissions in British Columbia (BC) 33 per cent below 2007 levels by 2020 and 80 per cent below 2007 levels by 2050 (Greenhouse Gas Reduction Targets Act, S.B.C., 2007).

The legislation requires that each public sector organization (which includes the provincial government and other provincial public sector organizations) be carbon neutral from 2010 onwards and that the provincial government be carbon neutral for the 2008 and 2009 calendar year in relation to GHG emissions from travel of public officials (Greenhouse Gas Reduction Targets Act, S.B.C., 2007). To comply with this regulation the provincial government and public sector organizations must document actions taken to minimize GHG emissions and apply emission offsets to net all remaining emissions to zero (Greenhouse Gas Reduction Targets Act, S.B.C., 2007).

All emission offsets used in order to comply with this regulation must be acquired from the Pacific Carbon Trust on terms and conditions approved by BC's Minister of Finance (Greenhouse Gas Reduction Targets Act, Carbon Neutral Government Regulation, B.C. Reg. 392/2008). BC's Ministry of Environment has established an emission offsets regulation that sets out requirements for GHG reductions and removals from projects or actions to be recognized as GGRTA Offsets (Greenhouse Gas Reduction Targets Act, Emission Offsets Regulation, B.C. Reg. 393/2008). The detailed guidance document for the regulation is expected in 2009 (Ministry of Environment, 2009).

Standard authority and administrative bodies

The BC Ministry of Environment serves as the regulatory authority for the BC emission offsets regulation.

The Pacific Carbon Trust is a provincial Crown corporation with a mandate 'to deliver quality BC-based greenhouse gas offsets to help clients meet their carbon reduction goals and to support growth of this industry in BC' (Pacific Carbon Trust, 2009). The Pacific Carbon Trust is the designated organization from which provincial public sector organizations must acquire emission offsets to meet their compliance obligations (Greenhouse Gas Reduction Targets Act, Carbon Neutral Government Regulation, B.C. Reg. 392/2008).

Regional scope

At this time, the BC emission offsets regulation only applies to GHG emission reduction activities in the Canadian province of British Columbia.

Recognition of other standards/links with other trading systems

Currently there are no links with other trading systems. The GGRTA includes provisions to enable linkages with other offset systems, and to ensure that the adoption of other regulations is not restricted (Greenhouse Gas Reduction Targets Act, S.B.C., 2007).

Market size and scope

Tradable unit and pricing information

All emission reductions and removals will be expressed in terms of metric tons of CO_2e (Greenhouse Gas Reduction Targets Act, Emission Offsets Regulation, B.C. Reg. 393/2008).

Participants/buyers

Provincial public sector organizations are required to participate in the emission offsets regulation to comply with the GGRTA. Communities in BC are also welcome to participate, and most have voluntarily committed to becoming carbon neutral through reductions and the purchase of offsets. The Pacific Carbon Trust is also preparing to acquire offsets for other clients, including businesses, NGOs and individuals who wish to offset emissions (Pacific Carbon Trust, 2009).

Current project portfolio

The Pacific Carbon Trust, as of July 2009, has signed agreements to purchase offsets related to 15 projects that are expected to generate over $300,000MtCO_2$e of offsets over a five-year period starting in June 2009 (Pacific Carbon Trust, 2009). These 15 offset projects are fuel-switching and energy efficiency project types. Offset project information is available at: www.pacificcarbontrust.ca/Home/BCOffsetShowcase/tabid/92/Default.aspx.

Offset project eligibility

Project types

There are no current project type restrictions.

Project locations

All offset projects must be located in British Columbia (Greenhouse Gas Reduction Targets Act, Emission Offsets Regulation, B.C. Reg. 393/2008).

Project size

There are no project size restrictions.

Start date

Offset projects must have a start date no earlier than 29 November 2007 (Greenhouse Gas Reduction Targets Act, Emission Offsets Regulation, B.C. Reg. 393/2008).

Crediting period

Currently, all offset projects will expire ten years after the validation date unless otherwise ordered by the Director of the Climate Change Branch of the Ministry of Environment (Greenhouse Gas Reduction Targets Act, Emission Offsets Regulation, B.C. Reg. 393/2008). At the end of this period, projects may be validated for another ten-year time frame, providing project proponents submit a new project plan for validation. These submissions will be considered as new projects that must also meet the regulatory requirements.

Longer crediting periods, referred to as 'validation periods' are anticipated for forestry projects (Ministry of Environment, 2009).

Co-benefit objectives and requirements

The regulation does not specify objectives or requirements concerning co-benefits of the project.

Additionality and quantification procedures

Additionality requirements

As specified in the emission offsets regulation, all projects must meet the following additionality criteria:

* baseline scenario must comply with relevant regulations;
* baseline scenario must incorporate all relevant incentives and grants;
* financial implications of the baseline scenario must suggest it would occur if the project is not carried out;
* demonstration that the project faces financial, technological or other barriers that are overcome, or partially overcome by the incentive of the reduction being recognized as emission offsets (Greenhouse Gas Reduction Targets Act, Emission Offsets Regulation, B.C. Reg. 393/2008).

Quantification protocols

An optional list of approved protocols will be developed and made available (Ministry of Environment, 2009). At present, project developers are encouraged to make use of recognized protocols and adapt them as necessary to the BC context (Ministry of Environment, 2009). The Director of the Climate Change Branch of the Ministry of Environment also has the authority to designate mandatory protocols related to any aspect of carrying out a project including: selection of sources, sinks or reservoirs; baseline scenarios; quantification of GHG; and monitoring of GHG sources, sinks and reservoirs (Greenhouse Gas Reduction Targets Act, Emission Offsets Regulation, B.C. Reg. 393/2008).

Permanence

Permanence of carbon sequestration or carbon capture and storage projects is addressed by requiring the development of a risk mitigation and contingency plan to ensure that the GHG reduction achieved will endure for either at least 100 years or a period comparable to the atmospheric effect of a non-sequestration project GHG emission reduction (Greenhouse Gas Reduction Targets Act, Emission Offsets Regulation, B.C. Reg. 393/2008). The risk mitigation and contingency plan may include: a plan for maintenance and protection of sinks, description of legal means for long-term protection, a plan for monitoring any reversal, a description of arrangements to address the risk of reversal, a description of discounts applied in the calculation of project reductions, and a description of any arrangements made to replace credits in the event of a reversal (Greenhouse Gas Reduction Targets Act, Emission Offsets Regulation, B.C. Reg. 393/2008).

Project approval process

Validation and registration

Offset project plans must be validated by a validation body in a manner consistent with ISO 14064–3 (Greenhouse Gas Reduction Targets Act, Emission Offsets Regulation, B.C. Reg. 393/2008).

Until 1 July 2010 a team that includes a person authorized to act as an auditor of a company and at least one qualified professional (as defined in the regulation) will be able to act as a validation or verification body (Greenhouse Gas Reduction Targets Act, Emission Offsets Regulation, B.C. Reg. 393/2008). After 1 July 2010 validation and verification bodies will need to be accredited, in accordance with ISO 14065, by a member of the International Accreditation Forum to use ISO 14064–3 (Greenhouse Gas Reduction Targets Act, Emission Offsets Regulation, B.C. Reg. 393/2008).

Monitoring, verification and certification

Before offsets can be recognized under the regulation, an offset project report must be submitted to a verification body for review (Greenhouse Gas Reduction Targets Act, Emission Offsets Regulation, B.C. Reg. 393/2008). The verification body must verify the offset project report in a manner consistent with ISO 14064–3 (Greenhouse Gas Reduction Targets Act, Emission Offsets Regulation, B.C. Reg. 393/2008).

The same requirements for the validation body apply for the verification body and are described above.

Registries and fees

Under the BC regulation, project proponents must include in the project plan an assertion that they have ownership of the GHG reduction. Additionally, one of the requirements for the recognition of a GHG reduction as an offset is that the reduction has not previously been recognized as an offset under GRRTA or in another offset program (Greenhouse Gas Reduction Targets Act, Emission Offsets Regulation, B.C. Reg. 393/2008). Pacific Carbon Trust tracks offsets retired on behalf of clients on its website.

Selected issues

Detailed guidance for British Columbia's emission offsets regulation is under development.

EPA Climate Leaders

www.epa.gov/stateply

Unless referenced otherwise, the information in this section is based on the above website and personal communications.

Overview

Type of standard and context

Climate Leaders is the US Environmental Protection Agency's (EPA) voluntary greenhouse gas (GHG) emission reduction program. Launched as an industry–government partnership in 2002, it provides guidance to companies that develop climate change strategies and recognizes their efforts (US EPA, 2009b). The program's goal is to focus corporate attention on cost-effective GHG reduction and energy efficiency projects within the boundary of the organization through support and assistance from the US EPA (US EPA, 2009b).

Partner companies complete a corporate-wide inventory of the six major GHGs using the Climate Leaders GHG Inventory Guidance and set a corporate-wide GHG emission reduction goal to be achieved over 5–10 years. They also maintain an Inventory Management Plan, which institutionalizes the process of collecting, calculating and maintaining high-quality, corporate-wide GHG data through an annual reporting process with the US EPA (US EPA, 2009b). Thus, companies create a documented record of their emission reductions and receive EPA recognition as corporate environmental leaders (US EPA, 2009b).

Each partner works individually with the US EPA to set its respective reduction goals based on the emission sources and reduction opportunities within the company (US EPA, 2009b). To achieve the goal, the company may choose to develop its own GHG mitigation offset projects or to purchase GHG reductions certified through existing regulated or voluntary markets, provided that the project adheres to approved EPA methodologies. Performance-based GHG accounting protocols for offset projects were released in mid-August 2008 to provide guidance to companies using offsets to meet their goals (US EPA, 2009b). Partners may also use green power purchasing and Renewable Energy Credits (RECs) to reduce their indirect electricity emissions and meet their goals under the program.

Standard authority and administrative bodies

The US EPA administers the Climate Leaders Program. US EPA staff provide each program partner with technical assistance as they develop, update and document their Inventory Management Plan (IMP) and complete or adjust their base year inventory.

Regional scope

The Climate Leaders program is limited to industries with operations in the USA. Program partners must report US-based emissions and may optionally include their international emissions as well.

Recognition of other standards/links with other trading systems

Climate Leaders partners may meet their emission reduction goals through the purchase of offset credits from regulated or voluntary markets (US EPA, 2009b). The criteria for purchasing offset credits are outlined in the Screening Criteria, which include provisions to ensure that the offsets are real, additional, permanent and verifiable (US EPA, 2009b). Purchased offset credits are required to be quantified using offset protocols or accounting guidance approved by the US EPA Climate Leaders program. The US EPA reviews the purchased offset credits before deciding on their eligibility for meeting a partner's GHG emission reduction goal.

Market size and scope

Tradable unit and pricing information

Under the Climate Leaders program, offset credits are referred to as 'external GHG reductions' and are measured in units of metric tonnes of CO_2e (US EPA, 2007). No pricing information is available. Program partners may purchase offset credits from regulated or voluntary markets, where prices vary by program, or develop offset projects themselves.

Participants/buyers

There were 281 program partners in the Climate Leaders Program as of June 2009 (US EPA, 2009b). They represent a broad range of industry sectors including cement, forest products, pharmaceuticals, utilities, information technology and retail, with operations in all 50 US states (US EPA, 2009b).

Current project portfolio

No information is yet available. The EPA program administrators report that projects are being developed under the Climate Leaders methodologies; however, neither a Climate Leaders registry nor a compiled report has been developed.

Offset project eligibility

Project types

The EPA has developed a set of offset protocols for specific project types based on the performance standard approach, including landfill gas, manure management, captured methane end use, reforestation/afforestation, transit bus efficiency and boiler replacement for commercial and industrial projects (US EPA, 2009b).

The program's partners are generally limited to projects that use the offset protocols developed by the EPA. They can purchase or generate GHG reductions from other offset projects but must provide the US EPA with the 'performance standard' methodology and data used to calculate the purchased GHG reductions (US EPA, 2009b), which the EPA then reviews and approves.

Project locations

Offset project protocols are currently applicable to the US. Project developers able to develop a performance standard for an international project type can propose one, provided adequate country-specific data sets are available.

Project size

All project sizes are eligible, but commercial boiler replacement projects have specific size restrictions. (Commercial boiler replacement projects must have an input capacity of between 300,000 and 8 million British thermal units (Btu) per hour.)

Start date

Offset projects must have started on or after 20 February 2002. Exceptions may be made for projects developed by partners through state or other federal GHG programs.

Crediting period

The crediting period for Climate Leaders offset projects has not been specified.

Co-benefit objectives and requirements

Climate Leaders offset guidance document specifies that projects 'should be evaluated for any significant non-GHG impacts, both positive and negative ... including but not limited to: economic development, sustainability, technology transfer, public participation, and capacity building' (US EPA, 2009a).

Additionality and quantification procedures

Additionality requirements

Offset program protocols use a 'performance standard' methodology to assess additionality. Depending on the project type, emission performance may be defined as an emission rate, a technology standard or a practice standard (US EPA, 2007). Offset projects are required to achieve performance emission reductions that are significantly better than business-as-usual practices determined from similar, recently undertaken or planned practices in a similar geographic region (US EPA, 2007).

Quantification protocols

The project protocols developed by the US EPA are based on a top-down performance standard approach. Quantification protocols for eligible project types are consistent with the Greenhouse Gas Protocol: The GHG Protocol for Project Accounting (see WBCSD/WRI GHG Protocol for Project Accounting in Chapter 6).

Leakage and permanence

Project-specific guidelines regarding leakage and permanence are addressed in the protocols for each project type. If it is determined that leakage may result in significant emissions, these emissions must be quantified and included in the calculation of reductions; however, a specific quantification methodology is not required. The EPA states that 'all associated activities determined to contribute to leakage should be monitored'.

Project approval process

Validation and registration

The US EPA reviews all proposed external GHG emission reductions from offset projects, generated or purchased, for eligibility in meeting the Climate Leaders reduction goal. The review is based on the project information provided by the program partner.

Monitoring, verification and certification

Protocols for monitoring offset projects have to be submitted to and reviewed by the US EPA during its review process for external GHG emission reductions (US EPA, 2007). Although third-party verification is widely recommended for purchased offset credits, third-party verification of offset credits used by partners to meet their GHG reduction goals is encouraged but not required. There is no process for certifying offsets under the Climate Leaders program.

Registries and fees

Although not a requirement, Climate Leaders partners are encouraged to retire their offset credits permanently on an appropriate registry (US EPA, 2007). There are no fees associated with the Climate Leaders program.

Selected issues

While offsets are only one component of the Climate Leaders program, it has developed offset project protocols that reflect nearly a decade of EPA research and review and provide an important contribution to improving methods and rigour in the growing domestic US offset market. Climate Leaders has placed emphasis on standardized and performance-based elements of protocols in order to increase predictability, lower costs and enhance consistency.

Climate Leaders is currently more of a framework than a complete offset system, as compared with voluntary market offset programs such as VCS, CAR or CCX. For example, Climate Leaders does not provide or require the registration of offset credits to track ownership of credits generated or provide another mechanism to ensure credits are not used in multiple contexts. Similarly, Climate Leaders protocols require accounting for permanence and leakage, but do not specify fully how these are addressed.

6

Greenhouse Gas Accounting Protocols

Greenhouse gas accounting protocols provide guidance on definitions of and procedures for accounting for GHG emissions and emission reductions at various levels, including at entity-wide and project level.

Unlike offset programs and standards, GHG accounting protocols do not define eligibility criteria or procedural requirements and have no associated regulatory bodies. However, they do form the basis for many offset standards and programs. The following GHG accounting protocols for offset projects are described in more detail below:

The World Business Council for Sustainable Development/World Resources Institute (WBCSD/WRI) Greenhouse Gas Protocol for Project Accounting.

The International Organization for Standardization (ISO) Standard 14064–2.

WBCSD/WRI GHG Protocol for Project Accounting

www.ghgprotocol.org

Unless referenced otherwise, the information in this section is based on the above website, personal communications and these sources: World Resources Institute (WRI) (2005); World Resources Institute (WRI) (2006b); World Resources Institute (WRI) (2007).

Overview

Type of standard and context

The WBCSD/WRI GHG Protocol Initiative has developed two separate protocols: the 'Corporate Accounting and Reporting Standard' covers accounting for corporate GHG emission inventories; and the 'GHG Protocol for Project Accounting' (GHG Protocol) is an offset project accounting protocol. The GHG Protocol is a program-neutral tool for quantifying and reporting GHG emission reductions from GHG mitigation projects and does not focus on verification, enforcement or co-benefits. This section discusses only the GHG Protocol. The current version was released in December 2005, after a four-year multi-stakeholder consultation process involving businesses, NGOs, academics and government representatives.

The GHG Protocol aims to:

- provide a credible and transparent approach to quantifying and reporting project-level GHG emission reductions;
- enhance the credibility of GHG project accounting through the application of common accounting concepts, procedures and principles;
- provide a platform for harmonizing different project-based GHG initiatives and programs.

The protocol was developed by the GHG Protocol Initiative, which was launched in 1998. The initiative was jointly led by the World Business Council for Sustainable Development (WBCSD) (www.wbcsd.org), a global association of some 200 companies committed to sustainable development, and the World Resources Institute (WRI) (www.wri.org), an environmental think tank, in partnership with a coalition of businesses, NGOs and governmental and intergovernmental organizations. The project protocol was finalized and published in December 2005.

Standard authority and administrative bodies

WRI and WBCSD are responsible for developing and updating the protocol and its additions. The protocol can be freely used by anyone and its use is not administered by any organization.

Regional scope

Not applicable.

Recognition of other standards/links with other trading systems

The GHG protocol is not a full offset standard or program in itself but is used or referenced by several GHG standards and programs, including ISO 14064–2 and the Climate Action Reserve. It has been developed as a flexible tool that can be easily adapted by GHG programs to match their objectives.

Market size and scope

Tradable unit and pricing information

Not applicable.

Participants/buyers

Users of the GHG Protocol include companies, institutions, government agencies, other standards organizations (see above) and project developers.

Current project portfolio

Not applicable.

Offset project eligibility

Project types

The GHG Project Protocol can be used to quantify GHG reductions for any project type. The protocol is supplemented by more specific guidelines for accounting GHG emission reductions in grid-connected electricity and land use, land-use change and forestry (LULUCF) projects.

Project locations

Not specified under the GHG Protocol.

Project size

Not specified under the GHG Protocol.

Start date

Not specified under the GHG Protocol.

Crediting period

The protocol does not specify the duration of the crediting period. It provides the following parameters for project developers to consider in determining a crediting period:

- the pace at which economic conditions, technologies or practices are changing;
- the point at which the underlying assumptions for a project's baseline scenario are likely to change significantly;
- whether the baseline emission estimates are static or dynamic (change over time).

Co-benefit objectives and requirements

The GHG Project Protocol does not address co-benefits such as environmental and social impacts because they are not directly related to GHG reduction accounting and quantification per se. It acknowledges the importance of these issues but leaves it to the users of the protocol to determine policies in this regard and to incorporate them into the requirements of their program or standards.

Additionality and quantification procedures

Additionality requirements

The GHG Protocol contains no formal requirements for additionality determination but it discusses additionality conceptually as it relates to baseline determination.

Quantification protocols

The GHG Protocol defines the baseline scenario as 'a hypothetical description of what would have most likely occurred in the absence of any considerations about climate change'. It suggests the following step-wise approach to choosing a baseline scenario:

1   Identifying possible 'baseline candidates', which are alternative technologies or practices within a specific geographic area and time period that could provide the same product or service as the project activity.
2   Assessing the identified implementation barriers (and optionally, the projected net benefits) of each baseline candidate and the project activity.
3   Using a comparative analysis to identify the most likely alternative for the baseline scenario.

The Protocol offers further guidance on the use of both project-specific and performance-based standards for estimating the baseline of a project. The protocol recommends use of the performance standard procedure when:

1   a number of similar projects are being implemented;
2   obtaining verifiable data on project activity alternatives is difficult;
3   the project developer intends to keep confidential data that would need to be revealed if a project-specific standard were used; and
4   the number of baseline candidates is limited or the GHG emission rate data for baseline candidates are difficult to obtain.

Project approval process

Validation and registration

Not specified under the GHG Protocol.

Monitoring, verification and certification

The GHG Protocol requires a monitoring plan for GHG emissions at the sources or sinks significantly affected by a project. It also requires monitoring of the data underlying key baseline assumptions, and a description of the quality assurance and quality control measures to be employed for data collection, processing and storage.

The guidance provided for developing a monitoring plan allows the use of direct (e.g. smokestack measurements) and indirect (e.g. fuel consumption data) measurements, both of which are subject to uncertainties. It recommends that the project developer be conservative, using data for quantification that reflect the uncertainties and that tend to underestimate the GHG reductions. It further recommends considering costs versus benefits in deciding whether to estimate emissions or monitor them directly.

Verification and certification are not defined under the GHG Protocol.

Registries and fees

Registries and fees do not apply to the GHG Protocol – the GHG Project Protocol is free and publicly available at www.ghgprotocol.org.

Selected issues

The GHG Project Protocol can be used as a building block for a fully fledged offset standard or program. As such, it is a valuable tool and has been used internationally by many regulatory and voluntary schemes.

ISO 14064 Part 2

www.iso.org

Unless referenced otherwise, the information in this section is based on the above website, personal communications and these sources: ISO (2006a); ISO (2006b); ISO (2006c).

Overview

Type of standard and context

ISO 14064 parts 1, 2, and 3 are policy-neutral, voluntary, GHG accounting standards. They were developed on behalf of the International Organization for Standardization (ISO) by an international working group of technical experts over the course of two years and launched in 2006. The ISO 14064 standard consists of three parts:

- The first part (14064–1) specifies requirements for organization level quantification and reporting of greenhouse gas emissions and removals.
- The second part (14064–2) details requirements for quantifying, monitoring and reporting emission reductions and removal enhancements from GHG mitigation projects.
- The third part (14064–3) provides requirements and guidance for the validation and verification of GHG assertions (e.g. declarations/claims).

More recently ISO 14065 has been developed. It specifies principles and requirements for auditors who undertake validation or verification of greenhouse gas (GHG) assertions.

Currently under development are ISO 14066 and ISO 14067. The former will give guidance on competence requirements for conducting greenhouse gas validation and verification engagements with guidance for evaluation; the latter will give guidance on the carbon footprint of products (ISO, undated).

All these ISO standards are GHG program-neutral. Most of the information in this chapter focuses on ISO 14064–2, which specifies a framework for the quantification, monitoring and reporting of greenhouse gas emission reductions or removal enhancements. Because it is program-neutral, ISO 14064–2 is not prescriptive about elements that apply to the policies of a particular GHG program (e.g. specific additionality criteria, project eligibility dates or co-benefits). These decisions are required to be made by the user of the standard (e.g. the GHG program administrator or regulator) when applying the standard. In addition, the standard requires that 'good practice guidance' be applied when applying decision-making criteria and procedures, thus creating additional consistency in application of the standard. The interpretation of the standard is guided through the application of six principles: relevance, completeness, consistency, transparency, accuracy and conservativeness.

Standard authority and administrative bodies

The ISO is the world's largest developer and publisher of international standards. It is a non-governmental network of national standards institutes in 161 countries. Standards are developed by ISO if a need is perceived by the industry or business community. The requirement is communicated to ISO through one of its national standards institutes and either the work is assigned to an existing technical committee or a new one is created. The technical committee comprises technical and business experts from the industry that has asked for the standard and other experts from national government agencies, testing laboratories, consumer associations, environmentalists and others. All experts are represented at the technical committee as national delegations, and chosen by the respective national standards institutes. Draft standards recommended by the technical committees are adopted if two thirds of the members are actively involved in their development and 75 per cent of voting members vote in favour.

ISO 14064 was drafted by the Technical Committee on Environmental Management and its subcommittee on Greenhouse Gas Management and Related Activities.

ISO's national members pay subscriptions to cover the operational cost of ISO's Central Secretariat. The subscription paid by each member is in proportion to the country's Gross National Income and trade figures. Another source of revenue is the sale of standards. ISO 14064 costs 98 Swiss francs, 118 and 130 for parts 1, 2 and 3 respectively.

Regional scope

All above-mentioned ISO standards are international.

Recognition of other standards/links with other trading systems

ISO 14064–1, 2 and 3 are designed to be GHG program-neutral and therefore intended to be used by GHG programs or standards. For example, the procedures of the Voluntary Carbon Standard (VCS) are based on ISO 14064–2 and 3 and the Canadian GHG Offset Protocols will be based on the ISO 14064–2 framework. In addition, the Climate Action Reserve is beginning to adapt their quantification protocols to ISO 14064 standards.

Annex A of ISO 14064–2 contains additional information in cases where the project proponent wishes to conform to the United Nations Framework Convention on

Climate Change (UNFCCC), Kyoto Protocol's Clean Development Mechanism (CDM) or Joint Implementation (JI) Mechanism.

Market size and scope

Tradable unit and pricing information

Because ISO 14064–2 is program-neutral, the tradable unit is not defined by ISO 14064–2 but by the program or standard that requires the use of the ISO 14064–2 protocol.

Participants/buyers

Both the voluntary and the compliance programs have incorporated the ISO guidelines into their program design (see above).

Current project portfolio

Not applicable.

Offset project eligibility

Project types

Because ISO 14064 is program-neutral, no restrictions on project types are defined under ISO 14064–2. If a GHG project is not implemented under a specific GHG program or standard, then it is up to the project developer to define the accepted project types. This holds true for all the parameters that are not specified under ISO 14064–2.

Project locations

Not specified under ISO 14064–2.

Project size

Not specified under ISO 14064–2.

Start date

Not specified under ISO 14064–2.

Crediting period

Not specified under ISO 14064–2.

Co-benefit objectives and requirements

The requirements for co-benefits are presented in general terms. For example, an Environmental Impact Assessment (EIA) is required if the host country or region requires the completion of such an assessment. ISO 14064–2 also specifies that relevant outcomes of stakeholder participation and consultation be presented.

Additionality and quantification procedures

Additionality requirements

ISO 14064–2 requires that the GHG project must result in GHG emission reductions or removal enhancements in addition to what would have happened in the absence of that project. Because of its policy-neutral nature, the standard does not use the term 'additionality', prescribe baseline procedures or specify additionality criteria. These are all elements that are defined by the GHG program or regulation that requires the use of the standard.

ISO 14064 requires the project proponent to identify and select GHG sources, sinks and reservoirs relevant for the GHG project and for the baseline scenario. In order to be compatible with the broadest range of GHG programs, it does not use the term 'project boundary' but rather uses a lifecycle approach for the identification of GHG sources, sinks and reservoirs that are considered for quantification, monitoring and reporting.

The guidelines for additionality tools generally assume a project-specific approach. However, the requirements of the GHG program take precedence over specific ISO 14064–2 requirements, which allows performance standards to be used where this is prescribed by the GHG program.

Quantification protocols

Since ISO 14064–2 is designed to be program-neutral, baseline procedures are specified in general terms, allowing flexibility for GHG programs or regulations to adopt more prescriptive procedures. The standard offers guidance on and sets out general requirements for how to determine a project baseline and requires that the principles of conservativeness be applied when determining the baseline scenario to ensure emission reduction or removal enhancements are not overestimated.

Furthermore, ISO 14064–2 requires that the baseline, quantification and monitoring methods of project-level GHG emissions and removals be defined before quantification of emission reductions or removal enhancements. This is to ensure that project proponents are required to fully justify their baseline and describe their project before proceeding to quantification.

Project approval process

Validation and registration

ISO 14064–2 states that the project proponent should have the GHG project validated and/or verified. The use of the word 'should' instead of 'shall' makes this requirement non-mandatory. Such requirements are usually elements of a GHG program. If a GHG project has not been linked to a specific GHG program, then the project proponent has to decide on the type of validation and/or verification (first-, second- or third-party verification) and the level of assurance (e.g. high or moderate) required against the GHG assertion. ISO 14064–3 specifies the principles and requirements for validation and verification of GHG assertions (ISO, 2006b).

Under ISO 14064–2, the use of third-party auditors is strongly recommended, but only required if GHG emission reductions are to be made public. In these cases project proponents must provide a GHG report with a specified content or a third-party validation or verification statement prepared in accordance with the procedures in ISO 14064–3: *Specification with guidance for the validation and verification of greenhouse gas assertions.* ISO 14064–3 specifies the following for the validation and verification process including:

- selecting GHG validators/verifiers;
- establishing the level of assurance, objectives, criteria and scope;
- determining the validation/verification approach;
- assessing GHG data, information, information systems and controls;
- evaluating GHG assertions; and
- preparing validation/verification statements.

While ISO 14064–3 specifies similar requirements for both validation and verification, the objectives associated with project validation and project verification are usually different.

Monitoring, verification and certification

ISO 14064–2 requires the project proponent to establish and maintain criteria and procedures for obtaining, recording, compiling and analysing data and information important for quantifying and reporting GHG emissions and/or removals relevant for the project and baseline scenario (i.e. GHG information system).

The certification and crediting process, which may be under the authority of a GHG program and may vary among GHG programs, is not specified in ISO 14064–2.

Registries and fees

Not specified under ISO 14064–2.

Selected issues

ISO 14064–2 is designed to be used as a guideline for developing quantification methodologies and protocols. It has been integrated by several regulatory and voluntary schemes. ISO 14064–2 can be used with good practice guidance (e.g. CDM or IPCC methods) to ensure consistency with these existing quantification approaches. As such it is a valuable tool for streamlining procedures and providing guidance to project developers.

It is sometimes used as a stand-alone standard. Criteria and procedures are then defined by the project developers themselves. Because it is not specific in its requirements, the offset quality criteria vary depending on the program or the developer who defines the criteria. This means that ISO 14064–2 by itself cannot, nor is it designed to, guarantee offset quality.

7

Voluntary Offset Standards

Over a dozen voluntary offset standards have been developed in recent years. Their emergence is a reflection of the offset industry's response to offset quality concerns by offset buyers and the general public, as well as a sign of the maturation of the voluntary offset market (Hamilton et al, 2009). Standards in the carbon offset market are especially helpful because claims regarding offset products are particularly challenging for buyers to evaluate. Fully fledged carbon offset standards have three core components:

1   *Accounting and quantification procedures* aim to ensure that offsets are 'real, additional and permanent' and provide the methods for quantifying the number of offsets a project can generate. They specify the tests used to determine additionality and procedures to address uncertainty and leakage. They provide the methodologies for quantifying the baseline and project emissions, the difference between the two being the number of offset credits awarded to a project. Accounting rules may also include definitions of accepted project types and methodologies for validating project activities (Broekhoff, 2007a).

2   *Monitoring, verification and certification procedures* aim to ensure that offset projects perform as reported and follow the conditions specified in approved project documentation. Verification and certification rules are used to quantify the actual carbon savings that can enter the market once the project is up and running (Broekhoff, 2007b).

3   *Registration and enforcement systems* aim to ensure that contractual standards clearly identify ownership of the emission reductions and also define who bears the risk in case of project failure. Carbon offset registries track offset projects and issue offset credits for each unit of emission reduction or removal that is verified and certified. Registries are vital in creating a credible, fungible offset commodity. A serial number is assigned to each verified offset. When an offset is sold, the serial number and 'credit' for the reduction is transferred from the account of the seller to an account for the buyer. If the buyer 'uses' the credit by claiming it as an offset against their own emissions, the registry retires the serial number so that the credit cannot be resold. In this manner, registries reduce the risk of double counting, that is, to have multiple stakeholders take credit for the same offset (Broekhoff, 2007b). There are several registries currently operating in the voluntary market. They have been developed by governments, nonprofits and the private sector:

- American Carbon Registry, see www.americancarbonregistry.org
- APX Inc. administers offset registries for the VCS, the Gold Standard and the Climate Action reserve; see www.apx.com/environmental/environmental-registries.asp
- Caisse des Dépôts administers an offset registry for the VCS; see www.vcsregistry. caissedesdepots.com
- Chicago Climate Exchange Registry, see www.chicagoclimatex.com/content.jsf?id=501
- Markit Environmental Registry (formerly TZ1) administers offset registries for the VCS, the Climate Community and Biodiversity Standards (CCBS), the Plan Vivo and Social Carbon; see www.tz1market.com/registries.php.

The following GHG Project Offset Standards are described in more detail in this chapter:

Climate Action Reserve
Gold Standard
Voluntary Carbon Standard 2007
VER+
American Carbon Registry
Climate, Community and Biodiversity Standards
Plan Vivo
Social Carbon Methodology
Green-e Climate Protocol for Renewable Energy
Green-e Climate Program

Climate Action Reserve

www.climateactionreserve.org

Unless referenced otherwise, the information in this section is based on the above website, personal communications and these sources: WRI (2006a); State of California (2007); Climate Action Reserve (undated).

Overview

Type of standard and context

The Climate Action Reserve (formerly the California Climate Action Registry, see below) was launched in 2008. It is a national offsets program focused on the US carbon market.

The Climate Action Reserve (Reserve) establishes standards for quantifying and verifying GHG emission reduction projects, provides oversight to independent third-party verification bodies, and issues and tracks carbon credits called Climate Reserve Tonnes (CRTs pronounced 'carrots').

The California Climate Action Registry (California Registry) is the predecessor organization and legacy program of the Climate Action Reserve. It is a voluntary GHG registry established by the California State Legislature (www.legislature.ca.gov/) in

September 2000 to encourage and promote early actions to measure, manage and reduce GHG emissions. To support this goal, the California Registry developed a general reporting protocol, general verification protocol and a number of sector-specific reporting protocols to enable its members to voluntarily calculate and report entity-wide GHG emissions. The California Registry also produced a series of standardized, performance-based, project-specific protocols and accompanying verification protocols to quantify the emission reductions from GHG mitigation projects. For example, the first set of project protocols for quantifying and verifying forestry projects was launched in 2005 and these protocols were subsequently adopted by the California Air Resources Board (www.arb.ca.gov/homepage.htm) in 2007, which recognized the resulting emission reductions as early voluntary actions under the California Global Warming Solutions Act of 2006 (AB-32) (www.arb.ca.gov/cc/docs/ab32text.pdf). This act established a program of regulatory and market mechanisms to achieve real, quantifiable and cost-effective reductions in GHGs.

In 2007, CCAR worked with other regional non-governmental organizations to build and launch the Climate Registry (www.theclimateregistry.org/), a voluntary GHG registry for the North American region covering states in the USA, Native Sovereign Nations, Canada and Mexico. The last year for which the California Registry will accept emission reports is 2009 and thereafter its members will transition to the Climate Registry.

Standard authority and administrative bodies

The Climate Action Reserve is administered by employed staff with overall direction from a Board of Directors. The Board of Directors is comprised of representatives from state government, business, environmental organizations, academia and others.

The Reserve's operations are funded by account holder fees, CRT issuance and transfer fees, grants and sponsorships.

Regional scope

The Reserve provides services to companies and project developers in the USA and Mexico. Discussions are under way for further expansion throughout North America.

Recognition of other standards/links with other trading systems

The Reserve's GHG emission reduction program, including its project-specific protocols and its verifier accreditation and oversight program, has been approved under the Voluntary Carbon Standard (see VCS, 2007). The Reserve's Forest, Livestock and Urban Forest Project Protocols have all been adopted by the California Air Resources Board.

Market size and scope

Tradable unit and pricing information

Projects that achieve verified emission reductions are issued with a serialized Climate Reserve Tonne (CRT, pronounced 'carrot') per metric ton of CO_2e emissions reduced or permanently sequestered. Over a million CRTs have been issued and are available for trading, though many projects also sell their CRTs into the future before issuance. In early 2008, Pacific Gas and Electric Company announced it would purchase 200,000 short tons of GHG emission reductions from the Conservation Fund's Garcia River Forest project (PG&E, 2008). The price of US$9.71 per short ton of CO_2 for the purchase was approved by the California Public Utilities Commission (Woodall, 2008).

Participants/buyers

Climate Action Reserve account holders represent a variety of sectors, including environment, finance and business. Individuals, nonprofit organizations, government agencies and businesses may hold an account in the Reserve. Participating account holders, including project developers, traders and brokers and retailers are located throughout the USA and internationally.

Current project portfolio

As of July 2009, the Reserve had 75 total GHG emission offset projects, including 9 registered (completed verification) and 51 listed (accepted by the Reserve as eligible). Go to https://thereserve1.apx.com for an updated list of projects and their status.

Offset project eligibility

Project types

As of June 2009, the Reserve has adopted four performance-based project protocols defining the eligibility criteria and reduction quantification guidelines for carbon offset projects.

- The Livestock Project Protocol provides guidance to account for emission reductions associated with installing a manure biogas control system for livestock operations.
- The Forest Project Protocol provides guidelines for three types of forest projects: conservation or avoided conversion projects, conservation-based forest management projects involving the harvest and regeneration of native trees, and reforestation projects with native trees on land that has not been forested for at least ten years. The Forest Project Protocol was subsequently adopted by the California Air Resources Board, which recognized the resulting emission reductions as early voluntary actions under the California Global Warming Solutions Act of 2006 (AB 32).
- The Landfill Project Protocol provides guidance to account for GHG emission reductions associated with installing a gas collection and destruction system at a landfill.
- The Urban Forest Protocol provides guidance to account for GHG reductions from tree-planting projects by municipalities, utilities and universities.

Project locations

Currently, only forestry projects located in California are eligible for participation in the Reserve, but the updated Forest Project Protocol (expected adoption date in September 2009) expands the protocol nationwide. Livestock and landfill projects may be located anywhere in the USA or Mexico. Urban forest projects may be located anywhere in the USA. All future projects will be able to be located anywhere in the USA and discussions are ongoing about expanding all protocols to all North America.

Project size

At present, there are no limitations on project size in any sector, though very small projects are often not financially feasible.

Start date

For all project types (forestry, livestock, landfill and urban forest projects) the current start date for project eligibility is 1 January 2001 for projects in the USA and 15 August 2008 for landfill and livestock projects in Mexico. But as each project protocol undergoes review and update, the Reserve expects to adopt policies requiring that projects be listed (officially accepted) on the Reserve within six months of the start of operations. The Reserve released an updated version of its Landfill Project Reporting Protocol, version 2.0, in November 2008, including the new policy, but also provided a one-year grace period before implementation of the new policy. Upon the conclusion of the grace period on 17 November 2009, landfill projects must be listed with the Reserve within six months of the start of operations. The Mexican protocols also include this one-year grace period (beginning 1 July 2009) before projects must be listed within six months of their start date.

Crediting period

Distinct crediting periods apply for each project type:

- Livestock management projects must use the day their biogas control system started operating as the start date of their ten-year crediting period.
- For landfill projects, the crediting period is also ten years, beginning the day their gas control system began operation. This crediting period will end early if the landfill's emissions become subject to regulation.
- Forest projects have a 100-year crediting period and must be verified no less frequently than every six years and must submit annual monitoring reports.
- Urban forest projects have a 100-year crediting period and must be verified no less frequently than every six years.

Co-benefit objectives and requirements

It is Reserve policy that GHG projects must not create negative environmental externalities and that projects should result in environmental co-benefits whenever possible. The forest protocols specifically require projects to achieve environmental co-benefits.

Additionality and quantification procedures

Additionality requirements

Additionality requirements are standardized but specified by project type. Projects must not only demonstrate that the reductions go beyond what is required by law (regulatory surplus), but also that they go above and beyond common practice ('business-as-usual'). Additional project-specific requirements are outlined below.

- For forest management projects, additionality is defined as practices that exceed the baseline characterization, including any applicable laws and regulations. In the case of reforestation projects, additionality is further demonstrated by showing that the project area has not been forested for at least ten years. For conservation projects, it is demonstrated by showing that the project area would have been converted to a nonforest use without the protection provided under the project.
- Livestock methane abatement projects and landfill gas collection and combustion projects need to pass two tests to demonstrate additionality: a performance standard test and a regulatory surplus test. For both livestock and landfill projects, the performance standard test is done using a technology-based threshold that anticipates changes in technology in the sector (e.g. anaerobic digesters for livestock projects, and gas collection and combustion systems for landfill projects).
- For landfill projects, an additional practice-based threshold is used in the performance standard test – if the landfill was already collecting and combusting landfill gas with a non-qualifying technology, it cannot sell this as offsets. Only emission reductions from a new, qualifying system added at an existing landfill operation can produce offsets.
- For urban forest GHG reduction projects, the urban forest project must meet the performance standard test and the regulatory test. For utilities, the tree plantings are considered additional if they are not a power line replacement. Because it is not common practice for utilities to have residential tree-planting programs, all trees planted under these types of programs are considered additional and therefore are designated as eligible project trees. The performance threshold for municipalities and educational campuses is measured in terms of net tree gain: the annual number of trees planted by an entity minus the annual number of trees removed by an entity. Municipalities and educational campuses must maintain a stable population of existing trees and demonstrate net tree gain greater than zero. Trees that are planted to comply with federal, state or regulatory requirements may not be considered project trees.

Quantification protocols

Standardized baseline quantification and monitoring guidance is included in the project-specific protocols. These requirements are outlined below by project type.

Forestry project baseline scenarios are based on a characterization of the forest management practices that would have occurred in a project's absence.

Forestry project developers must monitor and report emissions from projects annually and submit a report that includes: information describing, quantifying and analysing any on-site activity-shifting leakage. Leakage may occur when a project activity changes the availability or quantity of a product or service, resulting in a change in the GHG emissions independent of the project's intended GHG impacts. The Reserve differentiates between two types of leakage – activity shifting and market leakage. Activity-shifting leakage is a displacement of activities from within the project's physical boundaries to locations outside it. Market leakage occurs when the project activity affects an established market for goods, causing substitution or replacement elsewhere, resulting in GHG emissions.

Project developers are also required to demonstrate that the project is maintaining a consistent amount of additional carbon stocks over time.

Livestock management project baseline scenarios are calculated based on the 'continuation of current practices', that is, the technology currently in use for a given geographical area, animal type and farm size. Projects are only eligible if the baseline scenario is an uncontrolled methanogenic process (such as an anaerobic lagoon).

Landfill project baseline scenarios include all uncontrolled methane emissions, excluding the portion of methane that would be oxidized by soil bacteria if the landfill does not utilize a synthetic cover material. Current regulatory requirements for capture of methane emissions can be incorporated into the baseline scenario as appropriate.

Urban forest project baseline scenarios are calculated based on a performance standard demonstration of 'better than business-as-usual'. GHG reduction credit calculations are based on the amount of annual project carbon sequestration in project trees minus the annual GHG emissions from motor vehicles and equipment related to tree planting, care and monitoring. The Urban Forest Project Protocol recognizes three approved approaches to quantifying the annual carbon stocks in eligible project trees, each of which is based on direct measurements of trees and approved urban tree carbon models (allometric equations).

Project approval process

Validation and registration

There is no required validation process for developers seeking to use the Reserve's protocols. Project developers must first open an account on the Reserve. The initial registration forms, known as listing documents, along with a fee are submitted online. The proposed project is evaluated by the Reserve and may be approved, denied or returned for revisions. If approved, the project is listed on the Climate Action Reserve and is eligible to be verified.

Monitoring, verification and certification

After the project activities are implemented, the project developer must hire an accredited verification body to verify that the emission reductions or removals have been achieved. Verification bodies are ANSI-accredited independent entities approved by the Reserve. The forestry, livestock, landfill and urban forest verification protocols provide verifiers with guidance on assessing the GHG stocks and emissions associated with projects in these sectors.

Once verification is complete, the verifiers upload their final report and opinion on the project's reductions. This project verification is then approved by the Reserve, at which point the project status is changed to 'registered' and the project developer's account will be credited with the appropriate number of CRTs. Credits for all project types are issued on an *ex-post* basis after verification has been completed and accepted by the Reserve. On payment of the issuance fee, the CRTs may be traded or retired.

Registries and fees

Project developers, brokers, traders, retailers or members of the public may open an account with the Climate Action Reserve at any time. The annual account maintenance fee is US$500 (this fee is waived for verification bodies).

Project developers may register a project by opening an account and paying a US$500 project submittal fee. The Climate Action Reserve charges an issuance fee of US$0.15 per metric ton of CO_2e and a transfer fee of US$0.03 per metric ton of CO_2e, paid by the seller.

Selected issues

The Climate Action Reserve has placed emphasis on standardized and performance-based elements of protocols in order to increase predictability, lower costs and enhance consistency. With the launch of its offsets registry, the Climate Action Reserve is respected as a national project registry that sets standards, accredits verifiers, and registers and tracks projects using advanced web-based software to serialize and transfer the issued emission reduction credits. With the exception of the forest protocols, which specifically require projects to achieve environmental co-benefits, the Reserve does not focus on enhancing co-benefits.

Climate Action Reserve credits are recognized by the VCS and it appears likely that they may qualify under criteria established in current proposals for US cap-and-trade legislation.

Gold Standard

www.cdmgoldstandard.org

Unless referenced otherwise, the information in this section is based on the above website and personal communications.

Overview

Type of standard and context

The Gold Standard (GS) is a voluntary carbon offset standard for renewable energy and energy efficiency projects. The GS can be applied to voluntary offset projects and to Clean Development Mechanism (CDM) projects. It was developed under the leadership of the World Wildlife Fund (WWF), HELIO International and SouthSouthNorth, with a focus on offset projects that provide lasting social, economic and environmental benefits.

The GS CDM was launched in 2003 after a two-year period of consultation with stakeholders, governments, non-governmental organizations (NGOs) and private sector specialists from over 40 countries. The GS Verified Emission Reduction (VER) standard was launched in 2006. The GS is presently endorsed by over 60 environmental and development NGOs. The stated goals of the GS are:

> *to help the CDM achieve its twin objectives of reducing compliance costs through project-based emission trading while at the same time fostering sustainable development in developing countries without generating additional emissions.*

> *In the voluntary market, the Gold Standard guarantees that offsetting emissions is not a zero-sum PR stunt, but real engagement with real impact.*

The objectives of the Gold Standard Foundation are to:

- help boost investment in additional sustainable energy projects;
- ensure significant and lasting contributions to sustainable development;
- provide assurance that investments have environmental integrity;
- increase public support for renewable energy and energy efficiency. (Gold Standard, undated a)

Standard authority and administrative bodies

The Gold Standard Foundation is a nonprofit organization. The operational activities of the GS are managed by the Gold Standard secretariat and include capacity building, marketing, communications, certification, registration and issuance, as well as maintenance of the GS rules and procedures. The secretariat currently has a core staff of 15.

The Foundation Board oversees the strategic and organizational development of the GS. The Board currently has six members. At least 50 per cent of its members must be recruited from the Gold Standard NGO supporter community and one member is at the same time the Chair of the Gold Standard Technical Advisory Committee (GS TAC, see below). In case of significant changes to the GS rules and procedures, the Board decides whether a Gold Standard NGO supporter majority is necessary to implement the change.

The Technical Advisory Committee (GS TAC) evaluates and approves projects and new methodologies for VER projects and is in charge of updating the GS rules and procedures. It is the equivalent of the CDM Executive Board (EB)/Methodology Panel for VER projects. The GS TAC currently has seven members, all acting in their personal capacities. GS TAC members are from the NGO community, multilateral organizations, aid agencies and the private sector, and all work for the GS on a pro bono basis.

The Gold Standard NGO supporters officially endorse the practices of the GS method and approve major rule changes (e.g. eligibility of project types). Gold Standard NGO supporters are consulted as part of the GS stakeholder consultations and are invited to take part in the project review process. They may also request an in-depth audit of GS projects at both the registration and the issuance stage.

The Gold Standard Auditors are UNFCCC-accredited Designated Operational Entities (DOEs) who carry out validation and verification of GS projects. DOEs are not allowed to carry out the validation and the verification of the same project, except for micro- and small-scale projects.

Regional scope

The GS is an international voluntary carbon offset standard. The large majority of projects are in non-Annex-1 countries, but Gold Standard projects also exist in, for example, New Zealand and the USA.

Recognition of other standards/links with other trading systems

The GS does not recognize any other voluntary standards, but the GS is recognized by the Green-e Climate. It is likely to be recognized by several other standards (e.g. VER+ and the Voluntary Carbon Standard) in the near future.

Market size and scope

Tradable unit and pricing information

Gold Standard offsets generally trade at a premium: average premium for GS VERs is 20–100 per cent above comparable VERs, and for GS CERs 5–25 per cent above regular CERs.

Average prices were: in 2008 US$14.4 (Hamilton et al, 2009), in April 2009 GS VER: €8.38 (07/08 vintage); €5.75 (future vintages) (*Carbon Finance*, April 2009).

Participants/buyers

GS Credits are purchased by buyers who place a high value on environmental integrity and strong co-benefits. These are buyers from the compliance market and voluntary buyers, such as NGOs, large corporate entities with strong corporate social responsibility (CSR) profiles, businesses and offset retailers.

Current project portfolio

As of May 2009, the Gold Standard Registry listed the following projects:

Gold Standard VERs: 3 validated, 20 registered, 7 issued, 76 listed
Gold Standard CERs: 5 validated, 7 registered, 4 issued, 91 listed
5 Gold Standard JI projects
Retired VER credits as of March 2009: 0.45MmtCO$_2$e
(Current project portfolio information changes rapidly. For the latest information, see the Gold Standard Registry at http://goldstandard.apx.com.)

Offset project eligibility

The latest version, Gold Standard v2.1, was released on 1 June 2009. The GS Requirements ('Requirements') present the fundamental principles and the rules of the GS certification in a concise way. The Requirements provide an 'at a glance' overview of the basic certification criteria for validators and project developers. The Gold Standard Toolkit describes the project cycle and provides examples and detailed instructions on the use of the GS. Based on experiences and recurring queries, the Toolkit will be updated to include the most relevant examples and guidance. The Toolkit comes with fixed templates (annexes) that are easily used to report information being passed between project proponents, validators, verifiers and the GS. All GS-related documents can be downloaded from the 'Technical Documents' section of the GS website.

Project types

The GS accepts renewable energy (including methane-to-energy projects) and end-use energy efficiency projects.

The eligibility of hydropower plants with capacity over 20MWe is evaluated on a case-by-case basis. All such projects must undertake a pre-feasibility assessment, which must include:

- the provision of a Compliance Report proving the project's compliance with World Commission on Dams (WCD) guidelines, to be validated by a DOE/AIE;
- a specific stakeholder consultation, including a site visit by local stakeholders (Gold Standard Toolkit Annex C, 2009).

Project locations

GS VER projects cannot be implemented in countries with an emission cap, unless GS VERs are backed by Assigned Amount Units (AAUs) being permanently retired.

Project size

The GS does not set a minimum project size. For GS CERs, CDM project size limits apply. Project size requirements for GS VERs are:

- micro-scale (<5000 tons CO_2 per year);
- small-scale (5000–60,000 tons CO_2 per year); or
- large-scale (>60000 tons CO_2 per year).

Start date

The earliest start date for retroactive crediting of GS VERs was 1 January 2006 and retroactive crediting is only permitted for a maximum of two years prior to the registration date.

The GS does certify CDM pre-registration credits for a maximum of one year prior to the project's CDM registration date under certain conditions:

- The project developer can provide proof that the final version of the PDD was submitted for validation to the DOE prior to 31 January 2008.
- The DOE must provide a verification report covering the GS VER period, either with the first verification of GS CERs or separately.
- The reasons for the delay between the start of project operation and the CDM registration have to be explained by the DOE as part of the verification report covering the GS VER period.

GS CERs will only be issued after the project has been successfully registered as a GS CDM project. Once the project has been registered as a GS CDM project, the normal GS rules apply.

Crediting period

Crediting periods are either one ten-year period or three renewable seven-year periods, except for validated pre-CDM GS VERs (see above).

Projects can opt in to GS crediting during the overall crediting period by submitting a GS-compliance verification report to the GS. Projects can opt out of GS crediting during the overall crediting period, but opting out is final and the project can no longer be communicated as a GS project.

Prior to opt in and after opt out, projects are permitted to seek issuance of credits from other standards. However, projects are not permitted to apply for the issuance of credits under different standards if this results in extending the overall crediting period of the project beyond the GS VER rules.

Co-benefit objectives and requirements

Both GS CER and GS VER projects must show clear sustainable development co-benefits, including environmental, social and economic benefits, as well as technological sustainability. The GS provides a sustainability matrix to help project developers develop their sustainability criteria. The GS requires that critical and sensitive sustainable development indicators as well as mitigation or compensation measures are monitored over the entire crediting period and that information on the status of the indicators is included in the verification reports.

Both the project developer and the stakeholders consulted assign scores of 'minus' (a major negative impact), '0' (neutral impact) or 'plus' (a major positive impact) to a broad set of predefined indicators covering all aspects of sustainable development. Scoring depends on the specific circumstances. The framework chosen for the scoring process is tailored to each project and must be clearly explained and justified.

Environmental Impact Assessment (EIA) requirements are the same for VER and CER for both small- and large-scale projects. For micro-scale voluntary offset projects, an EIA is required if the relevant local or national law prescribes an EIA or if stakeholders have concerns about environmental impacts for which no mitigation measures can be identified – in such a case, the project must be treated as a small- or large-scale project. If no EIA is required by the legislation, the project developer still has to provide a statement confirming that the project complies with local environmental regulation.

The GS requires two public consultation rounds for all projects. VER projects require a letter to the Designated National Authority (DNA) or, if no DNA exists, another relevant authority to communicate the development of the project as a GS voluntary offset project.

During the 60-day period prior to finalizing the validation process, stakeholders must have the opportunity to make comments on the GS Project Design Documents (PDDs). In contrast to GS CDM projects, no international stakeholder consultation is required for GS VER projects. However, all Gold Standard projects undergo two rounds of local stakeholder consultations. National GS NGO supporters and international GS NGO supporters with offices in the host country must be involved in stakeholder consultations in all cases.

Additionality and quantification procedures

Additionality requirements

The additionality requirements for both GS CERs and GS VERs are project-based and bottom up. The GS requires the application of the latest UNFCCC additionality tool. In addition, previous announcement checks are required for both CER and VER projects.

Quantification protocols

GS CDM projects can only use CDM EB-approved methodologies, which are bottom up and project-based. GS VER projects can choose to use the baseline methodologies approved by the Methodology Panel of the CDM EB, the CDM Small Scale Working Group or the United Nations Development Programme Millennium Development Goals' Carbon Facility. If no suitable methodology exists, GS VER projects can propose a new protocol to be approved by the GS TAC at a fixed cost paid by the project developer. The fees are US$2500 for small- and large-scale projects and US$1000 for micro-scale projects. Methodologies for the deployment of a fleet of small-scale biodigesters, as well as for energy efficient cooking stoves have so far been approved and implemented, and others are under review.

Project approval process

Validation and registration

Projects are approved by the GS TAC after it has reviewed and agreed all the required documentation. CER projects must additionally go through the CDM approval process. In general, the validation requirements for GS VER and GS CER projects are identical, but for VERs some requirements of the CDM have been simplified or removed. These include:

- simplified guidelines for micro-scale projects;
- broader eligibility of host countries;
- less stringent rules on the use of official development assistance (ODA);
- broader scope of eligible baseline methodologies;
- no need for formal host country approval.

All GS projects must be validated by a DOE. The GS provides support to DOEs in the form of a validation manual for each VER and CDM stream. The key validation requirements for GS projects are:

- a stakeholder consultation report;
- a completed PDD with the baseline and monitoring methodology and the sustainable development matrix;
- a validation report;
- acceptance of the GS terms and conditions.

GS CDM projects use CDM PDD and validation forms, with the additional GS-specific information on project type, stakeholder consultation and contribution to sustainable development provided as an annex. The GS provides templates and instructions for GS VER project verification documents.

Validation and verification procedures are often unreasonably costly for micro-scale projects. Hence, micro-scale projects pay a standard one-time fee to a validation fund (US$5000) and an annual fee to a verification fund (US$2500). The GS TAC uses a 'targeted random' selection method to select micro-sale projects for validation and verification. Actual validations and verifications performed by DOEs will be paid for via the GS validation and verification funds. Projects not selected for DOE validation and verification in this approach are validated and verified by the GS in-house, but may be required to undergo DOE verification in later years.

Monitoring, verification and certification

GS-specific verification is conducted by DOEs. It includes emission reduction data and the monitoring of sustainable development indicators. Monitoring reports have to be submitted yearly. Project developers monitor projects according to the monitoring plans provided in the PDD. Monitoring reports are submitted to a third-party auditor (a DOE). Except for micro-scale and small-scale projects, a DOE cannot validate and verify the same project.

The GS TAC, the GS secretariat and GS NGO supporters can request clarifications or corrective actions within a two-week period after submission of the verification report to the GS, before credit issuance of GS VERs or certification of GS CERs is initiated.

The verification report must demonstrate compliance with GS reporting criteria (especially sustainable development indicators (SDIs)). The SDIs must be monitored if they are:

- crucial for the overall positive impact on sustainable development;
- particularly sensitive to changes;
- generating stakeholder concerns.

Registries and fees

The GS Foundation launched an independent Gold Standards registry operated by APX Inc. in mid-March 2008. The registry tracks ownership transfers of GS VERs in the voluntary carbon market. It is a proprietary registry and the GS Foundation is the only entity to issue credits. CERs are registered in the CDM registry and will be tracked in the GS registry as well. The GS registry includes the GS Project Database and manages the transfer of documents during the certification process. The public has access to a number of reports and to project information.

The GS does not engage in project or credit transactions. The GS registry makes it possible to track the number of retired GS VERs and to review the number of GS VERs issued. However, buyers and intermediaries between the point of issuance and the point of retirement remain unknown to the GS. The ownership of retired credits can be made public if desired.

The Gold Standard Foundation has to date been funded through sponsorships, grants and fees. From 1 August 2009, new projects applying for the Gold Standard will no longer be charged a fee per credit certified, but instead will deliver a percentage of actual credits to the Gold Standard Foundation – 1.5 per cent of CERs and 2 per cent of VERs. This fee structure mimics the financing mechanism used by the UNFCCC for the adaptation fund. The offsets are purchased by Sindicatum Carbon Capital, an offset project developer, and the proceeds are delivered to the Gold Standard Foundation. The Gold Standard Foundation retains its independence and status as a nonprofit NGO.

Projects that are already operational may apply for retroactive registration to the GS. For this, they need to go through a '(retroactive registration) pre-feasibility assessment' for which the GS charges a fee of US$0.01 per VER for an amount of VERs equivalent to the expected annual volume of reductions (with a minimum fee of US$250).

Selected issues

The Gold Standard is generally accepted as a high quality standard, in particular with respect to co-benefits. It is the only voluntary standard that has all three of the following elements: (i) clearly defined additionality rules, (ii) requires third-party auditing and (iii) has a project approval body similar to the CDM EB.

Co-benefits

According to project developers, the project validation process is more intensive for GS projects, and co-benefit criteria impose added effort above the typical validation requirements. Project developers have reported that DOEs take this additional GS validation seriously and ask tough questions about the project's background data before filling in the GS sustainable development matrix.

The Gold Standard developed clear and detailed definitions of the stakeholder consultation process, in part to overcome criticisms of the CDM for lacking a well-defined process for involving stakeholders. However, the project types eligible for the GS generally do not face serious concerns from stakeholders. Improved stakeholder consultation is likely to be more important for CDM projects that would not qualify under the GS, such as large hydro projects.

Complex documentation

The GS sets more demanding requirements and has more complex documentation than most other offset programs. This makes validation and verification more stringent, and therefore at times more time-consuming and expensive. Some project developers might decide that the higher income from GS CERs and VERs does not justify the extra work.

Limited project categories

Currently, the GS only certifies offset reductions from renewable energy and end-use energy efficiency projects. This could significantly limit GS applicability in industrialized countries, if and as electricity, industrial and building CO_2 emissions are included in cap-and-trade systems. The Gold Standard is currently exploring potential methods for expanding its coverage to forestry projects.

Voluntary Carbon Standard 2007

www.v-c-s.org

Unless referenced otherwise, the information in this section is based on the above website and personal communications.

Overview

Type of standard and context

The Voluntary Carbon Standard (VCS 2007.1) is a fully fledged carbon offset standard. It focuses on GHG reduction attributes only and does not require projects to have additional environmental or social benefits. The VCS is broadly supported by the carbon offset industry (project developers, large offset buyers, verifiers and projects consultants).

VCS version 1 was published jointly in March 2006 by The Climate Group (TCG), the International Emissions Trading Association (IETA) and the World Economic Forum (WEF) Global Greenhouse Register. VCS 2007 was launched in November 2007 following a 19-member Steering Committee review of comments received on earlier draft versions. The Steering Committee was made up of members from NGOs, DOEs, industry associations, project developers and large offset buyers. The World Business Council for Sustainable Development (WBCSD) joined in 2007 as a founding partner of VCS 2007. VCS 2007.1 was launched in November 2008, with the main difference from the earlier version being the incorporation of guidelines for the development of projects in the agriculture, forestry and other land-use (AFOLU) sectors. The VCS will be updated yearly for the first two years and every two years after that.

Start-up funding for the VCS Association comes from the Climate Group, the IETA and the WBCSD, and additional fundraising is currently under way. Donations from commercial organizations are capped at US$31,600 per year. In the medium to long term, costs will be covered by levy charged at the point of VCU issuance.

Standard authority and administrative bodies

The VCS is managed by the VCS Association (VCSA), an independent, nonprofit association registered under Swiss law that represents the VCS Secretariat and the VCS Board. The VCSA is in the process of establishing a US entity headquartered in Washington, DC.

The VCS Secretariat is responsible for managing the VCS Program, which responds to stakeholder queries, manages relationships with registry operators and accreditation bodies, and supervises the VCS website and project database.

The VCS Board has a number of responsibilities. First, it is responsible for approving any substantial changes to the VCS. It also makes a final determination regarding the approval of other GHG standards (e.g. project methodologies, accreditation procedures, additionality performance standards) under the VCS and has the authority to suspend an approved program temporarily or indefinitely if changes are made to it that affect its compatibility with the VCS Program. Second, the VCS Board has the authority to approve accreditation bodies that will accredit validators and verifiers and also certifies registries that can join the VCS Registry System. Third, the VCS Board has the authority to sanction validators and verifiers as per the Terms and Conditions agreed to with these entities. Finally, the VCS Board makes final decisions on any appeals brought forward to the VCS.

The Technical Advisory Groups (TAGs) support the Board by providing detailed technical recommendations on issues related to the program and its requirements (e.g. the Agriculture, Forestry and Other Land Use TAG for biosequestration projects).

Accredited third-party auditors have the authority to validate and verify offset projects, validate new baseline and monitoring methodologies, validate additionality performance standards and, for AFOLU projects, validate market leakage and non-permanence risk assessments. They can only do this for the project scopes and geographies for which they are accredited, and they must be accredited either under an approved GHG Program or under ISO 14065: 2007 with an accreditation scope specifically for the VCS Program. Unlike the CDM, accredited third-party auditors can validate and verify the same project and give final project approval. Validators and verifiers working under the VCS must agree to the VCS Terms and Conditions, which require them, among other things, to replace VCUs that have been determined to have been issued in excess VCUs due to fraud or negligence.

Regional scope

The VCS is an international voluntary GHG offset standard.

Recognition of other standards/links with other trading systems

In early 2008, the VCS Program recognized the CDM and JI and in late 2008 it recognized the Climate Action Reserve. The VCS will evaluate and either fully adopt or adopt elements of other offset standards by commissioning a consultant to complete a detailed gap analysis of the two programs. The approval process will be based on the principle of full compatibility with the VCS Program, with acceptance required by the VCS Board. If another offset standard is fully adopted by the VCS, all their auditors and methodologies are automatically accepted by the VCS and credits certified by that standard can be fungible with VCS credits – the Voluntary Carbon Unit (VCU).

Market size and scope

Tradable unit and pricing information

VCS-approved carbon offsets are registered and traded as Voluntary Carbon Units (VCU). One VCU represents emission reductions of 1 metric ton of CO_2. VCUs (07 and 08 vintage) traded at €2.75–3.75 per tonne in the spring of 2009 (*Carbon Finance*, April 2009).

Standard users

VCS 2007.1 is expected to be used widely for the verification of VERs for the European and North American markets.

Current project portfolio

VCS 2007.1 was launched in November 2008 and the VCS Registry System was launched on 17 March 2009. As of 26 May 2009, there are 63 projects registered under the VCS, with 43 of them having issued 3,864,411 VCUs. All the registration and issuance information can be viewed at the VCS Project Database (www.vcsproject database.com).

Offset project eligibility

Project types

All project types are allowed under the VCS Program provided that they are supported by an approved VCS methodology or are part of an approved GHG Program. Exceptions include projects that are 'reasonably assumed' to have generated GHG emissions primarily for the purpose of their subsequent reduction, removal or destruction (e.g. new HCFC facilities) and projects that have created another form of environmental credit (e.g. a Renewable Energy Certificate). Renewable Energy Credits (RECs) are fungible with VCUs if the GHG program certifying the RECs has been approved under the VCS. In addition, projects that have created another form of environmental credit must provide a letter from the program operator to confirm that the credit has not been used under the relevant program and has now been cancelled to prevent future use.

Project locations

There are no project location restrictions for the VCS. Retirement of corresponding allowances is required for projects in countries or states/provinces that have established legislation to implement a cap-and-trade system.

Project size

There is no upper or lower limit on project size. The VCS does, however, classify projects into three categories based on their size:

- micro-projects: under $5000tCO_2e$ per year;
- projects: $5000–1,000,000tCO_2e$ per year;
- mega-projects: greater than $1,000,000tCO_2e$ per year.

The rules on validation and verification vary slightly depending on the project size category.

Start date

The project start date for non-AFOLU projects for the VCS 2007.1 is 1 January 2002. The project start date for AFOLU projects can be earlier than 1 January 2002, provided the following conditions are met:

- project validation and verification against the VCS have been completed by 1 October 2010;
- the project proponent can verifiably demonstrate that the project was designed and implemented as a climate change mitigation project from its inception;
- prior to 1 January 2002, the project applied an externally reviewed methodology and engaged independent carbon monitoring experts to assess and quantify the project's baseline scenario and net emissions reductions or removals.

For non-AFOLU projects, VCS 2007.1 validation has to be completed within two years of the project start date, or completed or contracted before 19 November 2008. In relation to validation contracts entered into before 19 November 2008, validation must be completed by 19 November 2009 and proof of contracting prior to 19 November 2008 must be provided. AFOLU projects starting on or after 1 January 2002 are not required to complete validation within a specific time frame.

VCUs from CDM pre-registration credits are allowed in accordance with the start date and crediting period rules. No further proof of additionality is required.

Crediting period

The earliest permissible start date for the project crediting period is 28 March 2006 for non-AFOLU projects and 1 January 2002 for AFOLU projects. For non-AFOLU projects and agricultural land management (ALM) projects focusing exclusively on emission reductions of N_2O, CH_4 and/or fossil-derived CO_2, the crediting period is a maximum of ten years, which may be renewed at most twice. For AFOLU projects other than such ALM projects, the crediting period is a minimum of 20 years and a maximum of 100 years.

Co-benefit objectives and requirements

The VCS does not focus on environmental and social benefits. It is sufficient for VCS projects to show that they are compliant with local and national environmental laws and project proponents are obliged to present in the VCS Project Description 'relevant outcomes from stakeholder consultations and mechanisms for on-going communication'. The requirements for stakeholder involvement are based on ISO 14064–2 requirements: ISO only briefly mentions co-benefits:

> *The project proponent shall describe the project and its context in a GHG project plan that includes the following ... (k) a summary environmental impact assessment when such an assessment is required by applicable legislation or regulation; (l) relevant outcomes from stakeholder consultations and mechanisms for on-going communication. (ISO 14064–2)*

Because adverse social impacts are more likely to occur in projects in the AFOLU sectors, the VCS does require that these projects 'identify potential negative environmental and socio-economic impacts and take steps to mitigate them prior to generating Voluntary Carbon Units (VCUs)'.

The VCS allows co-benefits to be tagged onto VCUs, thereby enabling community, biodiversity and other benefits to be added to the attributes of VCUs. Several of the REDD projects being developed under the VCS are being certified by the Climate, Community and Biodiversity Standard (CCBS) and there are several projects in the VCS Project Database that have also been certified under the Social Carbon Standard.

Additionality and quantification procedures

Additionality requirements

The VCS uses project-based, performance-based and positive technology list-based additionality tests. The project-based tests closely follow the CDM Additionality Tool procedures:

- *Step 1:* Regulatory surplus test – the project must not be mandated by any enforced law, statute or other regulatory framework. This criterion also applies to projects using the performance or positive list tests.
- *Step 2:* Implementation barriers test – the project must demonstrate that it faces either capital and investment return constraints or an institutional barrier that can be overcome by additional revenues from VCU sales, or that it faces technology-related barriers to implementation of the project.
- *Step 3:* Common practice test – the project must demonstrate that it is not common practice in the sector or region when compared with other projects that received no carbon finance and if it is found to be common practice, then the project proponent must identify barriers it faces that were not faced by the other projects. In order to demonstrate these criteria, the VCS advocates the use of guidance provided by the GHG Project Protocol for Project Accounting.

As an alternative to the project-based additionality test, project proponents can use performance tests or positive lists. With a performance test, a project can demonstrate that it is not business-as-usual if the emissions generated per unit of output it generates are below a benchmark level approved by the VCS Program for the product, service, sector or industry. Positive lists are based on the concept that a project could generate VCUs if it can demonstrate that the technology in question is not currently being used and probably would not be implemented without additional incentives, until a robust level of market penetration is achieved. To date, no performance standards or positive lists have yet been submitted to the VCS, and any such proposals would be approved through the double approval process and by the VCS Board.

Quantification protocols

The VCS accepts projects that use existing quantification methodologies approved either under the VCS Program or by another approved GHG program and it also approves new methodologies. At the time VCS 2007.1 was launched, all CDM baselines and monitoring methodologies had been approved for use under the VCS and all registry protocols were also approved.

For the most part, the VCS draws on guidelines provided in ISO 14064–2 to guide the development of a VCS Program methodology. The VCS Board approves new methodologies using a double approval process, which entails seeking an approval from two independent accredited auditors – one appointed by the project developer and the other appointed by the VCS Secretariat. The Board will approve the methodology/benchmark if there is unanimity between the two auditors and would reject it if there is disagreement between them. The project developer can appeal against the decision. If the decision is appealed against, the VCS Secretariat appoints an independent consultant to review the project proponent's claim. The VCS Board makes a final decision based on the review. The expenses for each review are paid by the project proponent.

Project approval process

Validation and registration

Validation is required under the VCS, but this can be done at the same time as verification. The VCS provides a template for both the validation and the verification report. Projects may choose to be validated either as an individual project or as part of a grouped project including two or more subgroups each retaining their distinctive characteristics. Group projects are only sampled by the project auditor. A project proponent contracts an accredited auditor of the VCS Program or of a VCS-approved GHG Program to validate the project. The auditor evaluates the project against the VCS validation requirements (see below) and prepares its report according to the VCS Validation Report template. The project is automatically approved if it is successfully validated by the auditor. Project validation requires projects to meet ISO 14064–3 validation requirements and to prepare a validation report that follows the VCS Validation Report template, including:

- a description of the project design;
- a description of the method used to calculate the baseline;
- a monitoring plan;
- a calculation of the GHG emission reductions;
- a calculation of the environmental impact;
- comments by stakeholders.

Monitoring, verification and certification

The emission reductions achieved by VCS projects can be verified by the same entity that validated the project. The VCS Board does not approve or reject projects (in other words, the VCS Board does not function like the CDM EB). Instead, the auditors who verify the projects approve the claimed emission reductions. The third-party auditor verifies the emission reductions and the accuracy of emission reduction calculations according to the requirements of ISO 14064–3. After a project has been validated and verified, the VCS Project Document and proof of title are submitted to the registry operator. Electronic copies of these documents are then put on the VCS Project Database and are made publicly available. A verification report is prepared following the same requirements as for the VCS Validation Report template.

Registries and fees

On successful verification, projects can issue VCUs by submitting the appropriate documentation to one of the three VCS registries – APX Inc., Caisse des Dépôts and Markit Environmental Registry (formerly TZ1) – who then check the documentation for authenticity, accuracy and consistency and make sure that the emission reductions have not been issued by other GHG programs. The registry operators then upload the required documentation onto the VCS Project Database, which completes a GPS search to make sure the project has not been registered before. Once all those checks are completed, the VCS Project Database issues VCUs with unique serial numbers to the registry that requested issuance.

An important feature of the VCS Registry System is the ability to transfer VCUs among the participating registries. That feature, however, is currently unavailable, though the VCSA expects that to be resolved in due course.

To minimize the risks of double counting, the project owner must also submit the following to the VCS:

- a letter confirming that the VCUs being registered have not been registered, transferred or retired previously;
- if emission reductions occurred in an Annex-1 country, a certificate from the national registry of the host country stating that an equal number of AAUs have been cancelled from that registry;
- emission reductions from renewable energy projects must show proof that they are not a result of activity to meet a regulatory renewable energy commitment or to generate Renewable Energy Certificates (or the RECs must be cancelled).

The registration fee for each VCU issued is €0.04. Account fees are set by each of the VCS approved registries.

Selected issues

The VCS aims to strike a balance between ensuring the integrity of offsets, simplifying procedures and keeping costs for project developers low. In some areas the VCS is quite innovative. This is especially true for its rules relating to biosequestration projects.

VCS Agriculture, Forestry and Other Land Use

The VCS Agriculture, Forestry and Other Land Use (AFOLU) rules are thorough and innovative in the way they address permanence concerns. Permanence issues are addressed through detailed rules on buffers, which include set asides sized for each project based on the risk profile of the project. The VCS also provides detailed guidelines for addressing leakage from AFOLU projects. The VCS is the first carbon offset standard to cover all the major land-use activities under a single verification framework. Only once projects have been implemented and credits generated will it be possible to fully evaluate the quality of the AFOLU offsets.

One of the potential risks of a buffer approach in a voluntary system is that projects may opt out at a later time. For instance, the cost of continuing monitoring and verification may outweigh the added benefits for a project developer over time. In such a case, the project developer may default and not have his project re-verified. If a significant number of project developers did so, VCS's pool of buffer credits might be used up quickly and not be available to replace defaulted credits. To address this potential threat the VCS plans to do regular 'true-up': an evaluation of all AFOLU projects. If the evaluation reveals increased project failure in one particular sector, activity type or region, the risk-based buffer assignment will be adjusted.

No separation of verification and approval of projects

The VCS does not have a separate accrediting board and projects can be validated, verified and approved by the same auditor. This is true for many of the voluntary standards, such as the VER+, CAR, CCBS and Green-e CPRE.

This reduces the standard's and project developer's administrative burden. Yet, the downside of this approach is that more decision-making power is given to DOEs. Given the pressures on auditors and given the conflict of interest (Schneider, 2007, 2009), the lack of an accrediting board to review projects and give final project approval could be a potential weakness of the VCS.

Approval of methodologies

There is pressure on auditors to approve their clients' methodologies in order to maintain a good relationship and not compromise future work opportunities. As has been shown in experience under the CDM (Schneider, 2007; Schneider and Mohr, 2009), this concern is difficult to address as long as the project developer pays for and can choose the auditor. The VCS is partly mitigating the fact that project developers and auditors have aligned interests by having two auditors approve a new methodology (the second of which is appointed by the VCSA). Moreover, the VCS requires that new methodologies and/or protocols be subject to a public consultation process and that the comments raised be duly taken into account.

Modular approaches

The VCS is fostering innovation by supporting the development of modular approaches to methodological development, whereby projects can draw from a toolkit of approved modules to construct new methodologies relevant to specific project characteristics. By covering a wide range of project activities under a comprehensive pre-approved suite of modules, transaction costs and approval uncertainties are likely to be reduced.

Co-benefits

The VCS requirements for stakeholder involvement are based on ISO 14064–2, which states these only in very general terms. Definitions of stakeholders, confidential information and 'sufficient opportunity' for comments appear to be left to the project developer to decide, though for AFOLU projects the VCS requires that these projects 'identify potential negative environmental and socio-economic impacts and take steps to mitigate them prior to generating Voluntary Carbon Units (VCUs)'. Nor are there specific procedures and rules on how stakeholder concerns are to be taken into consideration. For buyers who place value on these co-benefits, the VCS would not be a sufficient standard.

However, the VCS allows co-benefits to be tagged onto VCUs, thereby enabling community, biodiversity and other benefits to be added to the attributes of VCUs. Many of the AFOLU projects being developed under the VCS are being certified by the Climate, Community and Biodiversity Standard (CCBS), and there are several projects in the VCS Project Database that have also been certified under the Social Carbon Standard.

The future of the VCS

Given that the VCS 2007 is broadly supported by the carbon offset industry, it is likely to become one of the more important standards in the voluntary offset market and might very well establish itself as the main standard for voluntary offsets. VCS version 1 was criticized by many as too weak and too vague. VCS 2007 was developed after a two-year stakeholder consultation and has taken into account many of these criticisms.

VER+ (VERplus)

www.tuev-sued.de/climatechange
www.netinform.de
www.blue-registry.com
Unless referenced otherwise, the information in this section is based on the above websites and personal communications.

Overview

Type of standard and context

VER+ is a fully fledged carbon offset standard and closely follows the Kyoto Protocol's project-based mechanisms (Clean Development Mechanism (CDM) and Joint Implementation (JI)).

The VER+ standard was developed by TÜV SÜD, a Designated Operational Entity (DOE) for the validation and verification of CDM projects. It was designed for project developers who have projects that cannot be implemented under CDM, yet who want to use procedures similar to the CDM. The VER+ was launched in mid-2007. Revised version 2 of the VER+ standard was launched in May 2008. Any DOE or Accredited Independent Entity (AIE) accredited for corresponding scopes under UNFCCC may carry out validations and verifications for VER+ projects.

Standard authority and administrative bodies

TÜV SÜD certification body 'climate and energy' has four members who supervise and administer the VER+ standard's criteria. The same body also reviews all the CDM projects that TÜV SÜD audits as a DOE before the documents are submitted to the CDM Executive Board (EB).

Third-party auditors are CDM- and JI-accredited auditors. They are approved to validate and verify projects. In the validation and verification process, the auditing company is obliged to follow the requirements as defined by the Validation and Verification Manual (published by World Bank/IETA), in its most recent version. Unlike under CDM, but similar to VCS and GS, accredited third-party auditors can validate and verify the same project.

Regional scope

The VER+ is an international voluntary carbon offset standard. VER+ has offset projects worldwide.

Recognition of other standards/links with other trading systems

If a project that has been initially implemented under another standard seeks VER+ certification, a so-called 'equivalence check' is carried out. Based on validation and verification reports, the auditor in charge confirms that the already audited project also complies with VER+ requirements.

Market size and scope

Tradable unit and pricing information

VER+ offsets of 2007 and 2008 vintage traded at US$3.25 per metric ton in the spring of 2009 (*Carbon Finance*, April 2009).

Participants/buyers

VER+ is marketed to parties within countries that have not ratified the Kyoto Protocol, project owners of CDM and non-CDM projects and companies seeking to offset emissions and/or incorporate VER credits into their corporate or public climate change mitigation programs.

Current project portfolio

As of 1 June 2009 the BlueRegistry has registered 24 carbon projects, generating VER+ credits in the following countries: China, India, Russia, Turkey, Lithuania, Germany, Brazil, Chile, Fiji, Mexico and Peru. The Blue Registry lists more than 2.6 million VER+ credits and 400,273 VER+ offsets have been permanently retired.

Offset project eligibility

Project types

VER+ accepts all project types except HFC projects, nuclear energy projects and hydropower projects over 80MW. Hydro projects exceeding 20MW have to conform with World Commission on Dams rules. Land use, land-use change and forestry (LULUCF) projects, including those that reduce emissions from deforestation and degradation (REDD), are accepted if implemented with a buffer approach to address the risk of potential non-permanence.

Project locations

VER+ follows the same project criteria as JI but without limitation on the status of the host country. Hence, the host country can be an Annex-I, non-Annex-I or nonratification country.

The VER+ standard avoids conflicts of double counting by requiring the retirement of Assigned Amount Units (AAUs) by the authorities in charge of the host nation. Thus, the host country (which has ratified the Kyoto Protocol and assumed a reduction target) shall confirm that an equivalent amount of AAUs is set aside in the national account (registry) and is not used.

Project size

No restrictions apply.

Start date

Applications for retroactive VER+ accreditation can be submitted for start dates as early as 1 January 2005. Retroactive crediting has been limited such that credits are issued for two years back from the registration date and will be phased out by the end of 2009.

Crediting period

The crediting period of VER+ activities ends at the end of the latest agreed commitment period under the UNFCCC scheme. At the end of 2012, a brief check-up on the 'Kyoto status' of the host country will be carried out to avoid double counting with UNFCCC regimes. Once this review is carried out, the crediting period will be extended up to the end of the next commitment period (as defined by UNFCCC). At the end of this next commitment period (e.g. 2020), a revalidation is required. The maximum crediting periods are limited to 25 years for standard projects and 50 years for LULUCF activities.

CDM pre-registration credits

It is possible to generate VER+ credits before registering a CDM project without any further on-site audit. A registered CDM project has to have begun operating and reduced emissions prior to UNFCCC registration. The earliest starting date for this pre-CDM/JI crediting is the date of publication of the PDD on the UNFCCC website (Global Stakeholder Process) and is limited to two years. VER+ crediting may occur until CDM/JI registration. No separate PDD is needed for CDM or JI activities applying for VER+ credits for a crediting period prior to the one under UNFCCC.

Co-benefit objectives and requirements

If the project activity requires an Environmental Impact Assessment (EIA) due to national legislation, it must be submitted for project approval. If required by national law, a local stakeholder process must be carried out. Otherwise, the project developer can choose between performing a voluntary stakeholder process and submitting documentation in the VER+ Project Design Document (PDD), or justifying in the VER+ PDD that the project does not impact the vicinity.

As in CDM, the PDD is published for 30 days on the DOE's website and comments can be made via the website, which will then be considered in the audit process.

Additionality and quantification procedures

Additionality requirements

Additionality tests for VER+ are project-based.

VER+ projects are required to follow specific additionality rules of an approved CDM methodology, or, in all other cases, apply the most recent version of the CDM Additionality Tool.

Quantification protocols

All CDM-approved baselines and methodologies are allowed. The latest versions of the CDM methodologies must be used. If there is no existing CDM methodology that matches the project conditions, a project-specific methodology can be developed. This new methodology is reviewed on a project-by-project basis. The project methodology must be based on 'guidance on criteria for baseline setting and monitoring' as defined for JI activities.

Project approval process

Validation and registration

The requirements are similar to those of CDM but they do not require approval from the host country and include a completed PDD and a validation report. A UNFCCC-accredited auditor reviews the validation process and approves the project. The project can then be registered. The results of the validation (as well as verification at a later stage) are forwarded by the project's auditor to the BlueRegistry, where relevant information on VER+ projects is held and made publicly available.

A project-specific approach as defined for JI can be used for those project settings where a CDM-approved methodology is not available or fully applicable.

Monitoring, verification and certification

Verification is based on monitoring reports from the project developers and conducted by an auditor. The auditor also approves the verification report. All VER+ project documentation is submitted to the BlueRegistry. Unlike under CDM rules, an auditor is allowed to do validation and verification of the same project.

The first verification is required, at the latest, one year after registration of the starting date of the crediting period. For LULUCF projects, a first verification is required within five years from validation. For any VER+ activity, the frequency of the following verifications can be chosen by the project participants. Based on a positive verification statement, VER+ credits can be registered with BlueRegistry.

Registries and fees

In June 2007, TÜV SÜD launched its own BlueRegistry for VER+ credits.

If verification has been carried out by TÜV SÜD, then all VER+ credits are automatically registered in the BlueRegistry without additional costs. For projects and credits not verified by TÜV SÜD, there is a registration fee that covers incorporation into the BlueRegistry. TÜV SÜD charges a one-time subscription fee (€550) and a registration fee (€400 per year) for maintaining accounts. BlueRegistry charges €0.03 per transferred metric ton of CO_2e. The fee for permanent retirement and withdrawals of volumes less than 1000t is €150 and €150 + €0.03 per metric ton of CO_2e for volumes greater than 1000t.

In an effort to prevent project developers from registering their credits with multiple registries, VER+ includes in its contract a clause that stipulates that the credit holder shall refrain from double selling or registering. Agreements on the standardized interchange between registries are currently pending.

The VER+ is financed by funds from TÜV SÜD and by fees for the use of the BlueRegistry.

Selected issues

No separation of verification and approval of projects

VER+ does not have a separate accrediting board and projects can be validated, verified and approved by the same DOE. This is true for many of the voluntary standards, such as the VCS, CAR, CCBS and Green-e CPRE.

As mentioned earlier, this reduces the standard's and project developer's administrative burden. Yet, the downside of this approach is that more decision-making power is given to DOEs. Given the pressures on auditors and given the conflict of interest (Schneider, 2007, 2009), the lack of an accrediting board to review projects and give final project approval could be a potential weakness of VER+.

Currently, most of the VER+ projects have been audited by TÜV SÜD, the DOE that developed and manages VER+. A recent study by the WWF gave TÜV SÜD the second highest rating. Yet the performance of all evaluated DOEs was rated as fairly low: TÜV SÜD scored 65 out of 100 (Schneider and Mohr, 2009).

Co-benefits

VER+ does not focus on enhancing co-benefits. For buyers who place value on enhanced co-benefits, VER+ would not be a sufficient standard. VER+ could potentially be used in conjunction with a co-benefit standard such as Social Carbon or CCBS to ensure that a project delivers additional sustainability benefits.

The future of VER+

There are several reasons why project developers might choose VER+ over CDM. In comparison to CDM, VER+ provides more flexibility on methodologies, which speeds up validation and verification. A project-specific approach as defined for JI can be used for those project settings where a CDM-approved methodology is not available or fully applicable. Given the proliferation of standards, it remains to be seen how well the VER+ will be able to establish itself.

American Carbon Registry

www.americancarbonregistry.org

Unless referenced otherwise, the information in this section is based on the above website and personal communications.

Overview

Type of standard and context

The American Carbon Registry (ACR) was founded in 1997 as the GHG Registry, the first private voluntary GHG registry, by the environmental nonprofit Environmental Resources Trust (ERT). In 2007, ERT and its registry became part of Winrock International, a nonprofit based in the USA. The registry was relaunched as American Carbon Registry (ACR) in 2008.

ACR published its American Carbon Registry Technical Standard 2009 v.1.0 in July 2009, which outlines the eligibility requirements for registration of project-based carbon offsets. The American Carbon Registry Standard will incorporate the information of the ACR Technical Standard and will also include requirements for methodology validation and verification and other procedural requirements and information on general use of the American Carbon Registry. The ACR Standard is currently in the process of publication.

Standard authority and administrative bodies

The Director of ACR has ultimate decision-making power for ACR-related decisions. Technical decisions are made by lead team member experts in the subject matter.

ACR's standard and protocols are developed by staff of ACR's parent organization Winrock International, and by external consultants with specialized expertise not available internally. To date, standards have been a synthesis of project monitoring and verification protocols that have been written or vetted by Winrock. Winrock staff have authored and co-authored carbon protocols and methodology manuals and guidelines for a wide range of organizations including US Environmental Protection Agency, US Department of Agriculture (USDA), USDA Forest Service, US Agency for International Development, World Bank, International Tropical Timber Organization, United Nations programs, Intergovernmental Panel on Climate Change, Electric Power Research Institute and Climate, and Community and Biodiversity Alliance. Standards undergo internal and external peer review. Winrock has partnered nationally and internationally with leading environmental NGOs to develop its standard and protocols. Current and previous NGO partners include The Nature Conservancy, Wildlife Conservation Society, Conservation International, World Wildlife Fund, American Land Conservancy and Environmental Defense Fund.

ACR-approved verifiers can currently be chosen from a list on ACR's website or from verifiers who are approved under CDM, JI, VCS and CAR. Beginning in October 2010, the Registry will require that all verifiers be ANSI-certified.

Regional scope

ACR registers project-based carbon offsets from around the globe.

Recognition of other standards/links with other trading systems

The American Carbon Registry methodologies and protocols are all based on International Standards Organization (ISO) 14064.

ACR allows project developers to use methodologies and tools for GHG measurement from the Clean Development Mechanism (CDM), EPA Climate Leaders, Voluntary Carbon Standard (VCS) and WBCSD/WRI GHG Protocol, to the extent that they comply with the Registry's published standards.

Market size and scope

Tradable unit and pricing information

To date, ACR is the largest voluntary carbon market registry in terms of tradable project-based carbon offset tons. ACR has issued over 30 million project-based carbon offsets since 1997, and in 2008 was the most widely used voluntary carbon market registry in the world.

The American Carbon Registry holds serialized offsets called Emission Reduction Tons (ERTs). One 'ERT' represents the reduction or removal from the atmosphere equivalent to 1 metric ton of CO_2.

Participants/buyers

The main buyers of ERTs include corporate pre-compliance buyers, hedge funds, carbon retailers and nonprofit organizations.

Current project portfolio

As of July 2009, 22 projects were listed on the ACR website: www.americancarbonregistry.org/carbon-registry/projects

Offset project eligibility

Project types

ACT does not explicitly exclude any project types. All projects that meet the ACR Technical Standard are eligible for registration.

Current registered project types:

- afforestation/reforestation (in registration pipeline);
- carbon capture and storage;
- fuel switching;
- industrial gas;
- landfill gas;
- livestock waste management;

- renewable energy;
- transport.

Project locations

There are no restrictions on project location.

Current registered projects are located in the USA, Bolivia, Nicaragua and El Salvador.

Project size

There are no limitations on project size except for developing country indirect emissions from renewable energy projects, which have a limit of 100MW.

Start date

The American Carbon Registry requires all project types, with the exception of forest projects, to have a start date that is no earlier than 1 January 2000. Forest and land-use-change projects with a start date of 1 November 1997 or later are eligible for ACR registration. Forest and land-use-change projects with an earlier start date will be evaluated on a case-by-case basis.

Crediting period

ACR nonforest projects have a crediting period of ten years with opportunities for renewal. When the crediting period is over, project developers must re-verify the project, or cease to generate offsets from that project for ACR registration.

There are no restrictions on renewal as long as the project is verified to meet eligibility requirements.

ACR requires afforestation/reforestation projects to have a crediting period of 35 years or less, with opportunities for renewal. Improved Forest Management (IFM) and REDD projects to have a crediting period of ten years or less, with opportunities for renewal. There are no restrictions on renewal as long as the project is verified to meet eligibility requirements.

Co-benefit objectives and requirements

Co-benefits are not required, but are desirable. Additional certifications such as CCBS can be used with ACR Standards.

Additionality and quantification procedures

Additionality requirements

All projects must have a clear project action that is different from what likely would have happened in the absence of the project. ACR requires every project to pass either an approved performance standard and a regulatory additionality test or a three-pronged test of additionality in which the project must:

1   exceed regulatory/legal requirements;
2   go beyond common practice; and
3   overcome one of three implementation barriers: institutional, financial or technical.

Quantification protocols

ACR allows the use of specific protocols from the CDM, US EPA Climate Leaders and the VCS for calculating and updating baselines.

ACR also develops its own project protocols. ACR has published a forest carbon project standard, project-specific protocols for landfill methane, livestock waste management (biodigester) and industrial gas substitution, and has several other sector standards and protocols in various stages of development.

If no protocol exists for a particular offset project type, the project developer may submit a proposed methodology to ACR for validation. ACR evaluates the methodology through a peer review process. The developer may also work directly with the ACR to design a new methodology, which is also evaluated through a peer review.

ACR requires that all LULUCF projects calculate the baseline at the project start. Reforestation baselines are valid for the life of the project. REDD baselines are valid for up to ten years.

Project approval process

Validation and registration

The steps to submit a project for offset registration are:

1   Carbon offset project proponent submits PDD for review to determine eligibility.
2   If project passes eligibility screening, it is ready for independent verification from an American Carbon Registry approved verifier.
3   Once verified, the Registry issues and registers 'ERTs'.

Leakage

Project developers are required to follow guidelines in the approved methodology. ACR requires project developers to assess, account for and mitigate leakage, and provide documentation to support mitigation assertions. Project developers must deduct all leakage that reduces the GHG emission reduction and/or removal benefit of the project. ACR assesses leakage on a case-by-case basis.

Permanence

ACR requires projects to address the risk of reversal by use of one of the following:

•   an approved insurance product to guarantee offsets;
•   dedication of offsets to a buffer pool;
•   access to a secure source of replacement offsets.

Monitoring, verification and certification

ACR requires third-party verification with an ACR-approved verifier. Methodologies must be validated to be approved for use. Verification is project-specific against an approved (validated) methodology.

Registries and fees

In spring 2009 ACR announced a partnership with Markit Environmental Registry. Markit will provide an online registry infrastructure to the ACR. The registry is planned to go live in August 2009. Transaction fees depend on the type of transaction and vary between US$0.05 and US$0.12 per ERT transacted.

Selected issues

With over a decade of operational experience in carbon offset issuance, serialization and transparent online transaction reporting, ERT/ACR is a pioneer in creating a transparent system for carbon offset trading. According to ACR staff, ACR is the only registry to require all accounts to be public. Other registry systems allow for (and many account holders opt for) private accounts that are not viewable by the public.

Approval of projects

ACR does not have a separate accrediting board and projects can be validated, verified and approved by the same auditor. This is true for many of the voluntary standards, such as the VCS, CAR, VER+, CCBS and Green-e CPRE. However, ACR staff reviews each project before and after verification to ensure it meets ACR Standards and reserves the right to reject any project, even if it has been verified.

Co-benefits

While its host organization (Winrock) focuses on enhancing co-benefits, ACR methodologies themselves do not have specific co-benefit requirements. An exception to this is the forestry standard that does require the assessment of social and ecological effects and efforts to mitigate any negative effects. For buyers who place value on enhanced co-benefits of other project types, ACR would not be a sufficient standard. As with other voluntary programs noted above, ACR could potentially be used in conjunction with a co-benefit standard such as Social Carbon or CCBS to ensure that a project delivers additional sustainability benefits.

Climate, Community and Biodiversity Standards

www.climate-standards.org

Unless referenced otherwise, the information in this section is based on the above website, personal communications and CCBA.

Overview

Type of standard and context

Climate, Community and Biodiversity Standards (CCBS) is a project design standard that offers rules and guidance for project design and development. It is intended to be applied early on during a project's design phase to ensure robust project design and local community and biodiversity benefits. It does not verify quantified carbon offsets, nor does it provide a registry. The CCB Standards focuses exclusively on land-based biosequestration and mitigation projects and requires social and environmental benefits from such projects.

CCBS was developed by the Climate, Community and Biodiversity Alliance (CCBA) with feedback and suggestions from independent experts. CCBA is a partnership of non-governmental organizations, corporations and research institutes such as Conservation International, The Nature Conservancy, CARE, Sustainable Forestry Management, BP and Centro Agronómico Tropical de Investigación y Enseñanza (CATIE). The first edition was released in May 2005 and the second edition in December 2008.

Standard authority and administrative bodies

CCBA is formed by representatives from each member organization. The alliance currently has 12 members that make decisions about changes to the standards. It also works closely with project auditors, advising them on interpretation and application of the standards.

Working groups are comprised of alliance members and external advisors and are appointed when needed to address specific issues. Working group proposals for changes must be approved by the Alliance.

Third-party auditors are DOEs under the CDM for afforestation and reforestation: organizations that are approved to evaluate CDM projects or evaluators who are accredited under the Forest Stewardship Council. Validation and verification can be done by the same auditor. (The Forest Stewardship Council (FSC) is a nonprofit organization with a mission 'to promote environmentally appropriate, socially beneficial and economically viable management of the world's forests'. It certifies sustainably managed forestry operations and tracks their timber through the supply chain to the end product, which can then carry the FSC ecolabel.)

Regional scope

Projects using CCBS are worldwide.

Recognition of other standards/links with other trading systems

Since CCBS is focused on social and environmental impact and does not include a mechanism for generating emission reductions certificates, it is often used in conjunction with a carbon accounting standard such as the VCS or the CDM. A recent survey indicated that about 50 per cent of projects that are using or planning to use CCBS are or will be using it in conjunction with the VCS, about 25 per cent with the CDM.

Market size and scope

Tradable unit and pricing information

The CCBS is not a carbon accounting standard and does not issue or register carbon credits (see Recognition of other standards). Many CCBS projects fetch a premium price.

Some CCBS projects sell *ex-ante* credits. *Ex-ante* offsets are offsets that will occur in the future, *ex-post* offsets are emission reductions that have already occurred and usually have been verified by an auditor.

Participants/buyers

VER buyers: companies and institutions.

Current project portfolio

As of July 2009, a total of 10 projects have completed validation and 26 other projects have initiated the validation process. Of these 36 projects, 27 are in developing countries. Over 150 projects indicated intent to use the CCBS.

Offset project eligibility

Project types

CCBS focuses on land-based climate change mitigation projects and accepts the following project types:

- primary or secondary forest conservation;
- reforestation or revegetation;
- agro-forestry plantations;
- densification and enrichment planting;
- introduction of new cultivation practices;
- introduction of new timber harvesting and/or processing practices (e.g. reduced impact logging);
- reduced tillage on cropland;
- improved livestock management, etc.;
- actions to reduce emissions from deforestation and degradation (REDD).

Project locations

Projects can be located in industrialized and developing countries. The revised version of the standards (CCB 2008) includes rules to prevent potential double counting of Annex-1-based projects.

Project size

There are no restrictions on project size.

Start date

There are no restrictions on project start date but projects must have credible documentation for baselines from the start of the accounting period for carbon, community and biodiversity benefits.

Crediting period

CCBS has no rules on crediting periods because it is solely a project design standard.

Co-benefit objectives and requirements

CCBS projects must generate net positive impacts on biodiversity. The standard employs a screen to rule out negative impacts and requires that each project justifies net positive biodiversity benefits taking into account any off-site or indirect impacts. The second edition of CCBS has expanded its requirements for co-benefits. It stipulates that projects cannot have negative effects on high conservation values, including species included in the IUCN Red List (see www.iucnredlist.org/) of threatened species or species on nationally recognized lists and critical ecosystem services. Invasive species or genetically modified organisms cannot be used in a project. Impacts on biodiversity (positive and negative) must be monitored and the results made publicly available.

CCBS projects must generate net positive impacts on the social and economic wellbeing of communities and must mitigate potential negative effects caused by the project on site and off site. CCBS requires a 30-day public comment period. Stakeholder involvement is required and must be documented during all phases of project development. Stakeholders must have an opportunity before the project design is finalized to raise concerns about potential negative impacts, express desired outcomes and provide input on the project design. The project design must include a process for hearing, responding to and resolving community grievances within a reasonable time period. The net social and economic effect of the project must be positive, the impacts (positive and negative) must be monitored and the results made publicly available.

The biodiversity criteria require an evaluation of whether the project zone includes any of the following high conservation values and a description of the qualifying attributes:

- globally, regionally or nationally significant concentrations of biodiversity values;
- globally, regionally or nationally significant large landscape-level areas where viable populations of most if not all naturally occurring species exist in natural patterns of distribution and abundance;
- threatened or rare ecosystems;
- areas that provide critical ecosystem services (e.g. hydrological services, erosion control, fire control);
- areas that are fundamental for meeting the basic needs of local communities (e.g. for essential food, fuel, fodder, medicines or building materials without readily available alternatives); and

- areas that are critical for the traditional cultural identity of communities (e.g. areas of cultural, ecological, economic or religious significance identified in collaboration with the communities).

Additionality and quantification procedures

Additionality requirements

The additionality tests for CCBS are project-based and specified by individual methodologies.

CCBS requires:

Step 1: Regulatory surplus: Project developers must prove that existing laws or regulations would not have required that project activities be undertaken anyway. The standards also allow project developers to make claims when a law is in existence but is not enforced.

Step 2: Barriers: financial, lack of capacity, institutional or market barriers or common practice. Several additionality tests are required. The project proponents must provide analyses (poverty assessments, farming knowledge assessments, remote sensing analysis, etc.) showing that without the project, improved land-use practices would be unlikely to materialize.

Quantification protocols

CCBS relies on methods and tools developed by other organizations and standards for their baseline calculations. Projects must use 'IPCC's 2006 *Guidelines for National GHG Inventories for Agriculture, Forestry and Other Land Use* (IPCC 2006 GL for AFOLU) or a more robust and detailed methodology', i.e. updated from IPCC GPG.

The baseline calculations must be based on clearly defined and defendable assumptions about how project activities will alter carbon stocks and non-CO_2 GHG emissions over the duration of the project or the project accounting period.

Project approval process

Validation and registration

Once a project has been designed, a third-party auditor validates the project. After a review of relevant project documents, a site visit and taking account of the comments received during a 30-day public comment period, the auditor approves or rejects the project.

The CCBA responds to questions of clarification or interpretation from the auditors but does not review project documentation. The auditor issues an independent statement of conformance to CCBS, which is posted on the CCBA website with the final audit report.

There are 14 required criteria and three optional criteria. Gold Level status is earned by achieving any one of the optional criteria that require demonstration of climate change adaptation benefits, exceptional community benefits for the global poor or exceptional biodiversity benefits conserving sites of high biodiversity conservation priority.

Leakage

Decreased carbon stocks or increased emissions of non-CO_2 GHGs outside the project boundary resulting from project activities need to be quantified and mitigated. The project proponents must:

1   Determine the types of leakage that are expected and estimate potential off-site increases in GHGs (increases in emissions or decreases in sequestration) due to project activities. Where relevant, define and justify where leakage is most likely to take place.
2   Document how any leakage will be mitigated and estimate the extent to which such impacts will be reduced by these mitigation activities.
3   Subtract any likely project-related unmitigated negative off-site climate impacts from the climate benefits being claimed by the project and demonstrate that this has been included in the evaluation of net climate impact of the project.
4   Non-CO_2 gases must be included if they are likely to account for more than a 5 per cent increase or decrease (in terms of CO_2-equivalent) of the net change calculations (above) of the project's overall off-site GHG emission reductions or removals over each monitoring period (CCBA, 2008).

Permanence

Permanence is addressed by requiring that projects identify potential risks upfront and design in measures to mitigate potential reversals of carbon, community and biodiversity gains, including establishing buffer zones. Yet because CCBS is a project design standard, it does not have specific permanence requirements such as the issuance of temporary offsets.

Monitoring, verification and certification

To keep its CCBS validation, each project must be verified every five years. Verification includes a project document review by the auditor and a site visit to check on project implementation and monitoring results in addition to any changes in project design.

The validation and the verification can be done by the same auditor. All current CCBS projects are less than five years old and have therefore not yet been verified. The CCBA intends to develop and publish further rules and guidance on project verification.

The CCBS verification does not include a quantitative certification of the carbon benefits but is a qualitative evaluation that confirms carbon benefits as well as the environmental and social benefits of the project.

Registries and fees

Because CCBS is a project design standard it does not have a registry accredited for its offsets.

Cost for validation of a project ranges from US$5000 to 25,000. If the validation is being done in conjunction with CDM or VCS, the cost of CCBS validation is lower than for stand-alone projects, because many of the requirements for CCBS will already have been fulfilled through the CDM or VCS requirements (e.g. baseline calculations).

Selected issues

Project design standard

CCBS is intended to be used as a design tool to ensure that robust co-benefits will be delivered. Project design standards for forestry projects are especially valuable and important, since carbon verification standards typically do not come into play until many years after the project has been designed and after upfront investment has been secured.

The CCBS is a project design standard for enhancing co-benefits; it does not issue emission reductions certificates, include specific requirements for addressing issues of permanence, or provide an offset registry mechanism. Because of that CCBS should be used in conjunction with another fully fledged standard, such as VCS or CDM.

No separation of verification and approval of projects

Under CCBS, the auditors directly approve projects. Given the pressures on auditors and conflicts of interest discussed earlier, the lack of an accrediting board could be a potential weakness of the CCBS. This concern extends to many of the voluntary standards, including VCS, VER+, CAR and Green-e CPRE.

Co-benefits

CCBS emphasizes the social and environmental benefits of projects and has compiled a list of useful tools and guidelines to ensure and measure these co-benefits. Some of the criteria are quite specific (e.g. biodiversity rules), while others are defined in more general terms (e.g. stakeholder and capacity-building rules). Using general language to define requirements gives the project developer the flexibility to address the issue in a way that best fits the project, but it also leaves more up to the auditor's judgement when making the assessment. Quality of projects can therefore only be assured if auditors are truly independent and adhere to high standards in their work.

Issuance of offsets

CCBS is not a carbon accounting standard and does not issue or register carbon credits. While it can be used to validate carbon estimations, it is mostly used in conjunction with a fully fledged carbon accounting standard, primarily the VCS or CDM.

The CCBS do not mandate the use of a carbon accounting standard or specify which may be used. Projects may apply a separate standard that issues *ex-ante* credits or use the CCBS by itself and choose to sell *ex-ante* credits, sold prior to the actual emission reductions. *Ex-ante* credits, as noted for the Plan Vivo Foundation, create uncertainty with regard to how the risk for reversal is dealt with in the future.

The future of CCBS

CCBS has been steadily expanding its project portfolio. There are currently more than 150 projects being designed to meet CCBS.

Plan Vivo

www.planvivo.org

Unless referenced otherwise, the information in this section is based on the above website and personal communications.

Overview

Type of standard and context

Plan Vivo is an offset project method for LULUCF projects with a focus on promoting sustainable development and improving rural livelihoods and ecosystems. Plan Vivo projects work closely with rural communities and the system and standard emphasize participatory design, ongoing stakeholder consultation and the use of native species. The Plan Vivo Foundation certifies and issues currently only *ex-ante* offsets, although project developers can choose to sell *ex-post* offsets. *Ex-ante* offsets are offsets that will occur in the future, *ex-post* offsets are emission reductions that have already occurred and usually have been verified a third-party auditor.

The Plan Vivo System originated in 1994 as a research project in southern Mexico, which aimed to develop a framework enabling smallholders to engage in carbon sequestration activities through accessing funds from carbon markets. The system was developed by the Edinburgh Centre for Carbon Management (ECCM), a consulting company that focuses on climate change mitigation strategies and policies, in partnership with El Colegio de la Frontera Sur (ECOSUR), the University of Edinburgh and other local organizations with funding from the UK Department for International Development (DFID). The latest version of the standard was launched in 2008 and a new version is planned to be released for consultation in late 2009.

Standard authority and administrative bodies

Plan Vivo is currently managed by the Plan Vivo Foundation (formerly BioClimate Research and Development), a Scottish charity focused on environmental improvement and poverty reduction. The Foundation reviews and registers projects according to the Plan Vivo Standard, issues Plan Vivo Certificates annually following the submission and approval of each project's annual report and acts as overall 'keeper' of the Plan Vivo System, which is periodically reviewed in consultation with projects and other stakeholders. It also approves third-party validators and verifiers, and registers resellers of Plan Vivo Certificates. The Plan Vivo Foundation also occasionally conducts field visits to projects to monitor their progress and use lessons and experiences to update the Plan Vivo system as required.

Project developers are locally based NGOs that manage Plan Vivo projects and function as project developers ('project coordinators'). They coordinate sales with carbon buyers, coordinate continued monitoring and community consultation, and administer staged payments for ecosystem services to project participants based on achieved 'monitoring targets'.

Third-party auditors have to be approved by Plan Vivo and must be accredited by an international certification authority such as the CDM, ISO, Climate Action Registry, FSC or other forestry certification programmes. Auditors conduct project verification.

Regional scope

Plan Vivo currently has four registered projects, located in Mexico, Malawi, Uganda and Mozambique. Two more projects, in Malawi and Tanzania, are expected to be validated by the end of 2009.

Recognition of other standards/links with other trading systems

Plan Vivo does not currently work in conjunction with other standards.

Market size and scope

Tradable unit and pricing information

Plan Vivo currently certifies *ex-ante* credits. These are called Plan Vivo Certificates, and represent the future avoidance or reduction of 1 metric ton of CO_2, plus livelihood and ecosystem benefits. *Ex-post* credits are also accepted under Plan Vivo but currently all projects produce *ex-ante* credits.

Participants/buyers

Buyers of Plan Vivo Certificates are companies and individuals.

Current project portfolio

Plan Vivo currently has four projects (in Mexico, Uganda, Malawi and Mozambique) and several more are in various stages of development in Malawi, Rwanda, Ethiopia and Cameroon.

Offset project eligibility

Project types

Plan Vivo accepts the following project types: afforestation and reforestation, forest restoration; agro-forestry; forest protection and management.

Project locations

Plan Vivo projects are located in developing countries.

Project size

There is no minimum or maximum size limitation for Plan Vivo projects. Projects generally expand in size over a number of years as the project makes more sales and more smallholders or communities engage in the project, learn more about the notion of selling carbon as a commodity and see it working in practice. The current Plan Vivo projects range in size from a carbon offset potential of 10,000tCO$_2$/yr to 100,000tCO$_2$/yr.

Start date

In order to sell Plan Vivo Certificates, projects must first be registered as Plan Vivo projects.

The project start date is the date of implementation. Retroactive crediting is only possible if the project can demonstrate additionality under the normal process and also provide evidence that the project was designed as a carbon project from the outset and has gone through the necessary participatory planning process.

Crediting period

The exact payment schedule varies with each project, but normally involves payments over periods of 10–15 years.

Co-benefit objectives and requirements

Plan Vivo's focus is on improving the livelihoods of the rural poor and building capacity in developing countries to enable sustainable land management. The Plan Vivo Standard requires that all its projects provide additional benefits to the local environment and community through the development of sustainable land-use systems that meet local needs, the planting of native species and the promotion of improved livelihoods through diversification of income sources.

Additionality and quantification procedures

Additionality requirements

The additionality tools for Plan Vivo are project-based. Projects must go beyond regulatory requirements. Furthermore, Plan Vivo excludes commercial land-use initiatives likely to have been economically viable in their own right without payments for ecosystem services. Additionality must be demonstrated through an analysis of the barriers to implementing activities in the absence of the project. These could include, for example, lack of finances, lack of technical expertise or prohibitive political or cultural environments. In most cases, only native species, which are unlikely to be planted without financial incentives in many countries where seedlings are difficult to find, may be planted. Commercial forestry projects are excluded from participation.

Quantification protocols

Baselines are calculated at the project level and also modelled at the regional scale. Carbon sequestration potential, for the sale of *ex-ante* credits, is calculated on a per hectare basis for a specified length of time using information on the management regime, growing conditions, proposed species, growth rates and proposed planting densities.

Technical specifications that describe the methodologies for and carbon potential of each land-use system (e.g. boundary planting, species composition, etc.) are developed by projects and reviewed as part of the validation process and by peer reviewers. The Plan Vivo Foundation coordinates the peer review process and identifies suitable reviewers for technical specifications. Similarly to validators, they must have relevant experience of the project type and of carbon projects. All existing technical specifications are available in the project pages of the Plan Vivo website.

Project approval process

Validation and registration

Projects must first register a Project Idea Note (PIN), which involves a desk review of the project's eligibility and long-term viability. The project developer must describe the proposed project area and proposed activities and identify its sustainable development aims in consultation with the communities.

Projects can be registered as Plan Vivo projects once they have:

1   a Plan Vivo Foundation-approved set of technical specifications used for describing land-use activities, carbon accounting, prescribing risk and other management activities and monitoring indicators; noted analyses of leakage, additionality and permanence;
2   a Plan Vivo Foundation-approved Project Design Document that describes project governance and systems for evaluating and monitoring Plan Vivo projects, administering payments and community-led planning;
3   been validated by an expert reviewer with relevant experience in carbon quantification, the project type and community-based projects, chosen by Plan Vivo; validation involves an independent review of project documents and a field visit.

Leakage

Leakage at individual plot level
To minimize leakage in smallholder activities (i.e. where rural smallholders have agreements to plant trees on their land), each producer must show that they are not reducing their agricultural output below sustainable levels. In other words, a Plan Vivo project will not be registered unless the producer can live sustainably from its land under the plan and has identified management objectives beyond receiving carbon payments (e.g. sustainable timber production, fruits or other non-timber products, agro-forestry).

Leakage at project level
Leakage is assessed for each land-use activity in the technical specifications, with consideration given to local and regional trends, identifying potential leakage risks and mechanisms for controlling them. Unavoidable leakage must be estimated and deducted in the quantification of carbon credits.

Permanence

The Plan Vivo System contains a number of mechanisms that ensure permanence:

- Projects are initially assessed for their long-term viability, taking into account issues such as the organizational capacity and experience of all partners involved and the stability of the area.
- Producers selling carbon through the Plan Vivo System must enter into long-term sale agreements (contracts) with the in-country project coordinator, who ensures that payments are made following monitoring against measurable and realistic goals.
- Producers must hold land tenure agreements (or community concession or similar usufruct rights) to demonstrate long-term ownership of land.
- All producers are under obligation to replant where trees die, for example from disease or extreme weather events, or if they are harvested for timber.
- Projects are internally monitored by Plan Vivo through the approval of annual reports and site visits.
- Each project maintains an unsold reserve of carbon credits called a risk buffer. The level of the risk buffer is set by the Plan Vivo Foundation according to its risk assessment of the project (normally 10–20 per cent). The aim of the risk buffer is to cover any unexpected shortfall in carbon credits supplied to purchasers (e.g. due to extreme weather events, inaccuracies in baseline assumptions or producers defaulting on sale agreements).
- Projects must undertake third-party verification at least every five years.

Monitoring, verification and certification

Each project must develop its own internal Monitoring Protocol based on the monitoring of indicators prescribed in the project's technical specifications. Any change to the Monitoring Protocol must be reported to the Plan Vivo Foundation in the project's annual report. Specific requirements for each producer are set out in their individual sale agreements with the project coordinator. For example, a producer may receive 20 per cent of the total payment after completing 50 per cent of planting and a further 10 per cent after one year, provided they have completed 100 per cent of the planting.

Internal project monitoring is conducted throughout the crediting period by local technicians based on the protocol and indicators identified in the technical specifications approved by the Plan Vivo Foundation during project validation. All projects must conduct and submit annual reports to the Plan Vivo Foundation using the standard Plan Vivo Annual Reporting Template. This report contains a full update of the project's status and development, including sales and payments that have been made, the results of monitoring and outcomes of consultations. The Plan Vivo Foundation reviews each annual report and issues Plan Vivo Certificates after approval of the report. Approval of annual reports may be qualified by imposing corrective actions if the report shows the project failed to act in full compliance with the Plan Vivo System or Plan Vivo principles. The Foundation may choose to follow up corrective actions with site visits where it is deemed necessary. The local project coordinators monitor the work of each individual farmer and pay them when they are found to have reached their targets. The exact payment schedule varies with each project, but normally involves periodic monitoring and payments over periods of 10–15 years.

Projects must undertake third-party verification within five years of registration.

Registries and fees

Plan Vivo Certificates are issued, tracked and retired on an online registry independently managed by Markit Environmental Registry (formerly TZ1). Each Certificate has a unique serial number that can be traced back to the project and exact producer, which ensures there is no double counting of carbon credits.

Getting a project registered, reviewed and approved with Plan Vivo costs approximately US$10,000. The Foundation charges Certificate issuance fees of $0.35 per tonne, which includes a $0.05 fee for maintaining the registry.

Selected issues

The Plan Vivo Foundation works closely with rural communities and has motivated hundreds of rural participants to engage in more sustainable land-use practices. Because of Plan Vivo's grassroots approach, conservation and community benefits from projects can be high.

Permanence

Farmers who participate in Plan Vivo are paid in regular instalments over 10–15 years. Staged payments enable the participating NGOs to evaluate a farmer's performance and provide support and advice if needed. This strengthens the capacity-building aspects of a project and decreases the risk of project failure during the project's crediting period. In addition, Plan Vivo projects have a project buffer and where there are carbon losses reported in verification they are cancelled from the project buffer.

Once all payments have been made to the farmers, there are no repercussions for farmers who decide to cut their trees down. While Plan Vivo argues that the threat of non-compliance is largely mitigated through its project design and that there is an economic incentive for farmers to keep trees for fruit production, this approach challenges the permanence assurance of projects.

Ex-ante offsets and permanence

Plan Vivo's offset calculations are based on the assumption that the trees remain standing for decades after payments have ceased. Because Plan Vivo sells *ex-ante* credits, it is unclear who carries the risk if sequestration is reversed at a future point in time, once payments to farmers have ceased.

Ex-ante credit buyers can immediately claim the emission reductions, even though they may not occur until years from now. This creates several challenges: there is little incentive for the buyer to insist that such offsets be replaced in a case of non-compliance; and the buyer might never discover that the project has failed following the purchase. These concerns are true for any sales of *ex-ante* credits sold under any standard.

Ex-ante offsets and additionality

Ex-post credit projects require significant upfront investment for project implementation. It has been argued that *ex-ante* projects are more likely to be additional than projects that are able to secure enough upfront capital while waiting to generate revenue from the sale of *ex-post* offsets once they have been verified.

The future of Plan Vivo

Standards of this type usually remain small because community-based projects are more costly to implement than more centralized projects (e.g. hydropower) available on the globally traded carbon market. It unlikely that Plan Vivo will grow its portfolio beyond a handful of projects. Though notably, CDM has only three afforestation/reforestation projects currently registered, suggesting there have been challenges even for larger offset programs.

Social Carbon Methodology

www.socialcarbon.org

Unless referenced otherwise, the information in this section is based on the above website, personal communications and the following sources: TZ1 (2009); Instituto Ecológica (undated).

Overview

Type of standard and context

The Social Carbon Methodology (SCM) was developed by the Instituto Ecológica (Brazil) in 1998. Social Carbon (SC) is not a full offset standard. It is a methodology that focuses on enhancing co-benefits such as biodiversity and active participation of local communities. It is usually used in conjunction with another standard, such as the VCS or CDM.

Standard authority and administrative bodies

Instituto Ecológica (IE), a nonprofit, independent offset project developer based in Brazil, is the legal holder of the SCM trademark. The Instituto Ecológica is in charge of accrediting other organizations who wish to use the SCM. This procedure qualifies institutions to develop Social Carbon indicators and reports and guarantees that Social Carbon concepts and the fundamental steps of the Methodology are being adhered to by the Parties.

In 2008, IE formed a partnership with CantorCO2e (www.co2e.com/), an international offset project developer and offset trader. CantorCO2e formed the Social Carbon Company (www.socialcarbon.com/en), a for-profit carbon offset retailer based in São Paulo, who has been the main developer of offset projects using SCM. Social Carbon Company is the first organization accredited by Instituto Ecológica to apply Social Carbon Methodology.

Auditors of SCM projects are called Certifying Entities. Current projects have been audited by DOEs, yet SC also accepts auditors from full standards that have been accepted for use in conjunction with the SCM (e.g. VCS) and auditors that have 'proven experience in the validation/verification of projects with a scope of carbon credit commercialization in compliance (mandatory) and noncompliance (voluntary) markets' (Social Carbon, 2009a). SC plans to request Certifying Entities (auditors of Social Carbon) to sign an Accreditation Commitment Agreement with the Instituto Ecológica.

Regional scope

Currently, most SCM projects have been developed by the Social Carbon Company. All existing projects are located in Brazil; however, the SCM is not regionally specific and can be applied elsewhere.

Recognition of other standards/links with other trading systems

Because the SCM is a methodology for monitoring co-benefits of offset projects and not a full offset standard, it is usually used in conjunction with another full standard, such as the VCS. The VCS is usually used for VER projects, although SCM has been used in conjunction with the CDM as well.

Market size and scope

Tradable unit and pricing information

SCM-certified VERs (in conjunction with another VER standard) and CERs (in conjunction with the CDM).

Participants/buyers

Businesses, mostly VER buyers.

Current project portfolio

There are 25 projects currently registered with Social Carbon; 19 are active and 6 are pending.

Offset project eligibility

Project types

Because the SCM is usually used in conjunction with outside standards, Social Carbon does not set its own project type restrictions. Rather, projects must demonstrate that the project type complies with a Social Carbon-approved outside standard (e.g. VCS, CDM).

Project locations

The SCM can be applied to projects in any country, although all currently active and pending projects are located in Brazil.

Project size

Because the SCM is usually used in conjunction with outside standards, Social Carbon does not set its own project size restrictions. Rather, projects must demonstrate that the project type complies with a Social Carbon-approved outside standard (e.g. VCS, CDM).

Start date

Because the SCM is usually used in conjunction with outside standards, Social Carbon does not set its start date rules. Rather, projects must demonstrate that the project type complies with a Social Carbon-approved outside standard (e.g. VCS, CDM).

Application of the SCM begins with the 'initial diagnosis', an assessment of baseline social, economic and environmental conditions to establish a 'Zero Point' against which a project's future contributions to sustainable development will be measured. Although the methodology can be applied at any stage in a project's development, including after the issuance of credits, project credits are only eligible for accreditation once the initial diagnosis has been completed.

Crediting period

Because the SCM is usually used in conjunction with outside standards, Social Carbon does not set its own crediting period restrictions. Rather, projects must demonstrate that the project type complies with a Social Carbon-approved outside standard (e.g. VCS, CDM).

Co-benefit objectives and requirements

The Social Carbon Methodology is designed to ensure that offset projects make significant contributions to sustainable development throughout their lifetime. Initially SCM focused on forestry projects but the methodology can now be used for other project types. SCM uses a set of analytical tools that assesses the social, environmental and economic conditions of stakeholders affected by the project. Six aspects of each sustainability project are individually measured using the Social Carbon hexagon:

> Biodiversity Resource *represents the combination of species, ecosystems and genes that form biological diversity. Biodiversity Resource is the balance of the natural physical environment. The following aspects are relevant in this component: the integrity of natural communities, the way people use and interact with biodiversity, the state of conservation, pressures and threats imposed on native species, and the existence of overriding areas for conservation. In some projects where impacts over biodiversity cannot be measured in a direct way, this resource is replaced by the* Technological Resource, *which assesses the conditions of access to technological assets, including the innovation of equipment and processes, focusing on their contribution to economic, social and environmental development.*

Natural Resource *is the stock of natural resources (soil, water, air, genetic resources) and environmental services (soil protection, maintenance of hydrological cycles, absorption of pollution, pest control, pollination, among others), from which those resources derive.*

Financial Resource is the basic capital in the form of cash, credit, debt and other economic goods that are available or potential.

Human Resources are the skills, knowledge and capacities for work and life that people possess, in addition to good health. A Human Resource is the individual and all that he represents.

Social Resources are the working networks, social demands, social relations, relationships of trust and associations in social organizations.

Carbon Resource refers to the type of carbon project developed, encompassing the methodologies utilized, project performance and the involvement of stakeholders.

(Social Carbon, 2009b, p6)

Co-benefit criteria are established and monitored through the following process:

1   *Selection of Social Carbon Indicators for the Project:* Sustainability indicators are chosen in order to monitor the project's contribution to sustainable development during its expected lifetime. These indicators are project-specific and based on the description of the social and environmental impacts and/or benchmark analysis.
2   *Social Carbon Report:* The project developer must report how the selected indicators are measured and monitored. The report must include the results of a site visit and interviews with stakeholders. Annual reports are recommended, although other periods might be accepted, according to the periods of verification of emission reductions.
3   *Verification:* Periodic verifications must be carried out to assess the project's co-benefits. The project must show that at least part of the identified co-benefits are being developed and that the project has not lead to a decrease in sustainability benefits.

Additionality and quantification procedures

Additionality requirements

Because the SCM is usually used in conjunction with a full outside standard, Social Carbon does not set its own additionality criteria but relies on the outside standard to do so. If project developers choose to rely solely on SCM as the project standard, Social Carbon advises adoption of the additionality guidelines and standards established by the CDM Executive Board.

Quantification protocols

Because the SCM is usually used in conjunction with an outside standard, Social Carbon does not develop its own protocol criteria but relies on the full standard to do so.

Project approval process

Validation and registration

The Project Design Document must be validated and verified by an independent third party, based on the outside standard accepted by the Social Carbon.

The Social Carbon Report also needs to be validated and verified, and must:

• be based on the assessment of compliance with the Social Carbon Guidelines criteria;
• include a local visit for the collection of information and evidence;
• have as a result the Social Carbon Validation or Verification Report (Social Carbon, 2009b, p18).

Validation and verification of offset projects that use the SCM in conjunction with another standard should preferably be consolidated into a single validation or verification report.

Leakage

Leakage is not addressed in the SCM.

Permanence

Permanence is not addressed in the SCM.

Monitoring, verification and certification

The SCM recommends annual verification but longer intervals might also be accepted depending on the outside standard used.

Registries and fees

The SCM registry is managed by Markit Environmental Registry (formerly TZ1), an Environmental Registry service used by many other voluntary offset standards as well. SCM charges an issuance fee of US$0.02 and a transaction fee of US$0.05 per ton of CO_2e.

Selected issues

Co-benefits

The Social Carbon Methodology is one of several standards and methodologies that have been developed to strengthen co-benefits of offset projects (see CCBS, Plan Vivo and Gold Standard). Because the Social Carbon Methodology is an add-on standard for ensuring co-benefits, it should be used in conjunction with another fully fledged standard, such as VCS or CDM.

SCM's requirements for co-benefits are defined in general terms and do not include specific rules. As an example, the project developer is only required to provide a brief description of the potential positive and negative social, economic and environmental impacts (Social Carbon 2009b, p 19). Environmental impact assessments are only needed if required by law. No further in-depth evaluation of co-benefits is required.

No separation of verification and approval of projects

Under Social Carbon Methodology, as is the case for several other voluntary standards, auditors directly approve projects. Given the pressures on auditors and conflicts of interest (Schneider, 2007; Schneider and Mohr, 2009), the lack of an accrediting board can be considered a potential weakness of the standard.

The future of Social Carbon Methodology

Currently 20 out of the 25 projects listed on the Social Carbon registry are developed by the Social Carbon Company, owned by CantorCO2e, who commercialized and translated the Social Carbon Methodology. All the listed projects are fuel-switching projects in ceramic tile factories based in Brazil. It remains to be seen if Social Carbon Methodology will establish itself as a robust co-benefits standard.

Green-e Climate Protocol for Renewable Energy

www.green-e.org/getcert_ghg_re_protocol.shtml

Unless referenced otherwise, the information in this section is based on the above website, personal communications and the following sources: Bird and Lokey, 2007; Gillenwater, 2007.

Overview

Type of standard and context

The Green-e Climate Protocol for Renewable Energy (Green-e CPRE) is part of Green-e Climate, a certification program for carbon offsets sold to consumers in the voluntary offset market. All Green-e programs are administered by the Center for Resource Solutions (CRS), a nonprofit organization based in California.

The Green-e Climate Protocol for Renewable Energy (Green-e CPRE) is a voluntary GHG offset protocol that certifies eligible renewable facilities in the USA to sell GHG offsets.

> *The intention of this Protocol is to bring additional credibility to the market for GHG emission reductions derived from renewable energy project activities. By establishing clear guidelines, informed by stakeholders, on the greenhouse gas claims that can be made from*

> *renewable energy projects, the Protocol will help further the development of the voluntary market for renewable energy. The Protocol addresses the issues of tracking, additionality, double counting and double claiming in order to ensure that the greenhouse gas benefits from eligible renewable energy projects are real, surplus, measurable, verifiable and additional. (Green-e, 2007)*

Standard authority and administrative bodies

The Green-e CPRE is governed by the Green-e Governance Board and administered by the CRS. The Green-e Governance Board is comprised of environmental organizations, consumer groups, public policy advocates, regulatory agencies and offset market experts. To avoid conflicts of interest, market actors do not have a vote but they are represented through a non-voting seat.

Regional scope

The Green-e CPRE is specific to projects in the electricity sector in the USA.

Recognition of other standards/links with other trading systems

The Green-e CPRE is an endorsed program of the Green-e Climate certification program.

Market size and scope

Tradable unit and pricing information

Green-e Climate certified VERs are in units of 1 ton of CO_2e (metric or short ton according to the program certified). There is no pricing information currently available.

Participants/buyers

Buyers of Green-e Climate certified offsets are individuals, organizations and companies in the USA.

Current project portfolio

A list of renewable energy projects that have been approved under the Green-e CPRE can be found at www.green-e.org/getcert_ghg_re_protocol.shtml.

Offset project eligibility

Project types

The following project types are accepted under the Green-e CPRE:

1   wind power;
2   solar photovoltaics (PV) and solar thermal electric power;

3   hydropower from either new-generation capacity (see Start date below) on a non-impoundment, or new generation capacity on an existing impoundment. It must meet one or more of the following conditions:

- the hydropower facility is certified by the Low Impact Hydropower Institute;
- the facility is a run-of-the-river hydropower facility with a total rated nameplate capacity equal to or less than 5MW. Multiple turbines will not be counted separately and cannot add up to more than a 5MW nameplate capacity;
- the hydropower facility consists of a turbine in a pipeline or a turbine in an irrigation canal.
- geothermal electric generation facilities with no direct emission of GHGs;
- gaseous biomass from landfill gas methane, wastewater methane and digester methane derived from waste biomass fuels used to generate electricity. (No biomass in a liquid or solid state will be allowed. Animal wastes in solid state, agricultural biomass, energy crops, municipal solid waste and waste to energy are ineligible.)
- ocean thermal, wave and tidal power.

New and emerging technologies not included in the above list will be considered on a case-by-case basis by the Green-e Governance Board.

Project locations

Projects must be located in the USA.

Project size

Hydropower facilities have to be smaller than 5MW or be certified by the Low Impact Hydropower Institute. No size restrictions apply for other project types.

Start date

Eligible facilities cannot have been operational before 1 January 2005.

Crediting period

The maximum crediting period is 15 years.

Only GHG reductions resulting from generation of renewable energy that occurred on 1 January 2007 or later are eligible. In addition, a Green-e Climate certified product using the Green-e CPRE as its endorsed program may include only GHG reductions from renewable energy generation that occurred in the calendar year in which the certified offset is sold, the first three months of the following calendar year or the last six months of the prior calendar year.

Co-benefit objectives and requirements

In general, the Green-e CPRE does not require any additional co-benefits of the projects that seek certification. The exceptions are the Low Impact Hydropower Institute certification requirements of hydro projects.

Additionality and quantification procedures

Additionality requirements

The Green-e CPRE uses a top-down approach and requires three additionality tests: the legal, regulatory or institutional test; the timing test (see Start date above); and the performance and technology test.

- *The legal, regulatory or institutional test:*

The renewable facility is not eligible if:

1   It was mandated by a local, state or federal government agency or was required under any legal requirement or settlement.
2   It was built as a least-cost facility when compared with non-renewable energy facilities.

> *However, if a marketer or generator can demonstrate to the Green-e Governance Board that the revenue from the sale of RECs or GHG credits was a determining factor in the facility being determined the least-cost option, the facility is eligible for certified GHG reductions. The demonstration that the sale of RECs or GHG emission reductions deemed a facility least cost under an Integrated Resource Planning (IRP) process is only required for least-cost facilities under an IRP process. Green-e Climate is not requiring a financial additionality test on project eligibility. (Green-e, 2007)*

3   It is located within a region with a legally binding GHG cap set for the electricity sector and no GHG allowances are allocated to the facility or no other mechanism exists to credit greenhouse gas emission reduction benefits to the facility. The annual Green-e Climate recertification process will include verification that the facility still satisfies the Legal and Regulatory Test. Furthermore, regulatory changes may also trigger revisions to the protocol itself.
4   The owner of a renewable generation facility is reporting direct GHG emissions in a legally binding cap-and-trade program.
5   If allowances are allocated to the facility, the allowances must be retired on behalf of the purchaser in order for the facility to be eligible under this protocol. A facility that sells a share of its RECs in compliance markets is eligible for GHG emission reductions from the remaining share of its generation, provided that it meets all the requirements of this protocol.

- *The performance and technology test:*

The Green-e CPRE uses a sector-based performance and technology test to identify whether a specific technology (in this case net-zero GHG emitting electricity generation) is an additional activity in the USA. This sector-based approach is similar to the approach used by the Climate Action Reserve and the US Environmental Protection Agency Climate Leaders program for their offset protocols.

Quantification protocols

The Green-e Climate CPRE uses a top-down approach.

The emission reductions are calculated using a regional Baseline Emission Rate (BER). For baseload technologies (i.e. firm power activities including biomass, geothermal, ocean thermal and hydro), the BER reflects the emission rates of the planned capacity additions in the USA (the build margin); and for non-baseload technologies (i.e. non-firm power activities including solar, wind, wave and tidal) the BER is an average of the emission rates of the build margin and the currently operating grid-connected electricity generation facilities (the operating margin). (The build margin represents the emission reduction that occurred because the renewable generation was built instead of a business-as-usual plant, while the operating margin estimates the effect of backing down other generating facilities when the renewable energy facility is operating and generating power.) Baseload emission rates are developed for different regions. The non-baseload rate used has been developed by the US EPA eGRID program. The BER will be updated at least every three years and posted on the Green-e Climate website.

The approach taken to quantification was built out of recommendations made by the World Resources Institute.

Project approval process

Validation and registration

Every project approved under the Green-e CPRE has to go through an initial review, which establishes that the project meets the requirements of the Green-e CPRE. Depending on the characteristics of the facility, this can include interviews with project developers, review of federal, state and utility regulatory documents, specific reporting procedures to GHG registries, siting documents and/or contractual requirements, as well as details of how the project addresses additionality and other specifics of the facility being added to the Green-e Climate website.

Monitoring, verification and certification

Since the Green-e CPRE establishes common factors for each technology type depending on the region in which it is located, the emission reductions can be directly calculated from the electricity generation. To address the risk of double counting, Green-e CPRE has developed explicit reporting procedures for generators participating in GHG registries. In addition, contractual ownership has to be documented.

Registries and fees

Ownership of GHG emission reductions will be documented, in part through the use of electronic tracking systems for RECs. Current eligible tracking systems are ERCOT, NE-GIS, PJM-GATS, WREGIS and MRETS. The Green-e Climate Program will update this list as new tracking systems are developed. Generators wishing to participate in this program must have all generation reported to an eligible tracking system.

GHG registries

If the owner of the eligible facility participates in a voluntary or mandatory GHG registry, the renewable energy facility can only participate in this program if the generator owner reports to the registry that the electricity generated at the facility is attributed emission-equivalent to the GHG emission reductions sold in the voluntary market and certified by the Green-e program.

Fees

The fees for certifying facilities according to the Green-e CPRE are paid by the company that is selling Green-e Climate certified offsets from a specific facility. The company has to pay US$3000 annually, in addition to the US$6000 base certification fee, to certify projects according to the Green-e CPRE.

Selected issues

Additionality

The Green-e CPRE approves renewable electricity facilities that are eligible to sell emission reductions as part of the Green-e Climate program. The Green-e CPRE was developed partly in response to the emerging market practice of selling RECs as carbon offsets. (Green-e Climate's sister program Green-e Energy certifies RECs.) Offsets generated from renewable energy facilities face particular challenges in terms of establishing clear ownership and additionality. (For a more in-depth discussion on RECs see Box 7.1.)

The Green-e CPRE addresses the issues of ownership and double counting by using Renewable Energy tracking systems, requiring accounting of how the RECs/offsets have been sold and retired, and by having contractual documents that specify that all GHG emission reduction attributes are owned by the seller of the offset.

The Green-e CPRE uses a sector-based performance and technology test to determine additionality. The sector-based approach has the advantage of being transparent and reducing transaction costs for project developers. However, sector-based approaches can lead to the approval of non-additional projects. According to Green-e:

> *The data analysis documented that approximately 1 per cent of the new generation capacity added to the US generation sector in 2000–2005 (the last time period for which official data was available) was in response to market drivers (and not legal mandates such as [Renewable Portfolio Standard] RPS policies). In response to this the Green-e Governance Board, with input from stakeholders, judged that the construction of a renewable energy facility in the USA under today's market conditions is an additional activity as long as the other requirements of the Green-e Climate Protocol are met.*

This approach defines that any new renewable facility that is not under a legal mandate or a Renewable Portfolio Standard is additional. Yet revenue from the sale of offsets from such facilities provides only a small fraction of the total revenue stream. It is therefore questionable whether such a definition of additionality is stringent enough to ensure that no offsets from business-as-usual facilities are sold.

The future of Green-e CPRE

The future role for the Green-e CPRE in the offset market is unclear. The protocol states that: 'If policies enacted on a state, regional, or federal level impact the GHG emission benefits from renewable energy, this standard will be updated to reflect such changes.' It is likely that most or all electricity generating sources in the USA will be covered by a compliance program, such as a national cap-and-trade system. Under such a system, electricity generating facilities would no longer be able to sell offsets in the voluntary market, unless rules were enacted to address how voluntary markets could coexist with mandatory systems in a way that would preserve their environmental integrity and avoid double counting of offsets. As a model for how this may play out at the national level, Green-e is currently evaluating how renewable energy facilities located in the RGGI region can continue to play a role in the green power and emission reduction markets.

Green-e Climate Program

www.green-e.org/getcert_ghg.shtml

Unless referenced otherwise, the information in this section is based on the above website, personal communications and Green-e (2008a).

Overview

Type of standard and context

Green-e Climate is a certification program launched in 2008 for carbon offsets sold to consumers in the voluntary offset market. Green-e Climate was developed and is administered by the Center for Resource Solutions (CRS) (www.resource-solutions.org/), a nonprofit organization based in California. CRS was founded in 1997 to identify, promote and implement sustainable development solutions. In addition to Green-e Climate, CRS manages two other certification programs:

Green-e Energy (www.green-e.org/getcert_re.shtml) is the leading US independent certification and verification program for RECs. This Green-e program is not discussed further in this report.

Green-e Marketplace (www.green-e.org/getcert_bus_what.shtml) is a program that allows companies to display the Green-e logo when they have purchased a qualifying amount of renewable energy and passed verification standards. This program is not discussed further in this report.

Renewable energy certificates and carbon offsets

In the USA, renewable energy sales in voluntary markets have grown at rates ranging from 40–60 per cent annually for the past several years. Collectively, the compliance and voluntary renewable energy markets made up an estimated 1.7 per cent of total US electric power sales in 2006 (Bird and Lokey, 2007).

In the voluntary carbon offset market, Renewable Energy Credits (RECs) are being converted to and sold as carbon-offset equivalents. The US National Renewable Energy Lab surveyed US-based renewable energy providers and found that about 210,000 RECs were converted into carbon offsets in 2008 (Hamilton et al, 2009). Converted RECs, while historically often cheaper than other offsets, are controversial. To understand why, it is especially important to examine additionality and ownership issues (Gillenwater, 2007; Offset Quality Initiative, 2009).

RECs are designed primarily to track renewable energy production. In the USA, for example, many states have established Renewable Portfolio Standards (RPSs). RECs that are used in this type of a quota system do not have to be tested for additionality. In the voluntary markets, RECs do not function under a quota and therefore have to be additional in order to be considered equivalent to offsets, which are meant to compensate for other emissions elsewhere.

If RECs are converted to carbon offsets without any strict additionality testing, these offsets will tend to come from cheaper business-as-usual (BAU) projects, which by definition are economic without additional offset incentives. These BAU projects will tend to dominate the market. Truly additional projects will not be able to compete because they face additional costs or barriers. The sale of non-additional offsets in the voluntary market can potentially hamper truly additional projects and lead to increases in emissions.

Many national and subnational programs offer financial incentives for renewable energy projects (e.g. production tax credits, state/local tax incentives and/or guaranteed feed-in or net metering tariffs) that play a more important role in funding renewable projects than REC (or offset) revenue. In other words, if the presumption is that a retired REC should count as an offset, the threshold question is whether REC revenue was sufficient to make a project happen.

The very fact that RECs trade for as little as US$0.05/kWh in some parts of the country (equivalent to perhaps US$5/tCO$_2$), and that production tax credits are worth about US$0.08/kWh in the USA, casts some doubt. But the fact that the REC or offset revenue is small compared to the total revenue stream does not inherently make a project non-additional. It does imply, however, that only a small proportion of projects will be additional, and that more tests are needed to identify those that were pushed over the threshold by making the project feasible with the extra revenue.

Offsets from renewable energy facilities and RECs face challenges about who has the right to claim ownership of a particular emission reduction. Establishing ownership of offset reductions from renewable energy projects is especially difficult. For example, if a wind farm is built, the emission reductions could potentially be claimed by the wind farm owner, the utility (whose emissions will be reduced due to the new renewable facility, even if it does not own that new facility), the county, the state that the wind farm is located in or the end-user of the electricity. This lack of clear ownership is exacerbated with RECs, the attributes of which are often defined in general and ambiguous terms, which makes assigning ownership more difficult.

In addition, as part of the Green-e Climate program CRS developed the:

Green-e Climate Protocol for Renewable Energy (www.green-e.org/getcert_ghg_re_ protocol.shtml), a component of the Green-e Climate Program, which determines the eligibility of renewable facilities in the USA to sell GHG offsets through Green-e Climate (for details, see previous section).

Green-e Climate has a different focus and is complementary to all the other voluntary GHG offset standards described in this report. Green-e Climate is a certification and verification standard for retailers' offset products. It ensures that retailers have actually purchased and retired the types of offsets that they have sold, that there is full disclosure of project information, and that no false or misleading claims are made to customers. Green-e Climate endorses other existing GHG offset standards (see 'Recognition of other standards' below). Sellers who seek Green-e Climate certification for their sales of offsets must source from projects that are certified by one of the endorsed programs. Generally, retailers mix together offsets that originate from a variety of projects to create an end product that is sold to consumers. Green-e Climate certifies these retail products:

> *Use of the Green-e Climate logo requires an annual independent audit of the seller's supply and sales to ensure that there is no double selling of reductions sold as offsets; and a twice-annual marketing compliance review to ensure customers were told what they were buying in the form of a detailed product content label, which specifies information about their offset, including the project type, which endorsed program certified the project and the location of the project. (Green-e, 2008b)*

Standard authority and administrative bodies

Green-e Climate was developed and is administered by the CRS.

The Green-e Governance Board is an independent body with primary responsibility for oversight and policy setting for all Green-e Programs. The Green-e Governance Board is comprised of environmental organizations, consumer groups, public policy advocates, regulatory agencies and offset market experts. To avoid conflicts of interest, market actors do not have a vote but they are represented through a non-voting seat.

The Greenhouse Gas Subcommittee is a subcommittee of the Green-e Governance Board with primary responsibility for the independent oversight of Green-e Climate. It reviews stakeholder comments on proposed revisions to the Green-e Climate Program and provides input on such revisions to the Green-e Governance Board.

CRS collects comments from stakeholders when it is considering substantive changes to the Green-e Standards. The Stakeholder Committee is open to anyone and has traditionally included representatives from environmental organizations, consumer organizations, power marketers, renewable developers, GHG reduction project developers and marketers, regulators, energy and climate policy experts and other interested parties.

The Green-e Climate Marketers Advisory Committee (CMAC) is composed of representatives of the program's participant marketers. The CMAC makes suggestions to the Green-e Governance Board on program issues associated with the feasibility and practicality of various implementation options and details and makes recommendations for changes that improve the effectiveness of Green-e Climate. The CMAC does not have a vote on the Green-e Governance Board.

Regional scope

Green-e Climate has a US focus, but has endorsed several international standards (see below) and is open to certifying products sold anywhere.

Recognition of other standards/links with other trading systems

Through the use of the Green-e Climate Standard, the Green-e Governance Board endorses select offset standards to serve as eligible sources of supply for the Green-e Climate retail certification program. As of May 2009, Green-e Climate has endorsed four GHG offset standards. For an updated list see Green-e Climate endorsed programs at: www.green-e.org/getcert_ghg_endorsed.shtml. The endorsed programs and any specific restrictions are set out below:

Gold Standard (www.cdmgoldstandard.org/)
All Gold Standard VERs and CERs are eligible, with the following restrictions regarding hydropower production:

- Outside the USA, only hydropower projects with a capacity under 10MW are eligible.
- In the USA only hydropower projects creating emission reductions from new generation capacity on a non-impoundment, or new generation capacity on an existing impoundment, that meet one or more of the following conditions are eligible:
    - the hydropower facility is certified by the Low Impact Hydropower Institute (http://lowimpacthydro.org/);
    - the facility is a run-of-the-river hydropower facility with a total rated nameplate capacity equal to or less than 5MW. Multiple turbines will not be counted separately and cannot add up to more than a 5MW nameplate capacity; and/or
    - the hydropower facility consists of a turbine in a pipeline or a turbine in an irrigation canal.
- In the USA and Canada, the Green-e Governance Board will consider on a case-by-case basis GHG emission reductions resulting from new incremental capacity on an existing dam, where the 'new' output is equal to or less than 5MW. Green-e Climate will not certify GHG emission reductions from new impoundments of water.

Voluntary Carbon Standard (VCS) 2007(www.v-c-s.org/)
All VCUs certified under VCS 2007 are eligible with the following exceptions:

- VCS Agriculture, Forestry and Other Land Use (AFOLU) projects are eligible as long as the seller provides proof that the native species requirements under the Green-e Climate Standard are met.

- Projects that qualify as additional using the VCS Test 2: Performance Test are eligible if the applied performance standard explicitly lists the eligible technologies.
- Projects certified according to the previous version of the VCS that are grandfathered in under VCS 2007 are not eligible under Green-e Climate.
- For hydropower, the same rules listed above under the GS apply.

Clean Development Mechanism (http://cdm.unfccc.int/index.html)
CERs are eligible with the following exceptions:

- Due to permanence issues, CDM land use, land-use change and forestry projects are ineligible.
- No hydropower projects with a capacity over 10MW are eligible.

Green-e Climate Protocol for Renewable Energy (www.green-e.org/getcert_ghg_re_protocol. shtml)
All offsets certified under the Green-e Climate Protocol for Renewable Energy are eligible (see Green-e CPRE).

Market size and scope

Tradable unit and pricing information

Green-e Climate program tradable units are VERs and CERs. Pricing will vary according to the type of project, the standard used and the quantities purchased.

Participants/buyers

These are at present carbon offset retailers in North America, but in future offset retailers may be from any region.

Current project portfolio

As of May 2009, eight retailers are selling Green-e Climate Certified Products. For the most up-to-date list of retailers, see Green-e Climate Certified Carbon Offsets at www.green-e.org/getcert_ghg_products.shtml.

Offset project eligibility

Project types

Project type eligibility is defined by the endorsed standards and programs, with the restrictions outlined in the section Recognition of other standards (above). Nuclear power, large hydropower, biosequestration projects that do not address prevention or reversibility or non-permanence and biosequestration projects using non-native species are ineligible.

Project locations

Project location restrictions, as defined by the endorsed standards and programs, apply; there are no additional Green-e Climate limitations.

Project size

As defined by the endorsed standards, large hydropower projects are ineligible.

Start date

GHG emission reductions are only eligible if they are from projects that became operational on or after 1 January 2000 and if they meet the timing requirements of the endorsed programs. Exceptions might be approved if project additionality can be clearly established for projects with earlier start dates.

Crediting period

The following crediting periods are acceptable for endorsed programs:

- up to 15 years; or
- ten years with the option of one renewal; or
- seven years with the option of two renewals.
- Biological carbon sequestration or conservation projects may permit crediting periods of up to 50 years or the lifetime of the project management plan, whichever is shorter.

Exceptions can be approved if clear justification is provided for crediting period requirements that vary from these guidelines.

Co-benefit objectives and requirements

Green-e Climate does not generally require additional co-benefits beyond those which are required by the endorsed standards. One exception is the requirement for biosequestration projects to use native species.

Additionality and quantification procedures

Additionality requirements

The endorsed standards must require that all their projects pass a legal, regulatory or institutional test, as well as a timing test (see Green-e CPRE). In addition, all projects must pass one of the following additionality tests:

- common practice test and financial test (both required); or
- common practice test and barriers test (both required); or
- technology test and performance test (both required).

Quantification protocols

Not specified.

Project approval process

Validation and registration

Retailers

To use the Green-e Climate logo, a seller of Green-e Climate certified emission reductions must agree to undergo a twice-yearly marketing compliance review by CRS and an annual independent verification audit. If a seller is found to be out of compliance, the seller will either have to revise its marketing materials to meet the requirements within 30 days of receiving notice from CRS, or immediately desist from using the Green-e Climate logo or making reference to Green-e Climate in any of its marketing materials for this product.

There are two product types eligible for certification under Green-e Climate. A Fixed Mix Product has the same combination and proportion of GHG emission reductions from project type(s), location(s) and endorsed programs/standards (e.g. 45 per cent Gold Standard energy efficiency from India, 55 per cent VCS renewable energy from the USA) for all customers. Customized Mix Products allow the customer to choose a unique combination and proportion of GHG emission reductions from a specified list of project type(s), location(s) and endorsed program(s).

Endorsed programs and standards

The Green-e Governance Board evaluates and approves GHG Offset Programs and Standards that seek to be endorsed under the Green-e Climate Standard based on stakeholder feedback. GHG offset programs and standards cannot be endorsed without stakeholders having had the opportunity to comment.

Program requirements and procedures consist of:

- procedural and technical standards for the validation, monitoring and verification of GHG emission reduction projects;
- contractual standards for information disclosure and avoidance of double issuance and double counting of GHG emission reductions; and
- accounting standards that specify consistent methods for estimating baseline emissions, accounting for emission leakage and establishing project additionality.

All projects except small-scale projects require an initial validation.

Monitoring, verification and certification

Retailers

The verification protocol requires sellers offering a Green-e Climate certified product to demonstrate through the use of company contracts, invoices, reports from endorsed standards, reports from registries and billing statements that:

- the seller retired or transferred to customers GHG emission reductions in quantity and type sufficient to meet customer sales for each specific product;
- the GHG emission reductions came from eligible GHG emission reduction projects, certified by an endorsed program;
- the information provided to customers on the product content label is accurate; and
- by attestation, the seller has no knowledge of double counting, double selling or double claiming of the GHG emission reductions used to supply the certified product.

Endorsed programs and standards

All projects, except for small-scale projects, require an on-site verification of GHG emission reductions. On-site verification must subsequently occur at least every five to seven years.

Endorsed programs must either certify the verified GHG emission reductions based on a review and the approval of these verification reports, or require certification of the verified GHG emission reductions from an independent third-party auditor. The auditors have to be accredited by the International Organization for Standardization (ISO) standard 14065; the United Nations Framework Convention on Climate Change (UNFCCC); a national, state or provincial governmental accreditation program; or with the approval of the Green-e Governance Board's broadly accepted professional accreditation programs.

Registries and fees

All endorsed programs and standards must have registries in place to prevent double counting, double issuance and double selling and to ensure that GHG emission reductions are not registered more than once.

The annual base fee for Green-e Climate certification is US$6000 per year. Carbon retailers also pay a fee based on aggregate metric ton volumes of Green-e Climate sales. Such fees range from US$9000 per year for 100,000 metric tons to US$24,000 and up for upwards of 1 million metric tons.

Protocol for renewable energy

If the carbon retailer uses the Green-e Climate Protocol for Renewable Energy as an endorsed program, there is a single annual US$3000 certification fee in addition to the base and volumetric fees.

Endorsed program fee

The fee for each additional endorsed program certification is US$2000 per year. For a seller using one endorsed program for verification (as long as that endorsed program is not the Protocol for Renewable Energy), there is no additional endorsed program fee. For a seller using the Green-e CPRE and an additional endorsed program, the total fee is US$9000 in addition to any volumetric fees. For a seller using the VCS and the Gold Standard, the fee is US$8000 in addition to any volumetric fees.

Selected issues

The Green-e Climate Program is the first program to address retailer accountability for the voluntary market and fills an important niche for quality assurance. The Green-e Climate Program has been recently launched and there are no selected issues or lessons learned to cite here.

For selected issues on the Green-e Climate Protocol for Renewable Energy, see the previous section.

8

Carbon Offset Funds

Carbon funds, both public and private, vary widely in their focus and the nature of their investments. Some funds focus exclusively on purchasing carbon offset credits, while others invest in projects or companies that have the potential to generate carbon assets. A study in late 2007 estimated that there were 58 carbon funds in operation and projected that the number would reach 67 in 2008. The 58 funds were expected to have US$10.8 billion (€7 billion) in management in 2007 and to increase to nearly US$14.6 billion (€9.5 billion) in 2008 (Cochran and Leguet, 2007).

This chapter gives more detailed information about the World Bank's Carbon Finance Unit, which manages the largest pool of investments worth over US$2 billion (World Bank, 2007), and focuses predominantly on Clean Development Mechanism (CDM) and Joint Implementation (JI) offset credits.

World Bank Carbon Funds

www.carbonfinance.org

Unless referenced otherwise, the information in this section is based on the above website, personal communications and the following sources: World Bank (2006a); World Bank (2006b); World Bank (2007).

Overview

Type of standard and context

The World Bank's Carbon Finance Unit (CFU) manages carbon funds and facilities using resources contributed by companies and governments in industrialized countries to purchase project-based GHG emission reductions from projects in developing countries (non-Annex-I countries) and countries with economies in transition (EIT).

The World Bank's carbon finance initiatives are part of the Bank's mission to reduce poverty through its environmental and energy strategies. Through its work, the Bank endeavours to ensure that developing countries can benefit from international efforts to address climate change. The role of the CFU is to catalyse a global carbon market by reducing transaction costs, supporting sustainable development, strengthening developing country capacity and ensuring that the benefits of the carbon market reach the poorer communities of the developing world.

The World Bank started its carbon finance operations in 2000, launching the world's first global carbon fund, the 'Prototype Carbon Fund', with a mission to pioneer the project-based GHG emission reduction market within the framework of the Kyoto Protocol and to contribute to sustainable development. Since then, it has created nine additional funds and facilities (BioCarbon Fund, Community Development Carbon Fund, Italian Carbon Fund, The Netherlands CDM Facility, The Netherlands European Carbon Facility, Danish Carbon Fund, Spanish Carbon Fund, Umbrella Carbon Facility and Carbon Fund for Europe), taking the total assets in its ten funds and facilities to over US$2.3 billion (World Bank, undated). In September 2007, the World Bank's Board of Executive Directors approved the creation of two new carbon facilities: the 'Carbon Partnership Facility' and the 'Forest Carbon Partnership Facility'. The former will pilot ways to use carbon finance on a larger scale and over longer time frames, while the latter will do so in new areas such as avoided deforestation and reduction of forest degradation. The ultimate goal of these facilities is to help developing countries move towards low-carbon development paths.

Standard authority and administrative bodies

The emission reductions are purchased by the World Bank as the Trustee for one of the CFU's carbon funds. The CFU is responsible for the overall management of the carbon funds. CFU staff review project proposals, prepare project documentation for consideration by each fund's Participants Committee and contracts with the project entities for the purchase of emission reduction credits.

The Participants Committee for each fund is responsible for reviewing projects and authorizing the purchase of credits using the fund's resources. The committee comprises the contributors to the fund, or a subgroup of the contributors if there is a large number of participants in the fund.

The World Bank has also created a Host Country Committee to advise it on its carbon finance capacity building and training activities. This committee is comprised of representatives from countries that have signed a memorandum of understanding with the Bank to participate in the committee, or that host a CDM or a JI project supported by a Bank-managed carbon fund. At present, there are over 50 countries represented on this committee.

Regional scope

The World Bank Carbon Funds work internationally. Through the CDM and JI, the funds develop projects in both Annex-1 and non-Annex-I countries (as defined in the UNFCCC). Select carbon funds have a specific geographic focus. For example, The Netherlands European Carbon Facility focuses on the purchase of credits from JI projects located in countries with economies in transition that serve to meet The Netherlands' compliance obligation. Similarly, The Netherlands CDM Facility focuses on the purchase of credits from CDM projects located in developing countries. The other carbon funds/facilities look at projects in both Annex-I and non-Annex-1 countries.

Recognition of other standards/links with other trading systems

Projects developed through the World Bank Carbon Funds are required to adhere to the modalities and procedures of the Kyoto Protocol mechanisms. The purchase of emission reductions by World Bank funds is designed to enable the carbon fund investors, known as 'Participants', to meet their emission reduction targets either under the Kyoto Protocol (in the case of governments) or the EU Emission Trading System (in the case of European private entities whose installations are covered under the EU ETS).

Market size and scope

Tradable unit and pricing information

The World Bank Carbon Finance Funds purchase CDM Certified Emission Reductions (CERs), Joint Implementation (JI) Emission Reduction Units (ERUs) and temporary CERs (tCERs) for afforestation and reforestation projects, as well as Assigned Amount Units (AAUs). In some cases, they also purchase Verified Emission Reductions (VERs) with the aim of converting them into Kyoto-compliant units.

The World Bank's purchase price for the different Emission Reduction Units it buys is not publicly available. However, the Bank has published its approach to determining price ranges for Emissions Reduction Purchase Agreements (ERPAs). It starts with a benchmark price, which is comparable to that which other market players have paid for similar transactions, and then adjusts the premiums or discounts based on the risks involved and how that risk is shared between the seller and the World Bank. Prices vary over time, based on market supply and demand, as well as other factors such as project, regulatory and other risks, technology type, project location, project co-benefits, payment timing and other costs. The preference of fund participants for projects of a specific technology type, and other environmental and social benefits, may also have an impact on the price.

The World Bank Carbon Funds VER ERPAs aim to shift the Kyoto regulatory risks from the seller to the buyer. Thus, the price paid for VERs would typically be lower than for CERs (or ERUs), but the seller is guaranteed payment for independently verified emission reductions – whether or not these VERs fully convert to Kyoto assets (i.e. CERs, ERUs, tCERs and AAUs). Discrepancies in the quantity of ERs between the VERs schedule specified in the ERPA and the issuance of Kyoto assets can be due to differences in methodology (i.e. difference between the methodology used to determine the VERs in the ERPA and the methodology approved by the CDM Executive Board) or differences between the start dates of VER and CER generation (due to delays in registration of the project by the CDM Executive Board). The VERs not converted to CERs due to delays in registration (which determines the start of CER generation) compared to VER start date are transferred to fund participants, who may then sell them on the voluntary market or use them for other purposes.

Participants/buyers

The buyers, the fund participants (via the World Bank), include 16 governments and 66 private companies. The sellers of the emission reductions may include project entities in any Kyoto Annex-1 or non-Annex-I country.

Current project portfolio

As of 31 December 2008, the World Bank-managed funds and facilities have 186 projects in their portfolio with an estimated carbon asset value of more than US$2.3 billion (World Bank, undated). The geographic distribution of projects funded is dominated by projects located in East Asia and the Pacific – particularly in China (World Bank, undated). Latin America and the Caribbean, followed by Europe and Central Asia, make up the second and third largest shares (World Bank, undated). Ten projects have been signed in Africa, primarily for renewable energy (World Bank, undated). HFC-23 projects account for 54 per cent of the project portfolio, though this share has been declining as the number of renewable energy, energy efficiency and waste management projects rises (World Bank, undated).

Offset project eligibility

Project types

The World Bank Carbon Funds and Facilities have no project type restrictions. However, specific funds have been designated to provide funding for specific project or technology types. For example, the BioCarbon Fund (BioCF) focuses on land-use and forestry projects, while the Community Development Carbon Fund focuses on projects with community development attributes. The Netherlands CDM Facility prioritizes projects in the following categories: (i) renewable energy, (ii) clean, sustainably grown biomass (not from biomass waste), (iii) energy efficiency improvements, (iv) fossil fuel switch and methane recovery and (v) sequestration. Similarly, the Danish Carbon Fund prioritizes projects in the areas of wind power, co-generation, hydropower, biomass and landfills.

Project locations

The World Bank Carbon Funds have no overall project location restrictions beyond those existing for CDM and JI projects.

Project size

There is no upper limit on project size. However, the World Bank will typically not consider small-scale projects generating less than $50,000tCO_2e$ of emission reductions per year, a threshold it considers necessary for the project to be viable under CDM and JI, although there are exceptions.

Start date

CDM and JI project start date requirements apply.

Crediting period

CDM and JI crediting period requirements apply.

Co-benefit objectives and requirements

In addition to the CDM and JI rules, the World Bank requires that all projects comply with the World Bank Group's Environmental and Social Safeguard Policies. (See the World Bank's Safeguard Policies, http://go.worldbank.org/WTA1ODE7T0.)

Additionality and quantification procedures

Additionality requirements

CDM and JI requirements apply.

Quantification protocols

CDM and JI requirements apply. The World Bank Carbon Finance Unit has developed several methodologies for projects in its portfolio (see Selected issues).

Project approval process

Validation and registration

CDM and JI requirements apply. The World Bank works with CDM- and JI-approved independent auditors, called Designated Operational Entities (DOEs) under the CDM or Independent Accredited Entities (IAE) (under JI), to validate and verify projects within their portfolio.

Monitoring, verification and certification

CDM and JI requirements apply.

Registries and fees

Carbon assets are forwarded to the Fund Participants' accounts (in their respective national registries) on a pro rata basis, according to each participant's share in the Carbon Fund. In the case of CERs, the credits are transferred from the CDM registry, while ERUs are directly transferred from the national registry of the project host on issuance. The World Bank has developed a carbon asset registry system (CARS) to track the World Bank Carbon Funds' carbon assets and manage allocations to fund participants.

The Carbon Finance Unit (CFU) of the World Bank does not publish information regarding the fees it charges. However, the World Bank, as trustee of the Carbon Funds, manages the funds on a not-for-profit basis.

Selected issues

In the early years of the carbon market, the World Bank played a pioneering role by setting up the first carbon fund – the Prototype Carbon Fund. It also helped to develop many of the approved CDM methodologies in existence today. By 2006, the World

Bank had developed 27 per cent of all approved methodologies (World Bank, 2006b). More recently, it has contributed to the development of methodologies for programmatic CDM, as well as methodologies in the forestry and transportation sectors (World Bank, 2007) where CDM project development has been scarce, in part due to methodological issues.

Through the recent introduction of two new carbon facilities, the CFU aims to address some of the current challenges in the carbon market. These include efforts by the Carbon Partnership Facility to address the lack of investment in large-scale energy infrastructure with long-term emission reduction potential as a result of regulatory uncertainty beyond 2012; and efforts by the Forest Carbon Partnership Facility to address the problem of deforestation and degradation by valuing the carbon in standing forests by providing an incentive for its sustainable use (World Bank 2008b).

Despite its pioneering role in the creation of new carbon funds, the World Bank is not without its critics. One of the key issues raised is that the price premiums offered by some of the buyers in the carbon market, including by the World Bank-managed carbon funds, have not been sufficient to significantly improve the internal rate of return for renewable energy projects (Pearson, 2007). This criticism is debatable since the CFU is arguably not the price-setter for the CDM market. At the same time, however, the World Bank as a whole is uniquely positioned to drive financing towards renewable energy.

Further criticisms relate to the World Bank's lending activities, and not necessarily to its carbon finance activities in particular. Nonetheless, it is important to highlight them as the Bank embarks on efforts to mainstream valuing carbon into its lending activities. For example, it has been criticized for continuing to invest, and perhaps even increasing its investments, in emission-intensive projects such as coal-fired power or oil and gas development (FOE, 2005; Park, 2007).

In an effort to increase the Bank's funding to address climate change in developing countries, the World Bank announced two new Climate Investment Funds in July 2008. One of the funds, the Clean Technology Fund, will serve as the Bank's financing vehicle to accelerate low-carbon investments in developing countries. To complement this initiative, the CFU is reviewing specific ways in which the World Bank can integrate carbon finance into its other financial mechanisms to provide more effective support to low-carbon projects (World Bank, 2008a).

Glossary

Additionality

The principle that only emissions reductions from those projects that would not have happened anyway should be counted as carbon credits.

Afforestation

The process of establishing and growing forests on bare or cultivated land that has not been forested in recent history.

Annex-1 countries

The 36 industrialized countries and economies in transition listed in Annex 1 of the UNFCCC. Their responsibilities under the Convention are various, and include a non-binding commitment to reducing their GHG emissions to 1990 levels by the year 2000.

Annex-B countries

The 39 emissions-capped industrialized countries and economies in transition listed in Annex B of the Kyoto Protocol. Legally binding emission reduction obligations for Annex B countries range from an 8 per cent decrease to a 10 per cent increase on 1990 levels by the first commitment period of the Protocol, 2008–2012.

Annex 1 or Annex B?

In practice, Annex 1 of the Convention and Annex B of the Protocol are used almost interchangeably. However, strictly speaking, it is the Annex-1 countries that can invest in JI/CDM projects as well as host JI projects, and non-Annex-1 countries that can host CDM projects, even though it is the Annex-B countries that have the emission reduction obligations under the Protocol. Note that Belarus and Turkey are listed in Annex 1 but not Annex B; and that Croatia, Liechtenstein, Monaco and Slovenia are listed in Annex B but not Annex 1 (source: www.cdmcapacity.org/glossary.html).

Anthropogenic greenhouse gas emissions

Humans emit greenhouse gases (GHGs) and other warming agents into the atmosphere through the burning of fossil fuels, industrial and agricultural processes, and deforestation. These human activities raise the concentrations of these gases in the atmosphere, causing anthropogenic climate change.

Assigned Amount Unit (AAU)

A tradable unit, equivalent to 1 metric tonne of CO_2 emissions, based on an Annex-1 country's assigned carbon emission goal under the Kyoto Protocol. AAUs are used to quantify emission reductions for the purpose of buying and selling credits between Annex-1 countries.

Atmospheric greenhouse gas concentrations

Atmospheric concentrations of greenhouse gases are usually expressed in parts per million (ppm) or parts per billion (ppb). For example, atmospheric CO_2 emissions have risen from approximately 280ppm to 385ppm in the last 250 years. To determine the atmospheric concentration of a particular GHG, we can either directly measure it by taking air samples, or use a model to calculate it.

Baseline-and-Credit system

A system in which, unlike in a cap-and-trade system, there is no limit to the number of credits that can be produced. New credits are generated every time an offset project is implemented. Such offset projects can only be implemented in sectors or regions that are outside a cap.

Baseline and monitoring methodologies

A baseline methodology is the means to estimate the emissions that would have been created in the most plausible alternative scenario to the implementation of the project activity (called the baseline scenario).

A monitoring methodology is the means to calculate the actual emission reductions from the project, taking into account any emissions from sources within the project boundary. A monitoring methodology sets out how project proponents should develop and implement a monitoring plan for a particular project type, in order to gather the data required to calculate emission reductions from the project. (CDM Rulebook, undated)

Baseline emissions

An estimate of GHG emissions, removals or storage that would have occurred if the offset project or program had not been implemented (i.e. baseline scenario emissions).

Baseline scenario

A hypothetical description of what would have most likely occurred in the absence of a proposed offset project.

Biosequestration

Reduction of existing atmospheric CO_2 through capture and storage in plants and soils.

Boundary (for GHG assessment)

The project boundary encompasses all the primary emissions and sinks and significant secondary emissions and sinks associated with a GHG project.

Cap-and-trade

A cap-and-trade system involves trading of emission allowances, where the total number of allowances is strictly limited or 'capped'. Trading occurs when an entity has excess allowances, because of improvements made, and sells them to an entity requiring allowances because of growth in emissions or an inability to make internal emission reductions.

Carbon credit

Used interchangeably with the term carbon offset.

Carbon dioxide (CO$_2$)

This greenhouse gas is the largest human-caused contributor to climate change. CO$_2$ is emitted by the burning of fossil fuels and by deforestation and land management practices.

Carbon dioxide equivalent (CO$_2$e)

A measure of the global warming potential of a particular greenhouse gas compared to that of carbon dioxide over the time frame of 100 years. One unit of a gas with a CO$_2$e rating of 21, for example, would have the global warming effect of 21 units of carbon dioxide emissions (over a time frame of 100 years).

Carbon offset

A credit representing the reduction of 1 tonne of CO$_2$ equivalent that can be used by the buyer of the credits to claim the reduction, even though it has been achieved elsewhere.

Certified Emission Reductions (CERs)

Tradable units issued by the UN through the Clean Development Mechanism for emission reduction projects in developing countries. Each CER represents one metric ton of carbon emission reduction. CERs are categorized by the year, or vintage, in which they are generated. They can be purchased before the actual reduction occurs (see forward crediting). CERs can be used by Annex-1 countries to meet their emission goals under the Kyoto Protocol.

Chicago Climate Exchange (CCX)

A US-based, voluntary but legally binding greenhouse gas emission registry, reduction and trading system.

Clean Development Mechanism (CDM)

A provision of the Kyoto Protocol that allows developed countries (Annex 1) to offset their emissions by funding emission-reduction projects in developing countries (non-Annex 1).

Compliance market

The regulated market for carbon credits (specifically CERs, EUAs, AAUs and ERUs) used to reach emission targets under the Kyoto Protocol, the EU ETS or other mandatory markets. Also called the regulated or mandatory market.

Conference of Parties (COP)

The meeting of parties to the United Nations Framework Convention on Climate Change.

Crediting period

The period during which a mitigation project can generate offsets.

Crediting start date

See start date

Deforestation

Conversion of forested land to a non-forested land (eg pasture, cropland or development)

Designated operational entity (DOE)

An independent auditor, accredited by the CDM Executive Board, who validates CDM project activities, and verifies and certifies emission reductions generated by such projects.

Direct GHG emissions

Emissions from GHG sources or removals from GHG sinks that are owned or controlled by the project developer (WRI/WBCSD, 2005).

Double counting

Double counting occurs when a carbon emission reduction is counted towards multiple offsetting goals or targets (voluntary or regulated). An example would be if an energy-efficiency project sells voluntarily credits to business owners, and the same project is counted towards meeting a national emission reduction target.

Emission reductions (ERs)

The measurable reduction of release of greenhouse gases into the atmosphere from a specified activity or over a specified area, during a specified period of time.

Emission Reduction Units (ERUs)

A tradable unit, equivalent to 1 metric ton of CO_2 equivalent emissions, generated by a Joint Implementation (JI) project and used to quantify emission reductions for the purpose of buying and selling credits between Annex-1 countries under the Kyoto Protocol.

Emission trading

A provision of the Kyoto Protocol that allows Annex-1 countries to trade emission reduction credits in order to comply with their Kyoto-assigned reduction targets. This system allows countries to pay and take credit for emission reduction projects in developing countries, where the cost of these projects may be lower, thus ensuring that overall emissions are lessened in the most cost-effective manner.

Environmental integrity

Environmental integrity is used to express the fact that offsets need to be real, not double counted, and additional in order to deliver the desired GHG benefits. The term should not be confused with 'secondary environmental benefits', which is used to describe the added benefits an offset project can have (e.g. air pollution reduction and protection of biodiversity) in addition to emission reductions.

European Union Allowance (EUA)

Tradable emission credits from the European Union Emission Trading System. Each allowance carries the right for the holder to emit 1 metric ton of CO_2.

European Union Emission Trading System (EU ETS)

The EU ETS is a greenhouse gas emission trading scheme that aims to limit emissions by imposing progressively lower limits on power plants and other sources of greenhouse gases.

Ex ante

Ex ante refers to offsets that are sold and claimed by the buyer before the emission reductions have occurred. The exact quantities of the reductions are therefore uncertain. See also forward crediting and forward delivery.

Ex post

As opposed to *ex-ante* offsets, *ex-post* reductions have already occurred when the offsets are sold and their quantities are certain. *Ex-post* offsets have usually been third-party verified.

Forward crediting

The sale of *ex-ante* credits. At contract closure, the buyer pays for and receives a certain number of offsets for emission reductions or sequestration that will occur in the future.

Forward delivery

At contract closure, the buyer pays the purchase price for a certain number of offsets that have yet to be produced. Unlike 'forward crediting', the offsets are not delivered to the buyer until the emission reductions have occurred and have been verified.

Geosequestration

The underground injection of CO_2 emitted by fossil-fuel power generation. At this point, geological sequestration is still very costly.

Greenhouse gases (GHGs)

Gases that contribute to climate change. Those named in the Kyoto Protocol include carbon dioxide (CO_2), methane (CH_4), nitrous oxide (N_2O), hydrofluorocarbons (HFCs), perfluorocarbons (PFCs) and sulphur hexafluoride (SF_6). Not all global warming causing molecules are gases (e.g. soot and other particulates). Usually these are referred to as warming agents.

Host country

The country where an emission reduction project is physically located.

Indirect GHG emissions

Emissions or removals that occur as a consequence of project activity, but take place at GHG sources or sinks not owned or controlled by the project developer (WRI/WBCSD, 2005). Examples for indirect emission reductions include demand-side energy efficiency upgrades: the emission reductions occur at the power plant (because of lower demand) and not at the place where the efficiency measures have been taken.

Internal rate of return (IRR)

The annual return that would make the present value of future cash flows from an investment (including its residual market value) equal the current market price of the investment; in other words, the discount rate at which an investment has zero net present value. The IRR is often used to establish a project's financial additionality.

International Transaction Log (ITL)

A registry system that aims to ensure the validity of carbon credits issued under the Kyoto Protocol. Learn more at http://unfccc.int/kyoto_protocol/registry_systems/itl/items/4065.php.

ISO 14064

Standards for greenhouse gas accounting and verification introduced by the International Organization for Standardization in March 2006. ISO 14064 aims to help governments and businesses engage in effective emission reduction projects as well as participate in carbon trading.

Issuance

Issuance of CERs refers to an instruction by the Executive Board to the CDM registry administrator to issue a specified quantity of CERs for a project activity into a pending account in the CDM registry.

Joint Implementation (JI)

A provision of the Kyoto Protocol that allows those in Annex-1 (developed) countries to undertake projects in other Annex-1 (developed or transitional) countries (as opposed to those undertaken in non-Annex-1 countries through the CDM).

Kyoto mechanisms

The three flexibility mechanisms that may be used by Annex-I Parties to the Kyoto Protocol to fulfil their commitments through emission trading (Article 17). They include the Joint Implementation (JI, Article 6), Clean Development Mechanism (CDM, Article 12) and trading of Assigned Amount Units.

Kyoto Protocol

An international treaty that requires participating countries to reduce their emissions by 5 per cent below 1990 levels by 2012. The protocol, developed in 1997, is administered by the Secretariat of the UN Framework Convention on Climate Change. Learn more at http://unfccc.int.

Kyoto units

A variety of units, including AAUs, ERUs and CERs, which allows for the trading of carbon credits among Annex-1 countries to meet their Kyoto Protocol-assigned emission targets.

Land use, land-use change and forestry (LULUCF)

The term given to biosequestration projects such as reforestation and afforestation, and agricultural carbon sequestration.

Leakage

Leakage occurs when activities that reduce GHG emissions (or increase carbon in plants and soils) in one place and time result in increases in emissions (or loss of soil or plant carbon) elsewhere or at a later date. For example, a steel firm in a country covered by the Kyoto Protocol makes reductions by closing one facility and replacing its output with production from a steel plant operating in another country that does not have a GHG constraint. Similarly, a forest can be protected in one location and cause harvesting of forests elsewhere (California Air Resources Board, 2007).

Legal requirements

Any mandatory laws or regulations that directly or indirectly affect GHG emissions associated with a project activity, and that require technical, performance or management actions. Legal requirements may involve: the use of a specific technology (e.g. gas turbines instead of diesel generators); meeting a certain standard of performance (e.g. fuel efficiency standards for vehicles); or managing operations according to a certain set of criteria or practices (e.g. forest management practices) (WRI/WBCSD, 2005).

Millennium Development Goals (MDGs)

The MDGs commit the international community to an expanded vision of development, one that vigorously promotes human development as the key to sustaining social and economic progress in all countries, and recognizes the importance of creating a global partnership for development. The goals have been commonly accepted as a framework for measuring development progress.

Monitoring

Project developers are required to maintain records measuring the emission reduction achieved during the operation phase. Emission reductions are issued based on the monitoring report.

Non-Annex-1 countries

A group of developing countries that have not been assigned emission targets under the Kyoto Protocol and which are recognized by the UNFCCC as being especially vulnerable to the effects of climate change. Learn more at http://unfccc.int/parties_and_observers/items/2704.php.

Non-regulated market

See voluntary market.

Offsets

Offsets designate the emission reductions from project-based activities that can be used to meet compliance – or corporate citizenship – objectives vis-à-vis GHG mitigation (Capoor and Ambrosi, 2007).

Permanence

Permanence addresses the risk of reversal: the unexpected release of GHGs in a climate mitigation project. It is of especial importance in biosequestration, e.g. the destruction of a forest by fire, pests or illegal logging.

Point of regulation

The point of program enforcement at which specific emitting entities covered under a cap-and-trade program are required to surrender enough allowances to match their actual emissions within a compliance period (California Air Resources Board, 2007).

Pre-registered Certified Emission Reductions (pre-CERs)

A unit of GHG emission reductions that has been verified by an independent auditor but that has not yet undergone the procedures and may not yet have met the requirements for registration, verification, certification and issuance of CERs (in the case of the CDM) or ERUs (in the case of JI) under the Kyoto Protocol. Pre-registered emission reductions are often sold in the voluntary market.

Primary market

The exchange of emission reductions, offsets or allowances between buyer and seller, where the seller is the originator of the supply (e.g. project developer), and where the product has not been traded more than once.

Project-based system

See Baseline-and-Credit system.

Project boundary

The project boundary encompasses all anthropogenic emissions from sources of greenhouse gases (GHG) under the control of the project participants that are significant and reasonably attributable to the project activity.

Project design document (PDD)

A project-specific document required under the CDM rules that will enable the auditor to determine whether the project (i) has been approved by the parties involved in a project, (ii) would result in reductions of greenhouse gas emissions that are additional and (iii) has an appropriate baseline and monitoring plan.

Project start date

See start date.

Prompt delivery

At contract closure, the buyer pays the purchase price for a certain number of offsets that have already been realized and are delivered promptly to the buyer.

Reforestation

Replanting of forests on land that previously contained forests but that had been converted to another land use (California Air Resources Board, 2007).

Registration

The formal acceptance by an offset program authority of a validated project activity as an offset project activity.

Regulated market

See compliance market.

Regulatory surplus

An emission reduction is in regulatory surplus if it is over and above what is required by law, and not otherwise required of a source by current regulations or other obligations. (Climate Trust, undated b)

Renewable Energy Certificates (RECs)

A Renewable Energy Certificate represents 1 unit of electricity generated from renewable energy with low net greenhouse gas emissions. One REC represents 1 megawatt-hour.

Retirement

Retirement of offset refers to offsets that are taken out of the market. Retired offsets can no longer be traded.

Secondary market

The exchange of emission reductions, offsets or allowances between buyer and seller where the seller is not the originator of the supply and the transaction represents a secondary trade in the particular product.

Stakeholders

Stakeholders are the public, including individuals, groups or communities affected, or likely to be affected, by the proposed project activity or actions leading to the implementation of such an activity.

Start date

Start date refers to *project start date* and *crediting start date*. The project start date of an offset project is the earliest date at which either the implementation or construction of the project activity can begin (UNFCCC, 2007e). *Crediting start date* defines the date after which an offset project can produce offset credits. Project and crediting start date are usually defined by the standard or programme under which an offset project is implemented.

Temporary Certified Emission Reductions (tCERs)

A temporary certified emission reduction or tCER is a unit issued pursuant to Article 12 of the Kyoto Protocol for an Afforestation/Reforestation CDM project activity under the CDM, which expires at the end of the commitment period following the one during which it was issued. It is equal to 1 metric ton of CO equivalent.

United Nations Framework Convention on Climate Change (UNFCCC)

An international treaty, developed at the 1992 UN Conference on Environment and Development, which aims to combat climate change by reducing global greenhouse gas emissions. The original treaty was considered legally non-binding, but made provisions for future protocols, such as the Kyoto Protocol, to set mandatory emissions limits. More at http://unfccc.int/2860.php.

Validation

The assessment of a project's Project Design Document, which describes its design, including its baseline and monitoring plan, by an independent third party against the requirements of a specific standard, before the implementation of the project.

Verification

The act of checking or testing by an independent and certified party to ensure that an emission reduction project actually achieves emission reductions commensurate with the credits it receives (California Air Resources Board, 2007).

Verified or Voluntary Emission Reductions (VERs)

Reductions that, unlike CERs, are sold on the voluntary market. VERs are linked neither to the Kyoto Protocol nor to the EU ETS. VERs are sometimes referred to as Voluntary Emission Reductions.

Voluntary market

The non-regulated market for carbon credits (especially VERs) that operates independently from Kyoto and the EU ETS. Also called the non-regulated market.

Voluntary offsetting

Offsetting purchases made by individuals, businesses and institutions that are not legally mandated to do so.

Warming agents

See greenhouse gases.

References

Alberta Environment (2007a) 'Offset credit project guidance document: Specified gas emitters regulation', September, http://environment.gov.ab.ca/info/library/7915.pdf

Alberta Environment (2007b) 'Offset credit verification guidance document', September, www.environment.alberta.ca/1240.html

Alberta Environment (2008) 'Offset credit project guidance document: Specified gas emitters regulation', February, www.environment.alberta.ca/

Antinori, C. and Sathaye, J. (2007) 'Assessing transaction costs of project-based greenhouse gas emissions trading', Lawrence Berkeley National Lab, LBNL-57315, 25 January

Australian Government (2007) 'Report of the task group on emissions trading', Department of the Prime Minister and Cabinet, www.resourcesmart.vic.gov.au/documents/PMs_emissions_trading_report.pdf

Australian Government (2008a) 'Australian emissions trading scheme', www.climatechange.gov.au/emissionstrading/index.html

Australian Government (2008b) 'Carbon pollution reduction scheme: Australia's low pollution future', vol 1, December, www.climatechange.gov.au/whitepaper/report/index.html

Bird, L. and Lokey, E. (2007) 'Interaction of compliance and voluntary renewable energy markets', National Renewable Energy Laboratory, October, http://apps 3.eere.energy.gov/greenpower/pdfs/42096.pdf

Broekhoff, D. (2007a) 'Voluntary carbon offsets: Getting what you pay for', Testimony before the House Select Committee on Energy Independence and Global Warming, 18 July, http://pdf.wri.org/20070718_broekhoff_testimony.pdf

Broekhoff, D. (2007b) 'Draft Green-e GHG protocol for renewable energy: Electronic comment form', World Resources Institute, www.green-e.org/getcert_ghg_re_protocol.shtml

Bryk, D.S. (2006) 'States and cities should not join the Chicago Climate Exchange', Natural Resources Defense Council, http://hawaiienergypolicy.hawaii.edu/PDF/Appendix_I.pdf

California Air Resources Board (CARB) (2007) 'Recommendations for designing a greenhouse gas cap-and-trade system for California. Recommendations of the Market Advisory Committee to the California Air Resources Board', 30 June, www.climatechange.ca.gov

Cames, M., Anger, N., Böhringer, C., Harthan, R.O. and Schneider, L. (2007) 'Long-term prospects of CDM and JI', Federal Environmental Agency, Öko-Institut e.V., Freiburg, Germany, http://oeko-institut.org/oekodoc/583/2006–136-en.pdf

Canadian Standards Association (undated) 'GHG Clean Projects Registry: Schedule B GHG Clean Projects Registry Services Agreement', www.ghgregistries.ca/assets/rtf/Schedule_b_e.rtf

Capoor, K. and Ambrosi, P. (2007) 'State and trends of the carbon market 2007', World Bank Institute, Washington, DC, May, http://wbcarbonfinance.org/docs/ Carbon_ Trends_2007-_FINAL_-_May_2.pdf

Capoor, K. and Ambrosi, P. (2008) 'State and trends of the carbon market 2008', World Bank Institute, Washington, DC, May, http://wbcarbonfinance.org/docs/State_ Trends_FINAL.pdf

Capoor, K. and Ambrosi, P. (2009) 'State and trends of the carbon market 2009', World Bank Institute, Washington, DC, May, http://siteresources.worldbank.org/ EXTCARBONFINANCE/Resources/State_and_Trends_of_the_Carbon_Market_ 2009-FINALb.pdf

Carbon Finance (April 2009) www.carbon-financeonline.com

Carbon Offset Solutions (2008) 'Search projects', www.carbonoffsetsolutions.ca/

Chicago Climate Exchange (CCX) (2007) 'Overview', www.chicagoclimatex.com/content. jsf?id=821

Clean Development Mechanism (CDM) Rulebook (undated) http://cdmrulebook.org/404

Climate Action Reserve (undated) 'Climate Action Reserve Project Database', https://thereserve1.apx.com/ myModule/rpt/myrpt.asp?r=111

Climate, Community and Biodiversity (2008) 'Project Design Standards Second Edition', http://www.climate-standards.org/standards/pdf/ccb_standards_second_ edition_december_2008.pdf

The Climate Registry (2009) http://www.theclimateregistry.org/about/

Climate Trust (undated a) 'Oregon Power Plant Offset Program', www.climatetrust.org/

Climate Trust (undated b) 'Glossary', www.climatetrust.org/solicitations_glossary.php

Cline, W.R. (1992) *The Economics of Global Warming*, Institute for International Economics, Washington, DC

Cochran, I. and Leguet, B. (2007) 'Carbon investment funds: The influx of private capital', Caisse des Dépôts Mission Climat, Research Report, www.caissedesdepots.fr/ accueil.html, accessed 23 July 2008

Congressional Budget Office (2009) 'Potential impacts of climate change in the United States', May, www.cbo.gov/ftpdocs/101xx/doc10107/05-04-ClimateChange_forWeb.pdf

Cosbey, A., Parry, J., Browne, J., Babu, Y.D., Bhandari, P., Drexhage, J. and Murphy, D. (2005) 'Realizing the development dividend: Making the CDM work for developing countries', International Institute for Sustainable Development, Winnipeg, Manitoba, Canada, May, www.ieta.org/ieta/www/pages/getfile.php?docID=1102

Crossley, D. (2005) 'The white certificate scheme in New South Wales, Australia', Presentation for the Task 14 Workshop on White Certificates, Paris, France, 14 April, www.ewc.polimi.it/dl.php?file=White Certificate Scheme in NSW.pdf

Ellis, J. and Kamel, S. (2007) *Overcoming Barriers to Clean Development Mechanism Projects*, Organisation for Economic Co-operation and Development (OECD)/ International Energy Agency (IEA), Paris, France, May, www.oecd.org/dataoecd/51/ 14/38684304.pdf

Ellis, J. and Tirpak, D. (2006) 'Linking GHG emission trading systems and markets', Organisation for Economic Co-operation and Development (OECD)/International Energy Agency (IEA), October, COM/ENV/EPOC/IEA/SLT

Environment Canada (2008a) 'Turning the corner: Regulatory framework for industrial greenhouse gas emissions', Environment Canada, March, www.ec.gc.ca/ doc/virage-corner/2008–03/541_eng.htm

Environment Canada (2008b) 'Canada's offset system for greenhouse gases, guide for protocol developers', Environment Canada, August, www.ec.gc.ca/doc/virage-corner/2008–03/pdf/526_eng.pdf

Environment Canada (2009a) 'Canada's offset system for greenhouse gases. Overview', Environment Canada, June, www.ec.gc.ca/creditscompensatoires-offsets/92CA76F4 –7A25–42F4-A1E0-E8361655A09D/Offsets_Overview_June_11_ final_e.pdf

Environment Canada (2009b) 'Canada's offset system for greenhouse gases. Program rules and guidance for project proponents', Environment Canada, June, www.ec.gc.ca/ creditscompensatoires-offsets/44B33F4A-34E2–49CE-9D3E-0775600A2AE6/ Offsets_Projects%20June%2011_%20pdf.pdf

Environment Canada (2009c) 'Canada's offset system for greenhouse gases. Program rules for verification and guidance for verification bodies', Environment Canada, June, www.ec.gc.ca/creditscompensatoires-offsets/F86DD35D-2561–427D-9FA1– 9A292A437FC2/Offsets_Verification%20June%209_e.pdf

European Commission (EC) (2007a) 'EU action against climate change: EU emission trading, an open system promoting global innovation. European Commission', November, http://ec.europa.eu/environment/climat/pdf/bali/eu_ action.pdf

European Commission (EC) (2007b) 'Emission trading: EU-wide cap for 2008–2012 set at 2.08 billion allowances after assessment of national plans for Bulgaria', Press Release, 7 December

European Commission (EC) (2009a) 'Emission Trading System', EU ETS, http://ec. europa.eu/environment/climat/emission/index_en.htm

Fowler, R., Abatement Solutions – Asia Pacific (2007) 'World's best practice in project-based mechanisms for abatement of greenhouse gases, version 1.0'

Friends of the Earth (FOE) (2005) 'Power failure: How the World Bank is failing to adequately finance renewable energy for development', Friends of the Earth, http://action.foe.org/content.jsp?content_KEY=2957&t=2007_Global-Finance.dwt, accessed 21 July 2008

Garnaut, R. (2008a) 'Garnaut climate change review: Interim report to the Commonwealth State and Territory Governments of Australia', February, www.garnautreview.org.au/CA25734E0016A131/WebObj/GarnautClimateChange ReviewInterimReport-Feb08/$File/Garnaut%20Climate%20Change% 20Review%20Interim%20Report%20-%20Feb%2008.pdf

Garnaut, R. (2008b) 'The Garnaut climate change review: Final report', Port Melbourne, Cambridge University Press, www.garnautreview.org.au/index.htm

Gaye, F. (2007) 'Joint Implementation Supervisory Committee: Work accomplished and challenges ahead', United Nations Framework Convention on Climate Change (UNFCCC), 4 December, http://ji.unfccc.int/Workshop/4_December_2007.html, accessed 6 January 2008

Gillenwater, M. (2007) 'Redefining RECs (Part 2): Untangling certificates and emission markets', Princeton University Press, Princeton, NJ, August, www.princeton.edu/ ~mgillenw/REC-OffsetPaper-PartII_v2.pdf

Gold Standard (undated a) The Gold Standard Foundation, Geneva-Cointrin, Switzerland, www.cdmgoldstandard.org

Gold Standard Toolkit Annex C (2009) 'Guidance on project type eligibility', www.cdmgoldstandard.org/fileadmin/editors/files/6_GS_technical_docs/GSv2.1/ Annex_C.pdf

Goodell, J. (2006) 'Capital pollution solution?', *New York Times Magazine*, 30 July, http://query.nytimes.com/gst/fullpage.html?res=9E07E2D7143FF933A05754C0A 9609C8B63

Green-e (2007) 'The Green-e Climate Protocol for Renewable Energy', October, www.green-e.org/getcert_ghg_re_protocol.shtml

Green-e (2008a) 'Climate Standard Version 1.1', Green-e Climate Program, www.green-e.org/docs/climate/G-e%20Climate%20Standard%20V1–1.pd, updated 16 June 2009

Green-e (2008b) 'Green-e Climate overview', www.green-e.org/getcert_ghg_intro.shtml

Greenhouse Gas Abatement Scheme (GGAS) (2007a) 'Fact sheet: Creating NGACs from demand side abatement', January, www.greenhousegas.nsw.gov.au/documents/FS-DSA-Certs-02.pdf

Greenhouse Gas Abatement Scheme (GGAS) (2007b) 'Fact sheet: Offences and penalties', August, www.greenhousegas.nsw.gov.au/documents/FS-Sch-Offences-07.pdf

Greenhouse Gas Reduction Targets Act, S.B.C. (2007) 'The Revised Statutes and Consolidated Regulations of British Columbia', www.qp.gov.bc.ca/statreg/

Greenhouse Gas Reduction Targets Act, Emission Offsets Regulation, B.C. Reg. 393/2008 (2008), 9 December, www.env.gov.bc.ca/epd/codes/ggrta/pdf/offsets-reg.pdf

Greenhouse Gas Reduction Targets Act, Carbon Neutral Government Regulation, B.C. Reg. 392/2008 (2008), 9 December, www.env.gov.bc.ca/epd/codes/ggrta/pdf/offsets-reg.pdf

Hamilton, K., Bayon, R., Turner, G. and Higgins, D. (2007) 'State of the voluntary carbon markets 2007: Picking up steam', Ecosystem Marketplace and New Carbon Finance, 18 July, http://ecosystemmarketplace.com/documents/acrobat/Stateofthe VoluntaryCarbonMarket18July_Final.pdf

Hamilton, K., Sjardin, M., Marcello, T. and Xu, G. (2008) 'Forging a frontier: State of the voluntary carbon markets 2008', Ecosystem Marketplace and New Carbon Finance, 8 May, www.ecosystemmarketplace.com/documents/cms_documents/ 2008_ StateofVoluntaryCarbonMarket2.pdf

Hamilton, K., Sjardin, M., Shapiro, A. and Marcello, T. (2009) 'Fortifying the foundation: State of the voluntary carbon markets 2009', Ecosystem Marketplace and New Carbon Finance, 20 May

Hansen, J., Nazarenko, L., Ruedy, R., Sato, M., Willis, J., Del Genio, A., Koch, D., Lacis, A., Lo, K., Menon, S., Novakov, T., Perlwitz, J., Russell, G., Schmidt, G.A. and Tausnev, N. (2005) 'Earth's energy imbalance: Confirmation and implications. *Science,* 308: 1431–1434

Hepburn, C. (2007) 'Carbon trading: A review of the Kyoto mechanisms', *Annual Review of Environment and Resources,* vol 32, pp 375–393, http://arjournals. annualreviews.org/doi/pdf/10.1146/annurev.energy.32.053006.141203?cookieSet=1, accessed on 10 July 2009

ICF International (2006) 'Voluntary carbon offsets market: Outlook 2007', ICF International, London, UK, www.icfi.com/markets/energy/doc_files/carbon-offsets.pdf

Instituto Ecológica (undated) www.ecologica.org.br/ingles/index.html

Intergovernmental Panel on Climate Change (IPCC) (2006) '2006 guidelines for national greenhouse gas inventories, volume 4 agriculture, forestry and other land use', www.ipcc.ch/meetings/session25/doc4a4b/vol4.pdf

International Emissions Trading Association (IETA) (undated) 'Linking the EU ETS with emerging emissions trading schemes', www.ieta.org/ieta/www/pages/index.php

International Organization for Standardization (ISO) (2006a) 'Greenhouse gases, Part 1: Specification with guidance at the organization level for quantification and reporting of greenhouse gas emissions and removals', ISO 14064–1, www.iso.org/iso/iso_catalogue/catalogue_tc/catalogue_detail.htm?csnumber=38381

International Organization for Standardization (ISO) (2006b) 'Greenhouse gases, Part 2: Specification with guidance at the project level for quantification, monitoring and reporting of greenhouse gas emission reductions or removal enhancements', ISO 14064–2, www.iso.org/iso/iso_catalogue/catalogue_tc/catalogue_detail.htm?csnumber=38382

International Organization for Standardization (ISO) (2006c) 'Greenhouse gases, Part 3: Specification with guidance for the validation and verification of greenhouse gas assertions', ISO 14064–3, www.iso.org/iso/iso_catalogue/catalogue_tc/catalogue_detail.htm?csnumber=38700

International Organization for Standardization (ISO) (undated) http://www.iso.org/iso/catalogue_detail?csnumber=43278

IPART (2007) 'Introduction to the Greenhouse Gas Reduction Scheme', GGAS, www.greenhousegas.nsw.gov.au/overview/scheme_overview/overview.asp

Kollmuss, A., Zink, H. and Polycarp, C. (2008) 'Making sense of the voluntary carbon market: A comparison of carbon offset standards', Stockholm Environment Institute and Tricorona, World Wildlife Fund, Germany, March, http://assets.panda.org/downloads/vcm_report_final.pdf

MassDEP (2008) 'Determination on availability of GHG credits for sale at or below trigger price', www.mass.gov/dep/air/climate/ghgcfndg.htm

MassDEP (undated a) 'The Commonwealth of Massachusetts Department of Environmental Protection Notice of Public Comment Period', www.mass.gov/envir/mepa/notices/122407em/10.pdf

MassDEP (undated b) 'Attachment A: Final regulatory revisions to 310 CMR 7.00; and Attachment B: Final regulatory revisions to 310 CMR 7.29', www.mass.gov/dep/air/laws/ghgappb.pdf

Midwestern Greenhouse Gas Reduction Accord Advisory Group (2009) 'Midwestern Greenhouse Gas Reduction Accord: Draft final recommendations of the Advisory Group', www.midwesternaccord.org/Accord_Draft_Final.pdf

Ministry of Environment, British Columbia (2009) 'Greenhouse Gas Reduction Targets Act (GGRTA)', April, www.env.gov.bc.ca/epd/codes/ggrta/offsets_reg.htm

Ministry of the Environment, Japan (MOE) (2007) 'CDM/JI Manual 2007', Tokyo, Japan, http://gec.jp/gec/gec.nsf/en/Activities-CDMJI_FS_Programme-CDMJI_Manual

Natsource LLC (2007) 'Realizing the benefits of greenhouse gas offsets: Design options to stimulate project development and ensure environmental integrity', National Commission on Energy Policy, January, www.energycommission.org/ht/action/GetDocumentAction/i/3178

Natsource (undated) 'European Union Emissions Trading Scheme (EU ETS)', www.natsource.com/markets/index.asp?s=106, accessed 4 March 2008

New South Wales (NSW) (2009) 'Preparing for the energy savings scheme', Department of Environment and Climate Change and Department of Water and Energy, NSW, Sydney, Australia, May, www.greenhousegas.nsw.gov.au/Documents/ ESS-preparing-for-scheme.pdf

New South Wales Department of Water and Energy (NSW DWE) (2008) 'Transitional arrangements for the NSW Greenhouse Gas Reduction Scheme', NSW Government, April, www.dwe.nsw.gov.au/energy/pdf/sustain_greenhouse_gas_ consultation_paper_ nsw_ggas_reduction_scheme.pdf

New South Wales (NSW) Greenhouse Gas Abatement Scheme (GGAS) (2004a) 'Fact sheet: when can large users create LUACs', July, www.greenhousegas.nsw.gov.au/ documents/FS-LUAC-Certs-01.pdf

New South Wales (NSW) Greenhouse Gas Abatement Scheme (GGAS) (2004b) 'Fact sheet: When can forest managers create NGACs?', November, www.greenhousegas. nsw.gov.au/documents/FS-CS-Certs-01.pdf

New South Wales (NSW) Greenhouse Gas Abatement Scheme (GGAS) (2007) 'Fact sheet: Offences and penalties', August, www.greenhousegas.nsw.gov.au/documents/ FS-Sch-Offences-07.pdf

New South Wales (NSW) Greenhouse Gas Abatement Scheme (GGAS) (2009) 'GGAS newsletter', Issue 12, June, Sydney, NSW, Australia, www.greenhousegas.nsw.gov.au/ Documents/Newsletter_Issue12_Jun09.pdf

New South Wales (NSW) Greenhouse Gas Abatement Scheme (GGAS) (undated) 'Audit Panel: Overview', www.greenhousegas.nsw.gov.au/audit/members.asp

Nordhaus, W.D. (1994) *Managing the Global Commons*, MIT Press, Cambridge, MA

Offset Quality Initiative (2009) 'Maintaining carbon market integrity: Why Renewable Energy Certificates are not offsets', June, http://offsetqualityinitiative.org/OQI%20 REC%20Brief%20Web.pdf

Olsen, K.H. (2007) 'The Clean Development Mechanism's contribution to sustainable development: A review of the literature', *Climatic Change*, vol 84, pp 59–73

Oregon Energy Facility Siting Council (undated) 'Oregon carbon dioxide emission standards for new energy facilities', www.oregon.gov/ENERGY/SITING/docs/ ccnewst.pdf

Pacific Carbon Trust (2009) 'Pacific Carbon Trust', www.pacificcarbontrust.ca, accessed 3 July 2009

Pacific Gas and Electric Company (PG&E) (2008) 'New release: Pacific Gas and Electric Company's Climatesmart Program makes largest purchase of greenhouse gas emission reductions in California', San Francisco, CA, 26 February, www.pge.com/about/news/mediarelations/newsreleases/q1_2008/080226.shtml

Park, S. (2007) 'The World Bank Group: Championing sustainable development norms?', *Global Governance*, vol 13, no 4, pp 535–556

Passey, R., MacGill, I. and Outhred, H. (2007) 'The NSW Greenhouse Gas Reduction Scheme: An analysis of the NGAC Registry for the 2003, 2004 and 2005 compliance periods', Center for Energy and Environmental Markets (CEEM), 7 August, www.ceem.unsw.edu.au/content/userDocs/CEEM_DP_070827_000.pdf

Pearson, B. (2007) 'Market failure: Why the CDM won't promote clean development', *Journal of Cleaner Production*, vol 15, no 2, pp 247–252

Plan Vivo, www.planvivo.org/

Point Carbon (2008a) 'Australia, NZ eye emissions trading link', 27 February www.pointcarbon.com/

Point Carbon (2008b) 'Primary CER prices on the rise', 16 July www.pointcarbon.com/

Point Carbon (2009) *Carbon Market North America*, vol 4, 15 May

Point Carbon Research (2007a) 'Emissions Trading in the US: Is RGGI over-allocated?', *Carbon Market Analyst*, 17 August, http://int.pointcarbon.com/article 24032–509.html?articleID=24032&categoryID=509

Point Carbon Research (2007b) 'Voluntary carbon markets: Lost in transactions?', *Carbon Market Analyst*, 24 October, www.pointcarbon.com/research/carbonmarket research/analyst/1.262969

Point Carbon Research (2007c) 'RGGI should expand forestry offset options: Report', 18 December, http://int.pointcarbon.com/Home/News/All%20news/ article25992–703.html?articleID=25992&categoryID=703&larger

Regional Greenhouse Gas Initiative (RGGI) (2006) 'Analysis supporting offsets limit recommendation', RGGI Staff Working Group, 1 May, www.rggi.org/ docs/offsets_limit_5_1_06.pdf

Regional Greenhouse Gas Initiative (RGGI) (2007a) 'Regional Greenhouse Gas Initiative Model Rule', 5 January, www.rggi.org/docs/model_rule_corrected_1_5_07.pdf

Regional Greenhouse Gas Initiative (RGGI) (2007b) 'Overview of RGGI CO_2 Budget Trading Program', October, www.rggi.org/docs/program_summary_10_07.pdf

Regional Greenhouse Gas Initiative (RGGI) (undated) 'Regional Greenhouse Gas Initiative: Emissions and allowance trading', www.rggi.org/tracking

Regional Greenhouse Gas Initiative (RGGI) Resources Panel (2007) 'Summary of RGGI Stakeholder Workshop on GHG Offsets', workshop dated 25 June 2004, Pew Center on Global Climate Change, Resources for the Future and the World Resources Institute, www.rggi.org/docs/offsets_workshopsummary.pdf

Ruud, L., Siemens, F., Webber, L., Meyers Norris, P., Haugen-Kozyra, K., Gorecki, K., (2008) 'Alberta Offset System: First year retrospective', Climate Change Central http://carbonoffsetsolutions.climatechangecentral.com/files/microsites/Policy_Regul ation/July%203%20Discussion%20Paper%20(final).pdf

Salay, J. (2007) 'Joint Implementation and the EU Emissions Trading Scheme', United Nations Framework Convention on Climate Change (UNFCCC), 16 October, http://ji.unfccc.int/Workshop/15_October_2007.html, accessed 6 January 2008

Schlamadinger, B. and O'Sullivan, R. (2007) 'ViewPoint: LULUCF projects under JI, will they be impossible?', *CDM and JI Monitor*, 24 January, p 1

Schneider, L. (2007) 'Is the CDM fulfilling its environmental and sustainable development objectives? An evaluation of the CDM and options for improvement', Öko-Institut, Berlin, Germany, 5 November, http://assets.panda.org/ downloads/oeko_institut__2007____is_the_cdm_fulfilling_its_environmental_ and_sustainable_developme.pdf

Schneider, L. and Mohr, L. (2009) 'A rating of Designated Operational Entities (DOEs) accredited under the Clean Development Mechanism (CDM): Scope, methodology and results', Öko-Institut, Berlin, Germany, 27 May, www.tuvamerica.com/services/ DOEratingexcerpt.pdf

Sherry, Christopher (2008) Personal communication, June 2009

Social Carbon (2009a) 'Social Carbon Accreditation Procedure for Social Carbon Methodology Application', Version 1, March, www.socialcarbon.org/Guidelines/ Files/Accreditation_of_Organizations.pdf

Social Carbon (2009b) 'Social Carbon Guidelines: Manual for the Development of Projects and Certification of Social Carbon Credits', Version 3, May, www.socialcarbon.org/Guidelines/Files/socialcarbon_guidelines_en.pdf

State of California (2007) 'Press release: Gov. Schwarzenegger applauds climate action Reserve for joining first multi-state greenhouse gas tracking', 8 May, http://gov.ca.gov/press-release/6165/

State of New South Wales (NSW) Department of Water and Energy (DWE) (2008) 'Transitional arrangements for the NSW Greenhouse Gas Reduction Scheme consultation paper', NSW Government, Department of Water and Energy, Sydney, NSW, Australia, April, www.dwe.nsw.gov.au/energy/pdf/sustain_greenhouse_gas_consultation_paper_nsw_ggas_reduction_scheme.pdf

Sutter, C. and Parreño, J.C. (2007) 'Does the current Clean Development Mechanism (CDM) deliver its sustainable development claim? An analysis of officially registered CDM projects', *Climatic Change*, vol 84, no 1, pp 75–90

Tradition Financial Services (TFS) (2007) 'Global environmental markets. June 2007', www.tfsgreen.com/pdf/global-reports/2006/tfs-ger-05-06.pdf

Trexler, M. (2007) 'US demand?', Presentation at the Point Carbon 'Carbon Market Insights 2007' Conference, Copenhagen, 13–15 March, www.pointcarbon.com/events/recentevents/cmiamericas07/

Trinity Consultants (2006) 'Trinity Consultants newsletter', August, http://trinity consultants.com/mep.asp?p=456

TZ1 (2009) www.tz1market.com/social.php

United Nations Environment Programme (UNEP) RISØ Centre (2008) 'CDM pipeline', 11 June, www.cdmpipeline.org/

UNEP RISØ Centre (2009) www.uneprisoe.org

United Nations Framework Convention on Climate Change (1992) 'Full text of the Convention', UNFCCC, 9 May, http://unfccc.int/2860.php

United Nations Framework Convention on Climate Change (1997) 'Kyoto Protocol to the United Nations Framework Convention on Climate Change', UNFCCC, http://unfccc.int/essential_background/kyoto_protocol/items/1678.php

United Nations Framework Convention on Climate Change (UNFCCC) (2006a) 'Report of the Conference of the Parties serving as the meeting of the Parties to the Kyoto Protocol', 1st session, Montreal, 28 November to 10 December 2005, UNFCCC, 30 March, http://unfccc.int/files/meetings/cop_11/application/pdf/copmop1_provisional_agenda.pdf, accessed 5 January 2008

United Nations Framework Convention on Climate Change (UNFCCC) (2006b) 'Joint Implementation Supervisory Committee fourth meeting report – Annex 6: Guidance on criteria for baseline setting and monitoring', UNFCCC, September, http://ji.unfccc.int/Sup_Committee/Meetings/004/Reports/JISC04report_Annex_6 .pdf, accessed 6 January 2008

United Nations Framework Convention on Climate Change (UNFCCC) (2006c) 'Activities implemented jointly under the pilot phase', Seventh synthesis report, UNFCCC, http://unfccc.int/cooperation_support/activities_implemented_jointly/items/2307.php

United Nations Framework Convention on Climate Change (UNFCCC) (2007a) 'Annual report of the Joint Implementation Supervisory Committee to the Conference of the Parties serving as the meeting of the Parties to the Kyoto Protocol', UNFCCC, December, http://unfccc.int/resource/docs/2007/cmp3/eng/04p01.pdf, accessed 5 January 2008

United Nations Framework Convention on Climate Change (UNFCCC) (2007b) 'Joint Implementation management plan 2008–2009', UNFCCC, http://ji.unfccc.int/ Sup_ Committee/Meetings/008/Reports/Annex7.pdf, accessed 5 January 2008

United Nations Framework Convention on Climate Change (UNFCCC) (2007c) 'Provisions for Joint Implementation small-scale projects', UNFCCC, http://ji.unfccc.int/index.html

United Nations Framework Convention on Climate Change (2007d) 'Annual report of the Executive Board of the Clean Development Mechanism to the Conference of the Parties serving as the meeting of the Parties to the Kyoto Protocol', UNFCCC, Bali

United Nations Framework Convention on Climate Change (2007e) 'Methodological Tool: Tool for the demonstration and assessment of additionality Version 04', http:// cdm.unfccc.int/methodologies/PAmethodologies/tools/am-tool-01-v4.pdf

United Nations Framework Convention on Climate Change (UNFCCC) (2008) 'Small-scale CDM project activities', UNFCCC, http://cdm.unfccc.int/Projects/pac/ pac_ssc.html, accessed 2 July 2008

United Nations Framework Convention on Climate Change (UNFCCC) (undated a) Accredited Independent Entities, UNFCCC, http://ji.unfccc.int/AIEs/index.html

United Nations Framework Convention on Climate Change (UNFCCC) (undated b) 'Joint Implementation: Eligibility requirements', UNFCCC, http://ji.unfccc.int/ Eligibility/index.html

United Nations Framework Convention on Climate Change (UNFCCC) (undated c) 'Kyoto Protocol background: Joint Implementation', UNFCCC, http://unfccc.int/ kyoto_protocol/mechanisms/joint_implementation/items/1674.php

United Nations Framework Convention on Climate Change (UNFCCC) (undated d) 'Kyoto Protocol mechanisms: Joint Implementation', UNFCCC, http://unfccc.int/ files/essential_background/background_publications_htmlpdf/application/pdf/pub_ 07_mechanisms.pdf

United Nations Framework Convention on Climate Change (UNFCCC) (undated e) 'Guidelines for the users of the Joint Implementation Land Use, Land-Use Change and Forestry Project Design Document Form', Version 02, Joint Implementation Supervisory Committee, UNFCCC, http://ji.unfccc.int/Ref/Documents/LULUCF_ Guidelines.pdf

United Nations Framework Convention on Climate Change (UNFCCC) (undated f) 'Guidelines for the users of the Joint Implementation Project Design Document Form', Version 02, Joint Implementation Supervisory Committee, UNFCCC, http://ji.unfccc.int/Ref/Documents/Guidelines.pdf

United Nations Framework Convention on Climate Change (UNFCCC) (undated g) 'List of DOEs', UNFCCC, http://cdm.unfccc.int/DOE/list/index.html, accessed 29 December 2007

United States Environment Protection Agency (US EPA) (2007) 'Climate Leaders fact sheet', December, www.epa.gov/stateply/documents/offsets_factsheet.pdf

United States Environment Protection Agency (US EPA) (2009a) 'Climate Leaders Greenhouse Gas Inventory Protocol optional module guidance', EPA-430-F-09–046, January, www.epa.gov/stateply/documents/resources/OffsetProgramOverview.pdf

United States Environment Protection Agency (US EPA) (2009b) 'Climate Leaders', 25 June, www.epa.gov/stateply/

United States Environment Protection Agency (US EPA) (2009c) 'EPA analysis of the American Clean Energy and Security Act of 2009, H.R. 2454 in the 111th Congress', 23 June, www.epa.gov/climatechange/economics/economicanalyses.html

van de Ven, J.W. (2007) 'UNFCCC Technical Workshop on JI: Incentives and Barriers', UNFCCC, 16 October, http://ji.unfccc.int/Workshop/15_October_2007.html

Vanotti, M.B. and Szogi, A. (undated) 'Comments on Regional Greenhouse Gas Initiative (RGGI) draft Model Rule', United States Department of Agriculture Agricultural Resource Service, Florence, SC, www.rggi.org/docs/usda_ars_florence_sc.pdf

Voluntary Carbon Standard (VCS) Secretariat (2007) 'Voluntary Carbon Standard program guidelines', VCS, Geneva, Switzerland, 19 November, www.v-c-s.org/docs/Program%20Guidelines%202007.pdf

Wara, M. and Victor, D. (2008) 'A realistic policy on international carbon offsets', Program on Energy and Sustainable Development at Stanford University, Working Paper #74, http://iis-db.stanford.edu/pubs/22157/WP74_final_final.pdf

Washington State Legislature (2004) 'House Bill Report HB 3141', http://dlr.leg.wa.gov/billsummary/default.aspx?year=2003&bill=3141

Western Climate Initiative (2008) 'Design recommendations for the WCI Regional Cap-and-Trade Program', 23 September, http://westernclimateinitiative.org/the-wci-cap-and-trade-program/design-recommendations?format=pdf

Whitmore, J. and Shariff, N. (2007) 'Comments on Alberta's Offset System Project guidance document', The Pembina Institute and Toxics Watch Society of Alberta, 20 June, http://pubs.pembina.org/reports/Comments-Alb-offset.pdf

Woodall, B. (2008) 'PG&E carbon offsets fund California forest', Los Angeles, CA, www.reuters.com/article/environmentNews/idUSN2626310820080226, accessed 9 July 2008

World Bank (2006a) 'The role of the World Bank in carbon finance: An approach for further engagement', World Bank CFU, http://wbcarbonfinance.org/docs/Role_of_the_WorkBank.pdf, accessed 9 March 2008

World Bank (2006b) *Carbon Finance for Sustainable Development 2006*, World Bank, Washington, DC

World Bank (2007) *Carbon Finance for Sustainable Development 2007*, World Bank, Washington, DC

World Bank (2008a) 'Towards a strategic framework on climate change and development for the World Bank Group: Concept and issues paper (consultation draft)', World Bank, 27 March, http://siteresources.worldbank.org/DEVCOMMINT/Documentation/21712411/DC2008-0002(E)ClimateChange.pdf

World Bank (2008b) 'The World Bank Carbon Finance Unit', World Bank Carbon Finance Unit, http://web.worldbank.org/WBSITE/EXTERNAL/TOPICS/ENVIRONMENT/EXTCARBONFINANCE/0,,menuPK:4125909~pagePK:6416 8427~piPK:64168435~theSitePK:4125853,00.html

World Bank (undated) http://wbcarbonfinance.org/Router.cfm?Page=Funds&ItemID=24670

World Resources Institute (WRI) (2005) 'The GHG Protocol for Project Accounting', WRI/WBCSD, Washington, DC, http://pdf.wri.org/ghg_project_accounting.pdf

World Resources Institute (WRI) (2006a) *GHG Scheme Data Sheet: Climate Action Reserve Forest Project Protocol*, Washington, DC

World Resources Institute (WRI) (2006b) *GHG Scheme Data Sheet: WRI/WBCSD GHG Protocol for Project Accounting*, Washington, DC

World Resources Institute (WRI) (2007) 'The GHG Protocol initiative', www.ghgprotocol.org/, accessed 7 November 2007

WRI/WBCSD (2005) *The GHG Protocol for Project Accounting*, World Resources Institute, Washington, DC

World Wildlife Fund (WWF-UK) (2007) 'Emission impossible: Access to JI/CDM credits in phase II of the EU Emissions Trading Scheme', June, WWF-UK, www.wwf.org.uk/filelibrary/pdf/emission_impossible.pdf

Index